The Acquisition of Consumer Durables

A cross-sectional investigation

J F Pickering

with the research assistance of
B C Isherwood and R C Davies

A HALSTED PRESS BOOK

JOHN WILEY & SONS
New York – Toronto

English language edition, except USA and Canada,
published by
Associated Business Programmes Ltd
17 Buckingham Gate, London SW1

Published in the USA and Canada by
Halsted Press, a Division of
John Wiley & Sons Inc
New York

First published 1977

Library of Congress Cataloging in Publication Data

Pickering, J. F.
    The Acquisition of Consumer Durables

    'A Halsted Press book.'
    Bibliography: p.
    1. Durable good, Consumer—Great Britain. 2. Consumers—
Great Britain. 1. Title.
HC260.C6P53   1977   339.4'7'0941   76-53535

ISBN 0-470-99030-9.

Produced by computer-controlled phototypesetting
using OCR input techniques by
UNWIN BROTHERS LIMITED
The Gresham Press, Old Woking, Surrey
A member of the Staples Printing Group   78-1807
Printed in Great Britain by A. Wheaton & Co, Exeter

To Jane

Contents

Preface

This book reports the results of a detailed cross-sectional study of the consumer durable purchasing activities of a panel of households in Great Britain over the year April 1972 to March 1973. This constituted the latter part of an extensive research project, financed by the Social Science Research Council, on the use of attitude and intentions surveys in the prediction of the demand for consumer durables. The results of the earlier stages of the work, conducted with different samples, have been reported in a number of separate papers in the professional journals and are referred to in Chapter 1 and in the list of references at the end of this study.

The approach was based broadly upon the ideas initially pioneered in the USA by George Katona who advocated a more specifically behavioural approach to the study of this area of consumer activity than is normally found in most economics texts or indeed in many forecasting models. This suggests that the demand for consumer durables is influenced not only by the *ability* of consumers to make purchases of consumer durables but also by ebbs and flows in the confidence of consumers, that is in their *willingness* to buy. While measures of ability to buy are normally available through official statistical series, changes in consumer confidence need to be measured by means of regular sample surveys. The initial purpose of the research was therefore to investigate the possibility of developing, in the light of available survey techniques and knowledge of consumer behaviour, new ways of measuring consumer confidence and/or other forms of consumer expectation as an aid to forecasting the demand for consumer durables.

However, it also presented the possibility of undertaking a detailed investigation of the extent to which such variables also help to 'explain' the purchase behaviour of individual consumers. Consequently this book is based upon one of the few extensive cross-sectional studies of consumer durable purchasing behaviour that appear to have been carried out. Taking survey data on the circumstances, attitudes and expectations of the sample households recorded in March 1972 and the way in which these changed over the following year, the study investigates the extent to which these help to explain expenditures by the panel households on all consumer durables and also their acquisitions of particular durables over that year. In this way the underlying model, that the demand for consumer durables is a function of both the ability and the willingness of consumers to buy, can be tested cross-sectionally. In fact, where the demand for individual durables is concerned, the model is extended somewhat by considering also the *need* to make replacement purchases. This is done by incorporating survey data on informant views of the state of their existing durables.

While forecasters are rightly concerned with the performance of any predictive model in a time-series context, it is also arguable that cross-sectional validation of a model in the way attempted here is also desirable. Cross-sectional analyses normally yield lower overall coefficients of multiple determination than a time-series investigation and it is likely that explanations of the determinants of actual behaviour will be more complex in a cross-sectional analysis. Because of the operation of the 'cross-section : time-series paradox' it cannot necessarily be assumed that cross-sectional conclusions will be found to apply also to time series data. However, it is hoped that the results reported here will be considered to be of some interest in throwing new light on the influences on individual durable purchasing behaviour and also in showing how the new variables suggested for inclusion in regular consumer surveys to monitor changes in consumer expectations through time do relate to actual expenditures over a relatively short period.

The structure of the book is as follows: Chapter 1 reviews the conceptual background to the study. Chapters 2–4 describe the survey procedure, the characteristics of the sample and the changes in their circumstances over the survey year from April 1972 to March 1973. Chapter 5 is concerned with a discussion of the nature and structure of consumer confidence and Chapter 6 reports the results of attempts to explain variations between consumers in their expenditures over the survey year aggregated across the fifteen different consumer durables used in this study. Chapters 7–11 provide a more detailed analysis of the ownership and acquisition of individual consumer durables with, in Chapter 11, a disaggregated analysis of the significant characteristics of purchasers and non-purchasers of each durable considered separately. Chapter 12 offers a general overview of the research and its contribution to the understanding of that area of consumer behaviour with which it has been concerned.

This study was based at the University of Sussex and I am grateful for the facilities and encouragement provided there. The work could not have been undertaken at all without the financial support of the SSRC and the co-operation of the households who, five times in the course of a year, were prepared to give the detailed information about themselves, their attitudes and activities which forms the data base for this study.

A number of people contributed their skills to different parts of the overall research project, of which this book deals with only the latter part. Desmond Cohen, Bob Davies, John Harrison, Julia Hebden and Baron Isherwood participated in different stages of the work and made valuable contributions to its conceptual development. Baron Isherwood initially and later Bob Davies were the research staff engaged full-time on the phase of the work reported here. Chapter 7 of this book draws substantially on results initially reported by Bob Davies in a University of Sussex MA dissertation on priority patterning. Thanks are also due to David Hitchin and Henry Lucas who gave invaluable programming assistance, to Ken Lewis who helped to ensure that the computing was eventually completed, to Angela Pead who helped in the administration of the surveys, to Joy Lee Dillon who typed the final manuscript with skill and alacrity, and to Douglas Parker who has again helped with the proof reading. I am grateful to Julia Hebden, Michael Greatorex and Patrick Laycock for valuable comments on parts of the manuscript. They are not responsible for any shortcomings that may remain.

Because of the scale and complexity of the work involved, this has been a much more demanding piece of research than I initially envisaged. I therefore owe even more than my usual high degree of gratitude to my family – Jane, Rachel and Catherine – for tolerating the long hours spent on this work and for the many ways in which they have given such practical assistance and encouragement.

J.F.P.

1 *The behavioural economics of consumer durable purchasing*

The basis of the models and hypotheses underlying this investigation is to be found in the emphasis on the role of consumer expectations (attitudes, buying intentions etc) in influencing the discretionary activities of consumers, particularly the buying of motor cars and other consumer durable items such as televisions, refrigerators, etc. These ideas are most notably associated with the work (both theoretical and empirical) of George Katona and his colleagues at the Survey Research Centre, Michigan (see Katona 1975 for a general review of his work in this area). They bring together, in an effective way, the concepts and techniques of economics and psychology and in so doing appear to offer a particularly helpful approach to the understanding of this area of consumer behaviour.

It is observed that the consequence of economic growth has been to move the incomes of large proportions of the population, in the more affluent societies at least, away from subsistence levels of consumption. Other products are available which, not being basic essentials of food, clothing or housing, would be considered luxuries. The consumer therefore has a choice as to the way in which, having satisfied his need for the basic necessities of life, he should allocate the remainder of his income. In other words, the consumer has more discretion as affluence increases. But a consumer may not only choose between alternative ways of spending his income, he may also have to choose between spending and saving. It is now apparent that at least the short run marginal propensity to consume may be very volatile.

It is expenditures over which the consumer has greatest discretion that are considered likely to show the greatest fluctuations in expenditure levels. Household durables and cars (henceforward to be referred to simply as durables) are considered likely to show wide fluctuations in expenditure levels as a result of the greater discretion assumed to be available to the household in deciding whether and when to make a purchase. Consequently, short-term forecasts of the demand for consumer durables are often subject to wide margins of error (Cohen 1971; Odling–Smee 1968; Surrey 1971) and the value of improving the accuracy of forecasts in this area is likely to be greater than the overall significance of the share of these items in total consumer expenditure would otherwise suggest.

There are other forms of expenditure besides durables which are subject to high income elasticities of demand and for which it might also be argued that consumers are able to exercise discretion. Travel and holidays are often cited as examples that are subject to similar influences and could usefully be analysed in the same way. Although it is likely that from some points of view foreign holiday buying decisions may be subject to some of the same sorts of consideration, it is clear that consumer durables tend to have certain important features which mark them out as worthy of particularly close study.

A number of distinguishing features have been identified by commentators as particularly relevant in explaining the difficulty of forecasting effectively the demand for consumer durables. Purchases of durables are not regularly undertaken and because of their expense and the infrequency with which any durable is bought it is likely that a longer planning horizon will be involved before the purchase is completed than is the case with regularly purchased items. There is less scope for consumers to rely upon their own learning from the effects of previous purchases and the costs of an unwise choice may be high. 'Consumption' of a durable takes place over a considerable period of time and considerations of stock depreciation become particularly important. The ownership of a durable also often involves a commitment to future outlays on that item once the purchase has been paid for. Running costs can be particularly high, so too can the repair costs. This has prompted Ironmonger to make a distinction between the fixed costs of acquisition (the interest paid or foregone on the capital involved in the purchase) and the variable costs of use (depreciation, repairs, running costs) (Ironmonger 1972). Unlike other forms of purchase, the acquisition of durables is less likely to be financed out of current income. Often the price will be so high that accumulated savings will need to be drawn upon and consequently saving and durable purchasing are frequently found to be competitive activities (Ferber 1962; Pickering *et al* 1973a; Schipper 1964). The development of credit facilities through hire purchase, personal loans, credit cards etc, however, offers the opportunity to acquire a consumer durable before the household actually has the savings to pay for it.

It is also often suggested that because a durable does not have to be acquired for consumption within a certain limited time period, as for example with food, purchases can be delayed. Probably, it does not make much difference to a prospective first-time purchaser whether a deep freeze is bought this week or in two or three week's time. On the other hand, an owner of an item that had broken down and was irreparable might consider himself to be under almost as much pressure to make an immediate replacement purchase as he would be to buy food. Presumably it depends upon the household's perception of the utility that loss of the item would cause it to forego. Where there is an organised secondhand market for a product, an owner, feeling that the unit he owned was now becoming too old or unreliable, might again have discretion in deciding just when to trade it in and obtain a replacement.

These considerations perhaps help to suggest that there are certain features of those products that we term consumer durables that make a close relation between changes in outlays and changes in incomes unlikely. Purchases may be brought forward or they may be delayed. While it might be the case that at the same time some people are speeding up their purchases and others are delaying them, the general evidence is that the behaviour of consumers does not balance out, but that at some periods consumers as a group seem more likely to speed up their purchases and at other times they appear much more likely to defer purchases. Hence durable expenditures are particularly volatile.

In order to try to explain this phenomenon, Katona advanced the thesis that discretionary expenditures were a function not only of the ability to buy an item (income etc) but also of the willingness of consumers to spend their money. Consumers, he argued, are subject to waves of sentiment which cause changes in the willingness to buy and this phenomenon is measurable by means of sample survey techniques. This thesis had strong foundations in psychology where the stimulus-response paradigm was well recognised and in which social structural factors and attitudes together were considered to be joint determinants of conduct. In this case, the stimulus may be an income increase, a price change or some other change in the objective environment. The overt behavioural response would be an increase or decrease in purchases. But both the nature of the response and the stimulus itself are influenced by intervening variables – the motives, aspirations and attitudes of the consumer and his perception of the stimulus. The intervening variables are therefore indicators of the willingness to purchase and because the mechanism influencing these is unstable, they need to be re-estimated frequently through regular surveys. All other things being equal, the higher the level of confidence, the greater the likely level of wants and the higher the level of expenditure (see Katona 1951, 1960, 1964, 1972, 1975). However, it should be emphasised that demand in this model is seen as a function of both ability and willingness to purchase and expectational information is likely to be only an ingredient in a forecast, not a forecast in itself.

The critical problem is therefore to find an appropriate combination of psychological variables that will measure changes in willingness to buy as an aid to forecasting changes in consumer demand. Two rather different types of expectational variable have been identified and used in various empirical investigations; both are to be found in Katona's own work. The most frequently used is a measure of general economic confidence or consumer sentiment. This is normally based upon answers to a small number of questions dealing, for example, with the financial position and expectations of the household, expectations about the change in business conditions or unemployment, whether the present is considered a good or a bad time to buy consumer durables. It is presented as an index measuring changes through time. Different methods of scoring the answers have been adopted in different countries and while it is normally assumed that all questions carry an equal weight, the Gallup Poll index in Britain uses principal component loadings as a means of weighting the individual questions in index construction.

While the questions in the consumer sentiment approach do not relate to specific products, the second form of expectational measure is based upon questions asking explicitly about the respondent's intentions to buy specific durables – cars, televisions etc. within a specified period of time up to one or even two years ahead. Clearly, there is likely to be some sort of relationship between the two types of indicator but it is not altogether clear how that relationship is to be understood. Katona and others have argued that buying intentions come rather late in the temporal link between the formation of attitudes and actual purchases (Strumpel *et al* 1969; Katona 1972) and that the lag is too short for intentions to be very useful in prediction. Juster has argued that both attitude and intentions surveys are needed since attitudes may be a determinant of the purchase rates of non-intending households and intentions surveys are needed to provide data on the proportions of the sample that are intenders or non-intenders. He suggested that 'intentions can be viewed as one among many dimensions of optimism or as probabilistic statements of future actions, while attitudes can be viewed as the fundamental psychological determinant of behaviour, or as one among many determinants of intentions' (Juster 1969 p.168).

In fact Juster has pioneered a major extension of the buying intentions approach, whereby instead of giving dichotomous answers to the question 'do you expect to buy . . .', respondents are asked to state on a numerical purchase probability scale the chances that they will buy a specified item. He has claimed that this is a more efficient predictor of purchases than a buying intentions question because it helps to overcome the problem that in intentions surveys the bulk of purchases are made by non-intenders whose mean purchase rates vary through time (Juster 1964; 1966).

In general, it appears that psychological measures of attitudes have not been very successful in predicting social behaviour, indeed it has been observed that many of the attempts to predict overt behaviour from attitude measures have resulted in 'spectacular failures' (Lemon 1973). In his review, however, Lemon did not deal with the relation between attitudes and economic behaviour where the predictive performance of attitudes seems to have been more encouraging.

The measure of attitudes whose predictive performance has been most frequently appraised is the Index of Consumer Sentiment constructed by Survey Research Center, Michigan. Here, numerous studies have indicated that the index does add significantly to the predictive performance of a time series forecasting model, especially for new car purchases, (Adams 1964; Adams and Klein 1972; Dunkelberg 1969; Friend and Adams 1964; Katona 1975; Mueller 1963; Smith 1975). Shapiro, however, has claimed that the improvement in predictive power resulting from the inclusion of the index in a forecasting model is only significant if the model itself is very naive (Shapiro 1972). Hymans has suggested that the index should first be 'filtered' to take account of the consistency of the direction of change in the index value over successive quarters (Hymans 1970). This has also been supported by Juster and Wachtel who emphasised that it is a large or persistent attitude change that is most important for prediction (Juster and Wachtel 1972b). They found that an anticipations model that combined both attitudes and intentions outperformed a fully specified objective forecasting model for cars and improved upon a fully specified objective model for the forecasting of expenditure on cars and all durable items. Katona has reported that a change in the index leads a change in behaviour by six to nine months (Katona 1964) and has claimed that the value of the index is in its indication of the direction, rather than the magnitude, of changes in confidence, and hence in expenditure. Juster has confirmed that the index does indeed forecast the turning points (Juster 1969; Juster and Wachtel 1972a).

Testing of the time series performance of similar indices of consumer confidence for other countries has been less extensive but such studies also support the use of such an index. A similar Canadian index was shown to have good predictive value not only in forecasts of car expenditure but also on other durables and even services (Shapiro and Angevine 1969; Angevine 1974). A German index also performed well in explaining car expenditures but was less useful in forecasting purchases of other durables (Strumpel *et al* 1969).

There is some debate as to whether cross-sectional tests are important in appraising the predictive performance of expectational variables. Katona's own position on this is interesting. He has emphasised that his approach is inductive and based on the study of individuals because it is the individual that acts and it is necessary to have a micro-understanding of the forces that fashion the aggregates (Katona 1951, 1975). However he has also claimed that explanation at the individual level is not necessary: 'Economics is concerned with an increase or a decrease in the total number of cars bought or to be bought in a given period, but not with whether or not John Smith or Jim Miller bought or will buy a car' (Katona 1972 p.562), and again 'the objective of micro-economic analyses is not the description of individual cases' (Katona 1975 p.50). Certainly, this is reassuring in view of the apparently stronger association between attitudes and purchases in time series than in cross-sectional analyses. It is also supported by Adams who commented on this phenomenon that 'the time series effect must be explained, at least in substantial part, in terms of relationships which do not have a basis in the micro-economic effect of attitudes' (Adams 1965 p.378).

Other commentators (e.g. Tobin 1959), however, would argue that reinterview tests are important and this is a view with which we would agree. Prediction of changes in economic aggregates is likely to be much more confident and reliable if it can be shown that the model on which it is based does have empirical validity in terms of individual responses. Of course, one should not expect there to be complete similarity between the results for the two types of test. For example, there may be some variable in respect of which different members of the population differ markedly and this may prove significant in explaining variations in behaviour between individuals. But if the values of this variable do not change through time its significance in a time series test will be much reduced or non-existent. Conversely, there might be an attitude which is held in more or less equal measure by all households but the values of which are prone to shift markedly through time and can be shown to be associated with shifts in behaviour. Here too then the cross-section into time-series transformation will not hold. In general, however, it seems likely that there will be at least some link between cross-sectional and time-series evidence, though equal explanatory performance in the two types of test is almost certainly not to be looked for.

In practice it has often been found that the cross-sectional explanatory performance of confidence variables has been disappointing (Adams 1965; Juster 1969; Tobin 1959). One possible explanation has been that to take a period of a year over which to observe behaviour in relation to attitudes expressed at the beginning of that year is too long a period of time to expect attitudes to continue to have an influence on individual behaviour. However, other investigations have suggested that there may indeed be a cross-sectional relation between attitudes and buyer behaviour. Klein and Lansing found that attitudes did help to discriminate between buyers and non-buyers (Klein and Lansing 1955) and Dunkelberg found that measures of attitudes and buying intentions were significant, together with incomes and information on whether the household had moved home, in explaining both expenditure levels and whether or not particular durables were purchased (Dunkelberg 1972). In an investigation based upon the first set of surveys in our own research, we found that various types of attitudinal and expectational variable did have explanatory power. They tended to be at least as important as socio-economic variables and together explained up to a quarter of the variance in recorded expenditures by households on consumer durables over a fourteen month period (Pickering and Isherwood 1975). They also contributed to successful discrimination between new and used car buyers and other types of consumer durable purchaser (Isherwood and Pickering 1975).

Rather less attention appears to have been paid to the possibility of refinements to the questions used in the construction of an index of consumer confidence. It has been shown that the variables used in the Survey Research Centre Index of Consumer Sentiment are highly intercorrelated (Adams 1965) and this suggests that the actual psychological field that is tapped by these questions is rather limited. In fact, the Survey Research Centre investigations do ask questions relating to a number of other possible aspects of consumer confidence. But it has been concluded that their inclusion in the index would not offer a consistent improvement in the performance of the index though they continue to offer considerable insight into the reasons for particular types of consumer behaviour (Katona 1974). We have, however, suggested that in further attempts to construct an index of consumer confidence it would be desirable to introduce questions relating to other variables which appear to be associated with purchase behaviour, to adopt a multipoint rating scale in order that more incisive answers can be given and to use principal components analysis as a means of weighting the various questions on which an index of consumer confidence is based (Pickering, *et al* 1973a).

Frequent, large-scale surveys of consumers are, of course, expensive and some attention has also been paid to the question of whether other, objective, economic variables can be used as a proxy for a sentiment measure. It has been suggested that the Index of Consumer Sentiment is a stable function of a limited number of objective financial and other

variables which could, therefore, be used in place of survey information
(Shapiro 1972) and that eighty per cent of the variance in the Index
values could be predicted using variables such as lagged personal
disposable income, changes in share prices and the ratio of prices
between quarters (Hymans 1970). Another attempt was made to
simulate such an index using a proxy for interest rates, the change in the
consumption deflator and the rate of overall unemployment. The
composite of these variables appeared to perform quite well but, on
balance, not as well as survey data (Angevine 1974). It has also been
claimed that employment conditions cover much of the variation in
attitudes (Adams and Green 1965).

That attitudes are related to some extent to recent developments in
objective economic variables is not to be wondered at and Katona has
argued that this is often the case (Katona 1960). But it seems clear that
the pattern of attitudinal response to particular changes in objective
variables cannot always be predicted, especially when a major change in
attitudes, and hence in behaviour, is about to occur. Consequently it
seems to be agreed that it is useful to survey directly changes in
consumer attitudes in order to pick up particular influences and changes
that are not readily predictable from objective economic variables (see
Adams and Green 1965; Angevine 1974; Katona 1960). It is also
appropriate to point out that if a wider psychological 'field' is tapped, as
suggested in an earlier paper (Pickering *et al* 1973a), the chances that
objective variables could be used instead may correspondingly decline.

The other main type of expectational variable that has frequently been
used for forecasting purposes is the measure of buying intentions for
particular durables or, as developed by Juster and used by others, the
purchase probability scale. In a time series context, it seems to be
generally agreed that intentions data are not significant when attitudes
are also included in a predictive model (e.g. Adams 1964; Adams and
Klein 1972; Friend and Adams 1964; Juster 1966; Mueller 1963;
Shapiro and Angevine 1969). Juster has suggested that this is due to the
fact that the mean achieved purchase rates of intenders and
non-intenders are not constant over time. Juster's subsequent work has
involved an appraisal of the performance of a series based on both
buying intentions data and, for more recent years, purchase probability
values. This has led him to conclude that such measures are related to
purchases but that they are less effective than attitudes at predicting
turning points (Juster 1969), that they do contribute to the explanation of
trend and cyclical movements in purchase rates, but that they are
sluggish in reflecting the full extent of the cyclical movement (Juster and
Wachtel 1972a). Since buying intentions and purchase probability data
are product-specific it might be anticipated that the quality of the

predictive performance will vary between different products. It has been suggested that intentions may be particularly useful when demand for the product is developing in a way that is different from the general trend in demand (Katona 1964) and that intentions are more reliable predictors in the case of items where demand is largely initial rather than for replacement purposes (Heald 1970).

Rather greater attention has been paid to the cross-sectional performance of intentions and probability data than has been the case with attitudes. The general position is that most commentators agree that measures of buying intentions do make a significant contribution in cross-sectional explanatory tests (Adams 1964; Dunkelberg 1969). However while higher proportions of intenders made purchases, it still remained the case that non-intenders accounted for the majority of purchases and of the variation of purchase rates (Juster 1966, Katona 1960, Theil and Kosobod 1968). It was in an effort to deal with this problem that Juster advocated the use of an eleven point probability scale. He has shown that such scales do have good predictive power, though they tend to underestimate the actual level of purchases (Juster 1964, 1966, 1969).

In a British study using purchase probability scaling it was found that the proportion of respondents actually making a purchase tended to rise markedly as the probability value increased but nearly two-thirds of all purchases were still made by households that had stated a zero purchase probability for that particular item (Gabor and Granger 1972/73). In our own earlier investigations of this question we found several reasons for concluding that purchase probability data had considerable cross-sectional predictive power (Pickering and Isherwood 1974). We found that purchase probabilities (other than for furniture) accounted for a high proportion of the variation in actual purchase rates among respondents. Purchase rates rose as subjective purchase probability values increased, purchasers had much higher mean purchase probabilities than non-purchasers and the number of units of an item actually purchased was reasonably well predicted using mean purchase probability values. Juster suggested that American purchase probability data under-predicted purchases. We found some evidence that this was so in the case of products that appeared to have short planning horizons, as evidenced by a high ratio of three month to twelve month purchase probabilities, but purchases were over-predicted where a low ratio of three to twelve month purchase probabilities indicated a long planning horizon or perhaps an indication of some interest in the product rather than a real expectation of purchasing in the reasonably near future. It was, however, still the case that rather more than fifty per cent of all purchases were made by respondents who had stated a zero purchase probability. To that extent it would appear that probability scaling still had not resolved the problem that a majority of purchases were made by 'non-intenders'. However, in a more extensive investigation of the ability to discriminate between different types of durable purchaser and especially the buyers of motor cars from other types of consumer, using various types of survey data, we found that stated probabilities of purchasing motor cars made a major contribution to the overall discriminatory power of the analysis (Isherwood and Pickering 1975).

There are two other approaches to the analysis of the demand for durables which have proved of interest to our work and upon which we have also attempted to build. The first is that concerned with the establishment of a consumer's priority pattern by measuring consumer preferences directly and, associated with it, the assessment using cross-sectional data of an order of acquisition, which may be viewed as a revealed preference indication of a priority pattern (McFall 1969; Paroush 1965; Pyatt 1964). This is a technique that is not appropriate for the handling of questions of replacement demand but it does help to build up a picture of the order in which consumer durables are accumulated. The evidence from most studies is that a reasonably unique order of acquisition can be identified. This would suggest that consumers do not normally exercise much discretion with regard to the order in which durables are acquired for the first time. However, this approach offers no evidence on the possible influences affecting the speed with which households acquire all the items in a given set of durables or on decision-making with regard to the timing of replacement purchases or the choice between replacing an existing product and making an initial acquisition of another durable.

Certainly the studies referred to above offered interesting insights into the apparent order in which different durables were added to the household's stock. Our earlier investigation of this technique allowed us to offer some extension to the statistical procedures advocated by Pyatt and led to further interesting conclusions (Hebden and Pickering 1974). We found that a set of leisure durables (black and white, and colour television, record player, tape recorder and caravan) did appear to be acquired in a fairly unique order, though higher social class respondents seemed likely to acquire a colour television rather earlier in the set than those in lower social class groups. Less unique patterns were found to exist when basic domestic utilities and household luxuries (vacuum cleaner, washing machine, refrigerator and spin dryer; and deep freeze, fridge/deep freeze, dishwasher and floor polisher respectively) were analysed. However, we did find that when the two groups were combined the domestic utilities were likely to be acquired before the household luxuries.

It has been argued (Pyatt 1964; McFall 1969) that only homogeneous products should be used to make up sets of goods for a priority pattern analysis. We did, however, test two heterogeneous sets (second car, colour television, deep freeze and dishwasher; and vacuum cleaner, first car, second car, colour television and deep freeze respectively) and found that in both cases reasonably unique orders of acquisition could be established. In the latter set we did however find some evidence of a life cycle effect, in that first cars and colour televisions were likely to be purchased earlier by those married less long, while respondents married for a longer time appeared to give a deep freeze a relatively higher priority.

As we have already indicated, this technique does not seem to be particularly suitable for forecasting purposes as such, but it does have considerable possibilities as a means of obtaining greater insight into consumer acquisition processes and as an aid in market segmentation. We also found that in some cases the 'probability' of acquiring a specified item next in the sequence became negative. This was a phenomenon that did not seem to have been encountered in Pyatt's investigations (it would not have been noticed in the other studies because their statistical outputs were insufficiently informative). While there are a number of possible statistical explanations that might account for this, in several instances we concluded that one durable item had become 'inferior' in terms of another item in the set and that households were abandoning the 'inferior' item in favour of a 'superior' one. It appeared, for example, that black and white televisions became 'inferior' in relation to colour televisions and fridge/deep freezes became 'inferior' in relation to deep freezes.

The concept of inferior goods in economics normally has a budget connotation. In the case of the results discussed here there is no direct cross-sectional budget influence. Rather it is suggested that two products may have the ability to satisfy similar types of want or provide a particular type of utility – visual entertainment, the opportunity to preserve foodstuffs etc. When the rival products are compared one may have greater ability to satisfy these wants than the other and so in this sense an inferior product is one that has less want satisfying power or, in other words, a lower rating in terms of the quantity of relevant characteristics. In the early stages of the acquisition of durables the effect of price differences or the unavailability of the 'superior' item may leave the consumer with little choice but to buy the 'inferior' product, but as household real income increases and product innovations occur so the opportunity to exercise a positive choice in favour of the product with superior characteristics becomes more attractive.

This leads on naturally to the final contribution to demand analysis on which this research has drawn. In an important work, Lancaster has argued that demand analysis should deal more explicitly with objective information about the characteristics of the product itself and has suggested that people should be considered as buying characteristics rather than goods as such (Lancaster 1966; 1971). In a study focussing particularly on new commodities Ironmonger has also adopted a similar position, arguing that consumers have various separate wants which may be satisfied by the particular characteristics of items that are purchased. Recognition that new commodities represent a change in the characteristics available in products means that the introduction of new commodities or of quality changes can be handled within a demand analysis framework whereas if the approach is based on the product, rather than its characteristics or want-satisfying powers, normal demand theory cannot handle this important phenomenon (Ironmonger 1972).

We have already shown how analysis based on the characteristics of a product helped in the explanation of the possible meaning of negative 'probabilities' of acquisition when a priority patterning approach was adopted to assess the uniqueness of the order of acquisition of different sets of consumer durables. In practice, a number of different types of characteristic may be identified for the same product. There may be objective characteristics – e.g. the power, accommodation, price etc. of a motor car on which Lancaster based his empirical tests of the efficiency of the characteristic mixes of a number of different types of car (Lancaster 1971). It is also likely that consumers will have perceptions about the characteristics of different products. Some of these may be related to objectively measurable features of the product while others may reflect more strongly subjective and social considerations.

Our interest in this study is not with brand choice but with decisions whether or not to buy particular types of consumer durable. We hypothesised that more favourable consumer perceptions of the characteristics of a product would indicate a greater likelihood that it would be purchased. This is one of the tests that we shall report later in this study. We did, however, also investigate, using data from our first set of surveys, whether different products could be distinguished on the basis of consumer perceptions of these characteristics (Pickering *et al* 1973b).

Thus our approach to the use of characteristics in demand analysis is different from that of Lancaster in that we emphasise psychological perceptions of products whereas Lancaster was concerned with comparing differences in objectively measurable characteristics between brands. In general it was found that the characteristics used were successful discriminators and the pattern of perceptions of the strength with which common characteristics were associated with each product indicated that the seventeen consumer durables used in that analysis could be classified into groups with similar patterns of strengths of characteristics. The groups identified were described as utilities (washing machine, furniture, cooker, vacuum cleaner, refrigerator, spin dryer); luxuries (fridge/deep freeze. floor polisher, deep freeze, dishwasher); leisure goods (caravan, colour television, tape recorder, record player, black and white television); car; and central heating. From this work it appeared likely that measures of subjective perceptions of the characteristics of a particular product and the change in these perceptions through time could also have a role in predicting likely rates of market penetration of new products.

It will be apparent that behavioural approaches to the analysis and understanding of consumer durable buying behaviour include a number of different emphases and are currently in a state of development. The purpose of the work reported in the following chapters is to test the general hypothesis that behavioural information derived direct from consumers has an important role in explaining cross-sectional variations in consumer durable buying behaviour. From this it is hoped that understanding of the factors influencing consumer discretionary buying behaviour will be enhanced and that a clearer indication may be available regarding the sort of influences that may prove to be relevant for time-series forecasting of the demand for consumer durables.

2 The survey methodology

Sample procedure

It was decided that the most cost-effective way of utilising the research funds available for this investigation would be to take a panel of households that would be personally interviewed at the start of the investigation and followed up at quarterly intervals for the following twelve months. In this way an extensive set of information about the households, their attitudes, expectations, changes in circumstances and their durable purchasing behaviour could be built up. In order to eke out the funds still further and to allow a larger initial sample size, arrangements were made for all follow-ups to be conducted by post and handled by the researchers themselves. It was recognised that there was a risk that this would depress and possibly bias the response. But we had experimented with a single postal follow-up after fourteen months in our earlier surveys and had been encouraged by the results.

The initial interviews and sample selection were the responsibility of a commercial market research company that had been selected on the basis of competitive tender for our earlier investigations. On the basis of the funds available it was decided that the achieved sample should be at least 600 and we gave guidance regarding the desired distribution of the sample. Our objective was to ensure that the distribution of the sample by income should reflect the contribution of different household income groups to total consumer expenditure on consumer durables as indicated in the *Family Expenditure Survey* reports. This meant that the sample would be skewed towards the higher income groups. In practice there is no method by which a researcher can establish income levels before making an initial contact with a household. Indications of the social class status of particular areas had to be used as the basis for sample stratification on the assumption that social class was a reasonable proxy for total household income. In fact the outcome of this sampling procedure was that representation of the higher household income groups was somewhat greater than we had intended and representation of the lower income groups, especially those with incomes in 1972 before £1500, was lower than had been hoped for. It is likely that this was due to a combination of influences including a greater reluctance of the lower income groups to participate, the imperfect relationship between social class status and household income and the consequences of the deliberate exclusion of families where the head of the household (HoH) was over sixty-five or a student.

The sample was drawn from a randomly selected sample of thirty parliamentary constituencies in Great Britain, and a wide geographical spread was obtained from the constituencies sampled. Within each constituency two wards were selected that met the stratification requirements and two starting addresses were selected at random from the appropriate electoral register. Interviewers called at all the addresses on a prescribed random walk from each starting address and worked to fill a specified social class quota requirement. Recalls were carried out on those found not to be at home at the time of the first visit.

In this way a reasonably random selection of households was made. Instructions were given that interviews were to include at least the head of the household though we did not mind if the spouse was also present. In order to increase the chances that the proportion responding to the postal follow-ups would be as high as possible, interviewers were instructed to explain at the outset the nature of the participation that would be involved in the follow-ups and only to interview those that were willing to co-operate over the whole year. In fact, it appears that very few people refused to participate because of the follow-ups, though rather more were unwilling to be interviewed because of the nature of the study or the length of the initial interview, which was expected to take at least one hour.

In all, 610 effective interviews were completed between 4 March and 23 March 1972. 332 interviews were conducted jointly with the male head of household and his wife, 242 with the male head of household only and thirty-six with the female head of household. The distribution of the respondents according to basic information about their socio-economic status is set out in Tables 2.1 and 2.2.

There are always a number of respondents who will not or cannot indicate their income levels. We went to considerable lengths, using jumbled letters relating to income levels on a prompt card to avoid the respondent having to state any sort of number in order to minimise non-response to this question. As a result rather less than seven per cent of respondents did not state their own income levels. This is an encouragingly low proportion. It is to be expected that a greater number

TABLE 2.1 Analysis of sample by household income and income of the head of the household

Income of Head of Household £	Household Income £									
	less than 1000	1000-1499	1500-1999	2000-2499	2500-2999	3000-3999	4000-5999	6000 and over	not available	Total
less than 1000	31	5	1	1	–	–	–	–	2	40
1000-1499	–	34	18	9	3	–	1	–	3	68
1500-1999	–	–	73	29	7	9	1	–	2	121
2000-2499	–	–	–	65	22	13	1	–	10	111
2500-2999	–	–	–	–	45	26	8	1	5	85
3000-3999	–	–	–	–	–	61	17	1	4	83
4000-5999	–	–	–	–	–	–	34	3	3	40
6000 and over	–	–	–	–	–	–	–	18	3	21
not available	–	–	–	–	–	–	–	–	41	41
Total	31	39	92	104	77	109	62	23	73	610

TABLE 2.2 Analysis of sample by age and
social class status of the head
of the household

	Social Class						
Age	A	B	C_1	C_2	D	E	Total
16-24	—	3	5	9	5	—	22
25-34	13	57	41	21	2	4	138
35-44	51	55	45	27	6	2	186
45-54	35	48	37	22	14	3	159
55-64	17	23	29	18	17	1	105
Total	116	186	157	97	44	10	610

Definition of social classes:

A   higher managerial, administrative or
professional
B   intermediate managerial, administrative
or professional
C_1 supervisory or clerical or junior managerial, administrative or professional
C_2 skilled manual workers
D   semi-skilled and unskilled manual
workers
E   those at the lowest level of subsistence

These definitions are those agreed by JICNAR
(Joint Industry Committee for National
Readership Surveys)

of respondents will be unable to assess their total household income but
it is again encouraging that as many as eighty-eight per cent of the
sample were able to answer this question. In the case of both the income
of the HoH and of the household, those failing to answer this question
were proportionately more likely to be in the age group
fifty-five–sixty-four and in social classes A or C_1. A detailed description
of the characteristics of the sample will be found in Chapter 3.

Response patterns

As our interest was particularly in the opportunity to study the durable
purchasing behaviour of the sample households over a period of time it

was clearly important to maximise the response rate to the postal questionnaires. There was unfortunately no possibility of offering any financial or other inducement to those participating to return the questionnaires and we had to rely entirely upon the goodwill of the panel and their interest in the subject for continued co-operation. All the follow-up questionnaires were sent out punctually on the working day nearest to 1 July, 1 October 1972 and 1 January and 1 April 1973. They were kept as short as possible though they still averaged four or more pages.

The pattern of responses is set out in Tables 2.3 and 2.4. 190 (thirty-one per cent) did not complete any postal questionnaires and were lost after the initial interview, despite attempts over the first six months of the postal reinterviews to obtain a reply. 300 respondents completed all four postal questionnaires and a further sixty-three completed the final questionnaire but had failed to return one or more of the intervening postal reinterview schedules. Of these, fifty-four missed

TABLE 2.3 Replies at each stage of the research

	Number of replies	
Survey I	Personal interview March 1972	610
Survey II	First postal follow-up July 1972	366
Survey III	Second postal follow-up October 1972	367
Survey IV	Third postal follow-up January 1973	359
Survey V	Fourth postal follow-up April 1973	363

TABLE 2.4 Analysis of individual response patterns to postal follow-ups

	Number	*per cent*
No response to postal follow-ups	190	31
Died/became untraceable during survey	11	2
Some follow-ups completed but not final questionnaire	46	8
Finished survey but one or more stages missing	63	10
Completed all four postal follow-ups	300	49

just one postal follow-up, this was more likely to have been the first follow-up than the second or third. In order to minimise the effects of a missing response a supplementary questionnaire was sent out with the next postal questionnaire after the non-response to cover basic factual information relating to the period for which no questionnaire had been completed at the time. In this way, a more or less complete picture about actual buyer behaviour can be assumed to have been compiled for 363 respondents, that is just on sixty per cent of the original panel. The number of completed questionnaires from each postal follow-up was also around 360.

The fact that so many people failed to complete one questionnaire but subsequently participated in later stages of the survey indicates that users of panel data will be able to sustain response rates if they persevere with reminders and further questionnaires to non-respondents. It suggests that forgetfulness and pressure of other events can be quite important reasons for non-response. The experience reported here also indicates that the chances of respondents dropping out were three times higher at the time of the first postal follow-up than at all other stages of the survey put together.

It is important to investigate the extent to which the propensity to complete or not to complete the postal questionnaires was associated with observable characteristics of the informant. Attention was paid to response by social class, age, income, geographical location and respondent attitudes. In order to keep the number of tables to manageable proportions only two analyses of response behaviour are recorded here. Tables 2.5 and 2.6 show that respondents in social classes D and E and with household incomes below £1,500 were more likely not to respond at all to the postal questionnaires and hence were less likely to complete the survey than respondents in the other social class groups. We also found that respondents who were unwilling or unable to state either the income of the HoH and/or the total household income were less likely to complete the postal questionnaires. In fact this was proportionately more noticeable in the case of failure to provide information on the income of the HoH where, since the respondent was the HoH, it can be assumed this was a direct refusal to answer the question. It seems therefore that it can be assumed that a refusal to provide income information will indicate that the chances of further co-operation from the informant will be lower than with those who were not apparently resistant to this question.

There is no evidence that the age of the HoH has any bearing on response rates. In contrast, however, there is evidence that respondents can be distinguished from non-respondents in respect of their attitudes and general expectations so far as the purchase of consumer durables was concerned. As will be explained in Chapter 5, all respondents were asked to complete a set of twenty-nine semantic differential scales dealing with their attitudes and expectations regarding various aspects of the general economic situation and the household's position and expectations and their anticipation of purchasing consumer durables. There were four respects in which reinterviewed respondents as a group differed significantly from non-respondents in their attitudes. Compared with those completing the postal follow-ups, those who failed to complete the survey were less likely to have reported at the first interviews that they expected to buy a motor car in the following twelve months, they were more likely to have reported that they were not saving up to buy any consumer durables, that they would not be able to finance durable purchases from their savings and to have indicated that durable purchases would be dependent upon a temporary increase in their incomes. In other words, non-respondents to the postal surveys were rather more likely to be those who had much lower expectations of making purchases of consumer durables and had lesser financial abilities to do so. We had, of course, emphasised that replies were needed from all members of the sample whether they had bought a durable item or not but it does appear that non-respondents were more

TABLE 2.5 Individual response patterns analysed by social class

	Social Class					Per cent
	A	B	C_1	C_2	DE	Number
No response to postal follow-ups	26	28	32	33	46	190
Died/became untraceable during survey	3	2	2	1	0	11
Some follow-ups completed but not final questionnaire	10	6	10	6	6	46
Finished survey but one or more stage missing	13	9	10	7	13	63
Completed all four postal follow-ups	48	55	46	53	35	300
Number	116	186	157	97	54	610

TABLE 2.6 Individual response patterns analysed by total household income

Total Household Income £

	less than 1000	1000- 1499	1500- 1999	2000- 2499	2500- 2999	3000- 3999	4000- 5999	6000 and over	not avail- able	Number
	percentages									
No response to postal follow-ups	61	46	27	31	27	24	19	30	41	190
Died/became untraceable during survey	0	0	3	3	1	2	2	0	1	11
Some follow-ups completed but not final questionnaire	3	8	12	3	9	10	10	9	5	46
Finished survey but one or more stage missing	6	3	12	10	10	10	15	13	8	63
Completed all four postal follow-ups	29	44	46	54	52	54	55	48	44	300
Number	31	39	92	104	77	109	62	23	73	610

likely to be drawn from those expecting to spend less on durables and who may therefore have felt that their answers were less likely to be of immediate relevance to the investigation. Since there is some correlation between social class and income on the one hand and durable purchasing expectations and attitudes on the other we cannot say with certainty which was the cause of the lower response rate among such people. It is also likely that the need to complete postal questionnaires will militate against the co-operation of those with less literary facility who may also be of lower socio-economic status.

All cases of non-response are unfortunate as they involve a loss of information, a waste of effort on the initial fieldwork and the inevitable uncertainty as to whether the information obtained from those who do respond is systematically biased and so is likely to weaken the confidence with which conclusions can be drawn from the available data. The effect of non-response in this investigation has been to heighten the skewness which we deliberately sought in the initial sample in order to over-represent the groups that spend more heavily on durables. Granted the size of the sample and the nature of the data it seems pointless to try to re-weight the observations in order to increase the importance of those groups that are under-represented. It should therefore be borne in mind that our observations over-represent those socio-economic groups that are known to spend the largest amounts per family on consumer durables but also that from the original sample those indicating a lesser likelihood of buying such items are under-represented in the postal follow-up information on actual buyer behaviour.

The existence of non-response has also posed a problem regarding the observations to be used at each stage of the analysis. In order to make the maximum use of all the information collected the decision has been to base the analysis on all informants at that stage where at all possible. Thus where a section requires information drawn only from the initial interviews the base for this analysis will be all 610 respondents. Where the analysis requires information from the postal surveys the base will be just those respondents who provided the requisite data, in practice this will often mean the 363 respondents completing the final postal survey.

Questionnaire content

Together the initial survey and the four postal follow-up questionnaires produced about 1000 different pieces of basic information, before any computations or conversions of the raw data had been undertaken. It is not therefore feasible to elaborate at this point each individual question. The Appendix at the end of the study reproduces the questions and the coding categories (p.235). The type of information collected can, however, be readily summarised under a number of separate heads.

1.   *Basic data on the socio-economic status of the informant and his household.* This covered questions relating to social class, age, marital status and the length of time the HoH had been married, the number of people in the household, whether the household income could be readily increased and if so by what method and by how much, the income of the HoH and the total household income. These questions were asked in the first survey only.

2.   *Financial position and expectations.* Use of credit in its different forms, methods of saving and the levels of saving and credit outstanding, whether households were saving up to purchase particular consumer durables, expectations regarding the levels of expenditure on durables over the next three and twelve months, likely changes in the informant's level of savings and usage of credit. These questions were asked in the first survey only.

3.   *Attitudinal data.* An identical battery of twenty-nine seven-point semantic differential scales was self-completed by each informant in each of the five surveys. These covered the respondent's personal financial and employment expectations, attitudes towards the economic condition of the country, attitudes to the purchase of durables and to savings, expectations regarding price trends and expectations of purchasing consumer durables.

4.   *Ownership of particular consumer durables.* The durables covered were black and white television, car, central heating, colour television, cooker, deep freeze, dishwasher, record player, refrigerator, tape recorder, vacuum cleaner, washing machine. Questions dealt with whether the item was owned and the number of each item owned, the age of the item and the length of time it had been owned, the way in which it was obtained, whether credit was outstanding on it, the chances that it would require major attention and if this did happen whether the respondent would repair, replace or abandon it. This information was collected in the first survey. In the fifth survey information was collected on the order in which the durables owned by the household had been acquired and on the one item not currently owned that the household would most like to acquire next.

5.   *Purchase probabilities.* In the first survey respondents were asked to indicate on a 0–10 scale the chances that they or a member of

their household would purchase specified durables within the following three, six or twelve months. In addition to the items mentioned in *4* (above) carpets and furniture were also included in the questioning and new and used cars were distinguished. In the postal surveys, buying expectations over the next twelve months were recorded on a seven point verbal scale.

6.   Perception of the characteristics of consumer durables. A battery of nineteen nine-point semantic differential scales on the characteristics of consumer durables, especially as they relate to the decision-making process, was completed for each item listed under *4* (above). In order to keep the number of scales to manageable proportions, each informant completed batteries relating to only six commodities. The items to be rated were randomly determined for each informant and the proportion of those completing the scales for each item who actually owned that item was very close to the proportion owning it in the sample as a whole.

7.   Durable purchase behaviour. In each of the postal follow-ups, that is surveys II–V, respondents reported which of the consumer durables constituting the key items in the survey they had purchased during the previous three months and the total amounts spent on these, net of any trade-in allowances. Qualitative explanations of the reasons for durable purchase decisions – both buying and deciding not to buy – were also recorded by the informant.

8.   Change in circumstances over the year. In each of the postal follow-ups, surveys II–V, information was collected on whether the income of the HoH and of the household as a whole and the level of the household's savings had changed over the previous three months. In the final survey similar questions were also asked relating to changes over the year as a whole together with questions dealing with other expenditures and events during the previous year.

With so many items of information it is clearly possible to go on almost indefinitely testing relationships between variables. The chapters that follow do not therefore report exhaustive tests of all possible associations though they do cover an extremely wide range of hypotheses that have been tested. In some cases negative findings, the failure to find support for a hypothesis, can be as interesting as a positive finding and these have been included where appropriate. A balance has to be struck between text and tables and it has often proved necessary to make statements without demonstrating the tabular information underlying the findings. Where an assertion is made that there is an association between two variables, this is made on the basis of appropriate statistical testing, though it also has to be recognised that routine identification of formal statistical associations has to be tempered by an awareness that the practical importance of an observation may not necessarily coincide with a measure of its statistical significance.

3   *The characteristics of the sample*

In this chapter we shall consider some of the basic features of the sample and the interrelations between variables that will be of particular relevance in the analysis reported in subsequent chapters. The discussion here relates to all 610 respondents.

Socio-economic status

The main socio-economic status variables with which we shall be concerned are social class, the age of the HoH, the length of time the HoH had been married, the number of people in the household, the income of the HoH, and total household income.

There tends to be a strong degree of association between some of the pairs of variables. The two income measures are highly correlated and social class is also correlated with income, rather more so with income of the HoH than with total household income. In our sample we also found that there was some association between social class and the age of the HoH; the length of time he had been married and the number of people in the household. This would not necessarily be found in larger samples. The distributions here indicate that those in the lower social class categories (especially social class D) tended on average to be slightly older and to have been married longer than those in other social class categories. Higher social class groups in this sample showed some tendency to have slightly larger households. Both income of the HoH and of the household were positively associated with household size, though the degree of correlation was low.

In several important respects there are examples of non-linearity in the distribution of variables. We find that for those in the thirty-five–forty-four age group, household size and income levels (both of the HoH and the household) were at their peak (see Tables 3.1

TABLE 3.1 Distribution of household size by age of head of household

Household size, percentages

	1	2	3	4	5-7	8 & over	Total	Number	Mean Value
16-24	4.5	40.9	45.5	9.1	0	0	100	22	2.6
25-34	2.2	24.6	24.6	33.3	15.2	0	100	138	3.5
35-44	1.6	10.2	11.3	40.9	36.0	0	100	186	4.3
45-54	4.4	23.9	26.4	30.8	13.2	1.3	100	159	3.4
55-64	9.5	47.6	25.7	11.4	2.9	2.9	100	105	2.7
Number	24	150	134	185	112	5		610	3.6

(Row group label: Age of Head of Household)

Note: mean values are calculated assuming that the mean size of the 5-7 group is six and that the mean of the 8 and over group is eight.

TABLE 3.2 Average income analysed by age of head of household

	Total household income		Income of head of household	
	£		£	
Age of HoH	Mean	Median	Mean	Median
16-24	1977	1800	1591	1500
25-34	2831	2450	2546	2275
35-44	3095	2800	2720	2530
45-54	2949	2640	2500	2250
55-64	2485	2085	2135	1875
Average overall	2850	2515	2547	2250

TABLE 3.3 Average income analysed by duration of marriage

	Total household income		Income of head of household	
	£		£	
Duration of marriage	Mean	Median	Mean	Median
0-4 years	2450	2460	2240	1975
5-9 years	3003	2460	2710	2260
10-20 years	2888	2750	2780	2535
Over 20 years	2902	2515	2510	2175
Average overall	2937	2600	2627	2300

Note to Tables 3.2 and 3.3 — the average value for the largest income group was assumed to be £7000, that for the smallest group was assumed to be £750. In all other cases the mid point of the income group was used. There were fewer observations used in calculating Table 3.3 as some of the informants were not married. This explains the difference in the overall averages compared with those shown in Table 3.2

and 3.2). As Table 3.3 indicates, a similar pattern is found to exist when incomes are compared with the duration of marriage. Here the peaking of incomes occurs for those married between ten and twenty years. Clearly this is not normally independent of the age of the HoH.

There is some suggestion in the data that second incomes (that is the difference between household income and income of the HoH) impart a smoothing effect on the level of total household income as compared with the variation in the income of the HoH alone. The evidence on this is not strong but is intuitively acceptable and is worth testing on a larger scale. If it were generally found to be the case the implications would be interesting. They would indicate that the largest contribution to total household income by the wife was likely to occur at the time when the income of the head of the household was relatively lower. In this way second incomes help to exercise a stabilising effect on total household income and could therefore be justification for viewing an existing total household income level at the start of marriage as not far from a permanent income in real terms even though at some stages in the life cycle it would be anticipated that the wife would not be working. In our final survey, we asked about the number of people in each household that had been working full time over the survey year. Relating this to information on the length of time the HoH had been married we found that the average number of people working full time per household was 1.7 for those married less than five years; 1.3 for those married five–nine years; 1.6 for those married ten–nineteen years and 1.7 for those married twenty or more years. This therefore gives further weak support for this hypothesis.

Financial circumstances

Questions about the financial position of a respondent are among the most likely to arouse antagonism. Consequently, cautious and, in some cases, not unduly probing questions were asked in this area. Information was obtained on whether the respondent had a bank account; the forms of savings used; an assessment of the size of the savings; how the level of savings had changed over the previous twelve months; the use of hire purchase and other credit facilities; what durable items were currently being purchased on HP and whether the household's income could be temporarily and readily increased and, if so, how.

Eighty-nine per cent of the sample had a bank account, those that did not were rather more likely to be in the lower social class and income groups and the HoH was likely to be either rather older than average and married a longer time or less than twenty-five years old. Table 3.4

TABLE 3.4 Percentages of sample using various methods of saving

Method	used by, per cent
Life assurance policies	61
Deposit account in bank	40
Building societies	38
Allow savings to build up in a current account	34
Post Office/savings bank	27
Shares/unit trusts	21
Save As You Earn (SAYE)	8

indicates the proportions in the sample using different modes of saving. An average of 2.3 modes was recorded for each household. Life assurance was easily the most frequently mentioned method, followed at some distance by bank deposit accounts, current accounts and building society accounts.

Life assurance policies as a form of saving were most likely to be used by higher social class and income groups and those with larger families. Unmarried HoHs were less likely to use life assurance as a form of saving. Bank deposit accounts were more likely to be used by those where the HoH was earning between £1500 and £3000 a year. They were less likely to be used by unmarried respondents. The use of bank current accounts as a form of saving tended to occur more frequently amongst households where total household income and that of the HoH were in the region of £2000–3000, and amongst those whose occupations would place them in social class B. Social classes A, B and C_1 were most likely to be depositing funds in building societies and this form of saving was also associated with cases where the income of the HoH was in the region of £2000–£6000. Accounts with the Post Office or a savings bank were used mostly by households with lower incomes, especially below £2000. The purchase of shares and unit trust units was particularly associated with social classes A and B and the proportion using this form rose as income levels increased. *SAYE*, perhaps as befits a more recent form of savings opportunity, was rather more likely to be adopted by those married a shorter period of time, though the proportions using this at all were so small that it would be unwise to place much emphasis upon this finding.

This information is not intuitively surprising. It confirms that share purchase, life assurance and, to a lesser degree, building society deposits are more likely to be forms of saving used by the higher income and social class groups. Those with incomes and occupations that would probably categorise them as the middle and lower middle classes are most likely to use bank accounts (current and deposit), as well as building society accounts. Post Office and savings bank accounts are more likely to be favoured by lower income groups.

Reliable measures of savings levels are particularly difficult to obtain. Not only do some respondents resent such questions but there are considerable definitional problems in establishing just what is to be understood to be included as savings. Does, for example, the capital appreciation on a house or accumulated pension contributions constitute savings? We attempted to deal with these problems in a neutral way by asking respondents whether they considered their savings were 'small (that is less than £100)'; 'medium (a few hundred pounds)' or 'quite large (over £1000).' No attempt was made to define 'savings' on the grounds that, as we were interested in explaining behaviour, one household's view as to what constituted savings could well differ from that of another.

This approach seemed to work well to the extent that fewer than seven per cent of respondents refused or were unable to answer the question on savings levels. Twenty-nine per cent of those who did answer said their savings were 'small', forty-two per cent said they were 'medium' and thirty per cent said they were 'quite large'. Savings levels tended to be larger in the case of households where the HoH was older and where there were fewer people in the household.

Recent changes in savings levels were also thought likely to have a bearing on subsequent discretionary behaviour. Respondents were therefore asked whether, and in what direction, their total savings had

TABLE 3.5 Change in total savings over previous twelve
          months

	per cent
Substantially decreased	8
Decreased	20
Remained the same	40
Increased	27
Substantially increased	5

changed over the previous year. Again, no attempt was made to dictate
to the respondent whether this should be answered in terms of a change
in the real value or the money value of the savings on the grounds that it
was more important to record the respondent's perception of the nature
of the change. The distribution of the responses is set out in Table 3.5.
Increases in savings were more likely to be reported by those in the
higher social class and income groups, especially where income (total
household and of the HoH) was above £3000. While a high income
increased the chances that savings would be reported to have risen, it did
not greatly reduce the chances that savings had fallen over the previous
year. This means therefore that those in the higher income groups were
less likely than the population as a whole to report an unchanged savings
level. Younger people were also more likely to experience changes –
one way or the other – in their savings and therefore were less likely to
report an unchanged level.

215 respondents stated that they had some credit outstanding, in the
form of bank credit or hire purchase contracts but excluding mortgage
debt. The distribution of the total amounts of credit outstanding is set out
in Table 3.6. Forty-nine respondents reported that they had both bank
credit and an HP debt, 119 had HP credit only and fifty-nine had bank
credit only. Nearly twenty per cent of those with a bank account also had
some bank credit outstanding. The users of bank credit tended to be in
the higher social class groups and where the income of the HoH was over
£2500 and total household income exceeded £3000. They also tended to
be younger, married less long but with larger families. Thus, the users of
bank credit were more likely to be those with good status as borrowers.
The members of the sample with HP commitments were also likely to be

TABLE 3.6 Total credit outstanding for households

Credit outstanding £	Per cent of households
0	61
1–50	11
51–100	7
101–500	15
over 500	3
Not answered	4

Note credit included HP and bank credit but not mortgage debt.

younger and with larger household sizes than the sample as a whole. Users of HP were most likely to be in social classes C_2, D and E, but there was a more even distribution of the proportions using HP when analysed by income level than was the case for users of bank credit.

The amount of credit outstanding rose as the income level increased but was also likely to be higher where the HoH was younger, married less long and/or had a larger household than the sample as a whole. The main features of the variation in the level of credit outstanding are set out in Table 3.7.

The average amount of credit outstanding of those with bank credit was £266 and for those with HP was £190. From this it would appear that bank credit was the source of larger sums and this would be consistent with the evidence that bank credit users were more concentrated amongst the higher income groups who would be expected to have a higher credit standing. However, the cases where a respondent had both bank credit and HP have not been separated from the rest so this conclusion must be tentative.

Hire Purchase contracts were reported, by the 168 respondents with some HP, to be outstanding on 222 items. Of these, there were forty-nine contracts relating to purchases of cars, twenty-six on furniture and carpets, eighteen on central heating and eighty-nine on the household consumer durable items covered in detail in this investigation. Ten were on other items including night storage or immersion heaters, bicycles, clothing, books and a caravan. There is not much clear-cut evidence that the use of HP on different items is closely associated with variations in the socio-economic status of the respondent. We did find, however, that HP on cars was most likely to exist where the income of the HoH was in the range £2000–£2499. People in the social class groups C_1 C_2 and D were more likely to have HP commitments on furniture. Respondents in the sixteen–twenty-four age group were more likely to have an existing HP contract on household durables though the number of observations here was not large. HP contracts on central heating were most likely to be held by those in the age range twenty-five–forty-four.

In general, the households using bank or HP credit were those with small savings. There were, however, a number of cases where it appeared households had deliberately chosen to use credit for a purchase rather than draw upon savings. Thus we found that thirteen per cent of the respondents with 'quite large' savings and twenty-one per cent of those with 'medium' savings had some bank credit and seven per cent of those with 'quite large' savings and twenty-eight per cent of those with 'medium' savings had some HP. The overall picture of the relation between total levels of credit outstanding and total savings is set out in

TABLE 3.7 Average levels of credit outstanding analysed by age, length of marriage of HoH, and total household income

Age Group	Average, all respondents £	Average, those with credit commitments only £
16-24	71	121
25-34	99	244
35-44	95	205
45-54	65	214
55-64	20	102
Length of marriage		
0-4 years	78	158
5-9 years	94	247
10-20 years	49	113
over 20 years	44	159

Total household income £ p.a.	Average, all respondents £	Average, those with credit commitments only £
less than 1000	57	150
1000-1499	55	152
1500-1999	54	176
2000-2499	66	180
2500-2999	78	175
3000-3499	101	230
4000-5999	135	336
6000 and over	156	408

Note These averages were based on the groupings of credit amounts shown in Table 3.6. The assumed value for the category 'more than £500' was £700.

Table 3.8. Here too the general pattern indicates that usage of credit was greatest where savings were lowest but in a number of cases it appears that households were accepting a level of credit that they could, if they so wished, have paid off from their savings.

Many households have more than one regular income earner and/or an ability to generate a ready increase in income either through overtime or through the wife working. Our prior investigations had indicated that this supplementary and possibly discretionary income was an important potential influence on consumer durable purchasing. We found that a high proportion of the sample claimed to have a certain amount of discretion over their household income levels. In all, 233 (thirty-eight per cent) said that their household income could be readily and temporarily increased, mainly by the HoH working overtime or by the wife going out to work. Of these, 105 said the HoH could work overtime and 111 said the wife could work. Twenty-two said the wife could work overtime and twenty-eight other answers were also given. (The number of methods stated exceed the number of respondents answering in the affirmative here as some indicated more than one way in which their income could be increased).

In general those in social classes A and B, those aged fifty-five and over and those in one-person households were less likely to think they could readily increase their income. The possibility of the HoH working

TABLE 3.8 Credit levels outstanding analysed by household savings levels (*percentages*)

| Total Credit Outstanding | Total Savings | | | |
	'small'	'medium'	'quite large'	Number
0	45	62	85	347
1-50	19	10	4	61
51-100	12	8	2	43
101-500	20	18	4	86
over 500	4	2	4	17
Total	100	100	100	
Number	167	251	136	554

Notes 'small' savings were indicated in the questionnaire to be savings of £100 or so, 'medium' savings were a few hundred pounds and 'quite large' savings were £1000 or more.

overtime was more likely to exist where the HoH was in social class C_2 or D or where his income was in the range £1000–1999 or total household income was in the range £1000–2499. The prospects of the wife working were more evenly distributed across all socio-economic status categories, though if anything those in social class A were slightly more likely to anticipate that the wife going out to work could constitute a way of obtaining an increase in the household's income.

The size of such prospective increases in incomes was variable. Fifty-two respondents thought they could increase their income by up to £5 per week, eighty-seven thought the increase could be in the range £5–10 a week, fifty-seven said £10–20, eighteen said £20–40 and two thought they could increase their income by over £40 a week. The average of the potential increases in income was about £11 a week. (Seventeen respondents were unable to indicate the extent of the increase they expected to be able to achieve.)

The average increase in income as a result of the wife going out to work was about £13 a week while the increase attributable to the effect of the HoH working overtime was about £9. When only households are considered where some such income increase could be readily achieved, we find that the average possible income increase was greater for the higher income and social class groups. However, when account is taken of the different proportions in each group who said they could achieve some income flexibility there is no strong association between the average income increase that could be achieved and any of the socio-economic status phenomena used for analysis in this chapter.

Financial expectations

The hypothesis underlying the research was that expectations have an important predictive role in explaining consumer expenditure that was not covered by other sorts of 'objective status' variables. Later chapters will consider the different sorts of expectations on which data were collected. Here it is useful to discuss the financial expectations of the sample. The variables concerned are expectations of changes in the household's use of bank and HP credit over the following three months, expectations of changes in the level of savings over the following twelve months, expected changes in levels of expenditure on consumer durables over the following three and twelve months and a comparison of the expected level with the level in the equivalent period over the past year. In addition, it is also convenient to consider here the respondent's expectation that he would move house during the following twelve months as house moving implies substantial financial commitments.

Ten per cent of the sample expected their HP commitments to decrease and nine per cent expected their use of bank credit to decrease. The proportions expecting an increase were five per cent and seven per cent respectively. This means that well over eighty per cent of the sample in each case anticipated no change in their use of either form of credit. Numbers are therefore too small to allow much meaningful identification of the characteristics of the people expecting a change in one direction or the other.

Forty-two per cent of the sample expected that their savings would remain unchanged over the following twelve months and forty-four per

TABLE 3.9 Expected changes in the use of bank credit and HP over three months and in the level of savings over twelve months *(percentages)*

Expected change	Use of bank credit 3 months	Use of HP 3 months	Level of savings 12 months
Substantially less	1	2	2
Less	8	8	12
The same	83	86	42
More	5	4	40
Substantially more	2	1	4

TABLE 3.10 Expected levels of expenditure on durables in the next three, twelve months *(percentages)*

£	3 months	12 months
0	67	28
1-50	8	10
51-100	9	15
101-200	7	15
201-300	2	9
301-500	4	11
501-1000	3	9
1001 and over	1	4

cent expected they would increase. Only fourteen per cent anticipated a fall in savings. While respondents in the higher social class groups were more confident than those in lower social class categories that their savings would rise, anticipation of a decline in savings seemed to be less closely related to social class. Younger HoHs were more likely to anticipate that their savings would increase and HoHs aged fifty-five or more were the most likely to anticipate a decline in savings. This is also reflected in the analysis by duration of marriage since those married twenty or more years were least likely to anticipate an increase in savings and more likely to expect a decrease in savings. Those married less than five years were also rather more likely than average to anticipate a decline in savings. Confidence that savings would rise was generally associated with higher income levels, though some high income households did anticipate a fall in savings.

Our previous investigations showed that opinions about the levels of funds that households had available to spend and that they expected to spend on consumer durables had an important role in predicting expenditure on consumer durables. Consequently, some measures of this were incorporated into our battery of attitude scales for this survey. However, we continued to ask informants how much they expected to spend on consumer durables over the following three and twelve months and how this amount compared with their expenditures on such items in the same period in the previous year. The broad distributions of the expectations are set out in Tables 3.10 and 3.11

The largest average expenditure levels were anticipated by those in higher income and social class groups and also by those who were younger and had been married a shorter period of time (see Tables 3.12 and 3.13). Both the ability to afford funds to spend on durables and a greater desire to do so in the early years of marriage could be reasonable

TABLE 3.11 Whether expected levels of expenditure on durables were more or less than in the equivalent period in the previous year (*percentages*)

	3 months	*12 months*
Substantially less	16	17
Less	22	23
The same	41	21
More	11	23
Substantially more	11	16

TABLE 3.12 Anticipated expenditure levels on durables for next twelve months analysed by age of head of household (*percentages*)

	Expenditure level £									Total	Median Value £
	0	1-50	51-100	101-200	201-300	301-500	501-1000	1001-2000	2001-5000		
Age of Head of Household 16-24	4.5	13.6	27.3	9.1	4.5	18.2	9.1	9.1	4.5	100	150
25-34	21.0	6.5	14.5	14.5	8.0	13.8	13.0	8.7	0	100	155
35-44	23.1	7.0	14.0	17.2	12.4	13.4	9.7	2.2	1.1	100	134
45-54	32.1	11.9	13.8	16.4	6.9	9.4	8.2	1.3	0	100	82
55-64	44.8	9.5	17.1	10.5	5.7	3.8	3.8	4.8	0	100	28

TABLE 3.13 Anticipated expenditure levels on durables for next twelve months analysed by total household income levels (*percentages*)

Total household income £	Expenditure level: £									Total	Median Value
	0	1-50	51-100	101-200	201-300	301-500	501-1000	1001-2000	2001-5000		
less than 1000	45.2	22.6	19.3	6.5	3.2	3.2	0	0	0	100	11
1000-1499	56.4	15.4	15.4	5.1	5.1	0	2.6	0	0	100	0
1500-1999	33.7	10.9	16.3	12.0	8.7	9.8	6.5	2.2	0	100	67
2000-2499	20.2	6.7	18.3	24.0	13.5	9.6	5.8	1.9	0	100	112
2500-2999	22.1	7.8	10.4	19.5	14.3	14.3	6.5	3.9	1.3	100	150
3000-3999	19.3	8.3	16.5	17.4	5.5	11.0	13.8	8.3	0	100	134
4000-5999	12.9	3.2	9.7	14.5	11.3	24.2	21.0	3.2	0	100	286
6000 and over	17.4	4.3	4.3	13.0	8.7	17.4	13.0	17.4	4.3	100	326

explanations of an expectation of high levels of expenditure. When a
qualitative approach was used, asking whether the anticipated spending
level would be higher or lower than in the equivalent period in the
previous year, a less clear-cut relationship with the socio-economic
status characteristics of the sample was found. Lower income or social
class groups were as likely to expect to spend more than in the previous
year as those in higher socio-economic groups.

The likelihood that a family will move house is a rather different sort
of expectational variable though it has major financial implications.
Eight per cent of the sample said they expected to move house in the
following year, eighty-one per cent said they would not move and
eleven per cent were uncertain. Those that said they were likely to move
were younger and often married less than five years. There was also
some evidence that those in the highest income and social class groups
were less certain that they would not be moving.

4   Developments during the survey year

Since the purpose of this study is to investigate and explain consumer durable purchasing behaviour over a specified period of time, it is necessary to describe in some detail the nature of the developments that took place over the survey year. In this chapter we shall report details of individual durable purchases and outlays, respondent perceptions of the changes in their financial circumstances and details of other activities and developments within the household that might have an influence on purchase behaviour. Some of this information is available on a quarterly basis and some relates to the year as a whole. In the next chapter changes in consumer confidence, again identified on a quarterly basis, will be considered. But first it is desirable to put these developments into a wider context by considering briefly the general economic situation during the survey year, from April 1972 to March 1973.

The general economic situation April 1972 to March 1973

The survey year began at a time of economic reflation. Hire purchase controls had been abolished and purchase tax rates reduced in the summer of 1971 and the March 1972 Budget had also been reflationary with income tax relief through increased personal allowances, increases in pensions and national insurance benefits and a reduction in purchase tax. The income and purchase tax changes were estimated to be likely to cost the Exchequer nearly £1400m in a full year and the initial effects were considered most likely to be reflected in an increase in consumers' expenditure (National Institute 1972). Granted the nature of the policy changes in 1971 and 1972 it was particularly likely that much of the boom in consumer spending would be concentrated on consumer durables.

It is not therefore surprising that we find that over the period April

1972 – March 1973 consumer expenditure at constant prices rose by eight per cent overall and whereas expenditure on food hardly changed in real terms, expenditure on all consumer durables rose by 28.6 per cent. This increase was no doubt partly funded and encouraged by the increase in money supply (M_3) which rose by 21.6 per cent over that period and by a substantial increase in hire purchase debt and bank advances. The index of industrial production rose by nine per cent and the unemployment rate fell from four per cent to 2.8 per cent. The proportion of operatives working overtime rose continuously over this twelve month period (after allowing for seasonal effects) and so too did the total number of hours of overtime worked. The index of wage earnings rose by 13.4 per cent and real personal disposable incomes increased by 7.6 per cent.

But economic booms also seem to bring with them economic difficulties. The balance of payments was moving rapidly into the red, especially on the visible earnings on the current account. The annual rate of increase of prices was also rapidly gaining pace. The Retail Prices Index rose by 9.2 per cent over the survey year, a figure which at that time was considered to be very high and the increase in food prices was in excess of fifteen per cent. In contrast, however, the index value for radios, televisions and other household appliances (though not for transport and vehicles) actually showed a small fall. The pound was floated in June 1972, a move which resulted in an effective devaluation against other currencies and a further effective devaluation occurred in November. In the latter part of 1972 rising import prices and wages further worsened the inflationary pressures.

In response to these developments, Bank Rate was raised on six occasions between April and December 1972, rising from five per cent to nine per cent before easing slightly to eight per cent by March 1973. Special deposits were called in by the Bank of England in November and December 1972. The Government announced anti-inflation policy proposals in September 1972 and in November 1972 a ninety day standstill on pay and prices was introduced. This was subsequently extended by sixty days to last until 31 March 1973, and in the case of prices it was extended to 30 April 1973 to cover the period of the changeover to Value Added Tax which took place on 1 April 1973.

Despite these policies, the level of consumer spending remained buoyant up to the end of the survey year. The National Institute reported that the high level of consumer spending in the first quarter of 1973 had been financed by a fall in the savings ratio (National Institute 1973) though the rush of wage settlements in the early autumn of 1972 to beat the imposition of the pay freeze might well have helped to sustain the buoyant level of consumer demand.

Changes in the circumstances of individual households during the survey year

Changes in financial circumstances

Table 4.1 indicates that, in keeping with the population as a whole, the majority of sample households reported that they had received an increase in their total incomes and that of head of the household, during the survey year. The proportion reporting an increase was higher in the first quarter (1 April to 30 June 1972) than in the latter quarters. This is presumably a consequence of the subsequent introduction of wage controls. In the light of this it is, however, rather surprising that in both the last two quarters, when the wage restraint policy was in force, more than one-quarter of the sample reported that the income of the household and of the HoH had increased. Over the survey year as a whole more than two-thirds of the sample reported that their incomes were higher than they had been a year before. While the majority of households experienced an income increase and most of the others succeeded in holding their incomes stable, a small proportion reported a decline in their incomes.

It would have been useful to know for certain whether these changes in incomes were appraised in real or money terms. Consideration was given to the possibility of asking questions that would make a distinction between the two concepts but it was decided that this would not be feasible, especially as the questions were asked on a postal questionnaire. It is likely that the vast majority of informants will have described their income change in money terms rather than in real terms. However, since our interest is primarily in the extent to which such perceptions have an influence on purchasing behaviour, it is arguable that it should be left to the individual informant to assess how he considers his own financial position has changed. In some cases his awareness may relate to monetary values only, in others it may be considered in real terms and measured against changes in the household's own cost of living, the general rise in the Retail Prices Index or compared against some other yardstick. Some research to establish the base against which people assess their own incomes or changes in incomes would be likely to be of considerable interest.

In an attempt to deal explicitly with changes in the real financial position of the household over the survey year, in our final questionnaire in April 1973 we also asked 'How do you assess your own financial position now compared with a year ago in *real* terms, that is after allowing for the effects of price increases?' In answer to this, six per cent reported that they were substantially worse off, thirty-one per cent said they were worse off, thirty-nine per cent said their financial position

TABLE 4.1 Changes in financial circumstances per cent of households

	Over 1st Quarter	Over 2nd Quarter	Over 3rd Quarter	Over 4th Quarter	Over Whole Year
Change in Income of the HoH					
Declined substantially	1	1	1	2	2
Declined	5	3	4	3	4
No change	52	67	66	70	26
Increased	40	27	26	25	62
Increased substantially	2	2	2	1	6
Change in Household Income					
Declined substantially	2	2	2	3	3
Declined	5	6	6	4	7
No change	47	57	63	64	22
Increased	43	33	27	28	61
Increased substantially	3	2	3	1	6
Change in Household Savings					
Declined substantially	5	3	4	5	5
Declined	20	19	19	25	26
No change	52	52	54	45	34
Increased	23	24	22	23	33
Increased substantially	1	1	1	1	1

was about the same, twenty-three per cent said they were better off and two per cent said they were substantially better off. This presents a very different picture from that given by the answers about income changes over the year set out in Table 4.1 and does tend to confirm that the questions about income change were more likely to have been answered in money rather than real terms. Table 4.2 shows the distribution of the answers on the change in the real financial position compared with changes in household income. As expected, informants generally were less likely to report an improvement in their real financial position than a rise in household income.

Changes in savings were somewhat more evenly distributed. Over the year as a whole, just over thirty per cent reported some decline and just over one-third reported that savings had increased. The quarterly patterns suggest that about half the sample tended to report unchanged savings each time with the balance more or less evenly distributed between those who reported an increase and those who reported a decrease.

By cross-tabulating this information with data on the key socio-economic characteristics of the informants we can establish whether there is any particular pattern of association between socio-economic status and change in financial circumstances. The socio-economic indicators used for this were social class, age of the HoH, the length of time the HoH had been married, the number of people in the household, the income of the HoH and of the household as a whole. The number of tabulations involved for this purpose (as with much of the analysis for this chapter) was extremely voluminous, so only the main findings are stated here. In general, we found that increases in incomes (both of the HoH and of the household) were significantly more likely to have been reported by those in higher social class groups, where the HoH was younger (aged less than forty-five) and married less long. Starting income levels were not significantly associated with the nature of the change in incomes. Total household incomes were more likely to have risen in larger families while the income of the HoH alone was more likely to have risen where the household size was smaller. Presumably larger families are more likely to have more than one income earner, so increasing the chances that household incomes will rise. Improvements in their real financial position were more likely to be reported by younger informants (aged up to thirty-five) and significantly less likely to be reported by older respondents.

Increases in savings were more likely to be reported by households with smaller families and those in higher social class categories. Savings were also more likely to have increased where the household reported

TABLE 4.2 Change in household income and in the real financial position of the household over the survey year

Change in household income over survey year	Financial position at end of survey year in real terms compared with one year before (percentages)					
	Substantially worse off	Worse off	The same	Better off	Substantially better off	Total
Declined substantially	36	55	9	0	0	100
Declined	12	58	23	8	0	100
Not changed	8	49	35	7	0	100
Increased	3	22	45	30	1	100
Increased substantially	0	9	23	46	23	100
per cent of sample	6	31	39	23	2	100

larger total savings at the beginning of the survey year. Increases in savings were more closely associated with high total household incomes than with the income of the HoH. This suggests that second incomes in a household exercise an important influence on the level of savings and hence, perhaps, on the ability to finance discretionary expenditures.

We also investigated whether the level of hire purchase and other credit commitments and the level of shareholdings had changed over the survey year. While a majority of informants reported no change (including those without credit commitments or shareholdings), twenty-four per cent reported an increase in their use of credit against thirteen per cent reporting a reduction, fifteen per cent reported an increase in their shareholdings and six per cent reported a decline. Although in general there is little clear association between socio-economic status and changes in either of these circumstances, an increase in the usage of hire purchase and other credit facilities was proportionately more likely to have been reported by families where the HoH was in the age range twenty-five–thirty-four.

If consumers know or are able to anticipate changes in their circumstances they may be better able to plan their spending decisions and may indeed anticipate future income increases in their present outlays. On the other hand those who experience unanticipated changes may behave in a way they themselves would not have predicted and in a way that knowledge of their characteristics would not have led us to expect. The influence of 'windfall' events – favourable or unfavourable – has sometimes been suggested as an explanation for the divergence between predicted and actual behaviour at the level of the individual household (Katona *passim*). Of our sample, sixteen per cent reported that over the survey year they had incurred heavy, unexpected expenses and six per cent had received large unexpected payments such as legacies or capital gains. Because such events are, by definition, uncertain, it is not surprising that no systematic association was found between these events and the socio-economic status of the informant.

Other changes in the household's circumstances may also be unexpected. Thirty-six per cent of the sample reported at the end of the survey year that the changes in their circumstances with respect to incomes, savings, use of credit and level of shareholdings had been unanticipated a year before. Of that 36 per cent, 11 per cent said the changes had been substantially less favourable than they had expected, 29 per cent said the changes were less favourable than expected, 30 per cent said the changes were more favourable than anticipated and six per cent said they were substantially more favourable. [The remaining 25 per cent of those who said that the changes were unanticipated, then indicated that their effect was about the same as had been expected. It is not easy to reconcile the two answers, perhaps they indicate that the change was not very significant either way, or that there had been unexpected developments but their overall effect was about in line with initial expectations.]

Generally, those with lower incomes and lower social class status were more likely to have reported unexpected changes in their circumstances over the survey year. The favourable changes were more likely to have been experienced by younger families and were also, predictably, associated with increases in incomes and savings over the survey year. Those who suffered a reduction in their incomes and savings were proportionately less likely to have anticipated the changes and it is interesting to note that they were also more likely to have been those who had reported at the beginning of the survey year that they could increase their family income by working overtime, by the wife working etc. This seems to suggest that while such 'discretionary incomes' may have an important influence on durable purchasing and savings decisions, where they occur total household incomes are less stable and predictable.

Changes in other circumstances

Many other activities and circumstances within the household may have an effect upon the purchasing of consumer durables. Buying a new house or receiving a credit card might stimulate purchases, while retiring from work or entering into other financial commitments and

TABLE 4.3 Proportion undertaking certain actions or experiencing a change in other circumstances during the survey year

percentages who:			
Moved house	8	Spent £100 or more on home decorations or improvements	40
Acquired a second car for the first time	6	Installed central heating	8
Acquired a third car for the first time	3	Entered into substantial and continuing new financial commitments	27
Took an overseas holiday	24	Retired from work	2
Received a credit card for the first time	28	Increased the size of the family	8

making other discretionary outlays may reduce the ability to buy durables. Consequently we investigated the extent to which other circumstances had changed for the sample households. The proportions are set out in Table 4.3.

In all cases a minority of the sample experienced each of the changes listed but the proportions spending quite sizeable amounts on decorations or home improvements, entering into new financial commitments, taking an overseas holiday and receiving a credit card for the first time were all quite large. In many cases, experience of such changes was not closely associated with any particular socio-economic characteristics of the members of the sample. However, overseas holidays and heavy outlays on home improvements were much more likely to have been undertaken by those in social class A. Younger and more recently married households were most likely to have increased their financial commitments, received a credit card for the first time and increased the size of their family.

It is possible to compare peoples' expectations of moving house at the start of the survey year with whether they did actually move during the survey year. Table 4.4 shows that those who expected to move were in fact proportionately much more likely to have moved than those who were uncertain or did not expect to move house during that year.

Durable purchasing over the survey year

Our interest in this section is with the level of purchases of consumer durables over the survey year. This may be measured in terms of the numbers of each individual durable purchased, the total number of items acquired or the level of expenditure on all items taken together. In an earlier paper based upon our previous research we drew attention to the problems of relying upon respondent recollections of the items they had

TABLE 4.4 Anticipation and actuality of moving house during the survey year per cent of households

| Expectation of Moving | Whether moved or not | | | |
	Moved	Not Moved	Total	Number
Will move	48	52	100	23
Uncertain	23	77	100	31
Will not move	3	97	100	308
Number	26	336		362

purchased over a whole year (Pickering and Isherwood 1974). In the present investigation it had been hoped that this problem might be overcome or at least reduced by sending out postal follow-up questionnaires every three months on which actual purchases and expenditures in the previous quarter would be recorded.

During the analysis of the results, however, it became apparent that there had been some tendency for the same purchase to be recorded in two consecutive quarters, thereby inflating both the number of recorded purchases and the reported levels of expenditure. The problem was further compounded by the possibility that some instances where the same item had been recorded as having been purchased in two consecutive quarters may well have been correct, for example, more than one carpet or item of furniture may well have been purchased in quick succession.

In an effort to deal with this problem, all questionnaires were checked by hand and obvious cases of double recording were removed and the appropriate adjustment was made to the stated expenditure level. This procedure was helped by the fact that verbal explanations of the reasons for the purchases were also recorded on the postal questionnaires (see Chapter 10). In all, it appeared that there were some seventy-three instances (about fourteen per cent of the total purchases recorded by the sample over the last three quarters of the survey year for which this analysis is possible) where the same purchase had been incorrectly recorded twice by a member of the sample. There were also a number of cases where the same household seemed actually to have purchased more than one unit of a particular durable in different quarters of the survey year. Such multiple purchases were most frequently of carpets, furniture and used cars. In fact, in some cases multiple purchases of an item were made in the same quarter – especially of carpets and furniture. These are counted here as a single purchase only.

Table 4.5 sets out the number of units of each item purchased quarter by quarter over the survey year and the proportion of households buying each item at some time or other during the survey year. It will be observed that the recorded number of purchases was highest in the first quarter. It is, of course, not possible to eliminate the effects of erroneous recording in this quarter of purchases that had in fact been made before the start of the survey year. From the evidence from the other quarters it therefore seems likely that this figure may be too high by thirty–thirty-five items but even so it appears that the overall number of purchases was slightly higher in this quarter than in later quarters. The rank ordering of the durables is the same when analysed by the total number of units purchased as by the proportion of households actually making a purchase of each item. Furniture, used cars and carpets were

TABLE 4.5 Acquisitions of consumer durables over the survey year

Number of units acquired

Item	1st Quarter	2nd Quarter	3rd Quarter	4th Quarter	Total for whole year	Per cent of households acquiring over whole year
Black and white television	8	7	2	7	24	6
Central heating	7	7	8	6	28	7
Carpets	33	20	22	28	103	23
Colour television	13	2	8	5	28	7
Cooker	9	8	8	15	40	10
Deep freeze	6	7	5	14	32	9
Dishwasher	4	1	0	2	7	2
Major furniture	39	26	30	35	130	27
New car	19	20	14	20	73	18
Used car	37	28	18	23	106	26
Record player	15	7	24	9	55	15
Refrigerator	3	5	6	4	18	4
Tape recorder	6	8	11	10	35	9
Vacuum cleaner	18	2	12	6	38	10
Washing machine	19	9	6	11	45	12
Total	236	157	174	195	762	

TABLE 4.6 Distribution of numbers of durable purchases reported by each household over the survey year

Number of Durable Items purchased	Per cent of households
0	15
1	30
2	23
3	16
4	9
5	5
6 and over	4

TABLE 4.7 Distribution of levels of expenditure on consumer durables over the survey year

Expenditure Level	1st Quarter	2nd Quarter	3rd Quarter	4th Quarter	Over Year as a Whole
£	percentage of households				
0	54	67	63	61	15
1-200	28	17	25	25	30
201-400	8	7	5	5	16
401-600	4	3	3	4	12
601-800	3	3	2	1	9
801-1000	1	2	1	1	6
1001-1200					2
1201-1400					3
1401-1600	3	2	2	2	4
1601-2000					2
2001 and over					2
Mean	£138	£115	£101	£103	£458
Lower Quartile	0	0	0	0	£70
Median	0	0	0	0	£278
Upper Quartile	£112	£80	£80	£86	£758

the most frequently purchased with, in each case, over 20 per cent of the sample buying these items. Purchases of dishwashers and refrigerators were very low. Many television sets are rented and so the details shown here of actual purchases of televisions would not represent fully the number of new acquisitions of these items.

On average, during the year each household purchased 1.8 different consumer durables from the fifteen used in this study and an average of 2.1 units in all. (The extent to which the number of units purchased exceeds the number of different items indicates the extent of apparent multiple purchasing of some durables). The number of different units purchased by each household ranged from none to nine, with fifteen per cent not purchasing any item and thirty per cent buying just one item over the survey year (see Table 4.6).

Table 4.7 indicates the distribution of expenditures on all the items covered in the survey for each quarter and over the year as a whole. Outlays on cars were reported net of trade-in allowances. In each of the quarters, over half the sample made no such expenditure. The mean expenditure in the first quarter appears to have been a little higher than in the succeeding quarters and may be influenced to a small extent by the recording of some purchases that had in fact been made before the start of the survey year. There was no significant correlation between expenditures by individual households in successive quarters. The majority of households reported expenditure on consumer durables in one or two quarters only: fiften per cent of the sample made no purchases over the survey year, thirty-five per cent made a purchase in one quarter only, thirty-four per cent made purchases in two of the four quarters, fifteen per cent made purchases in three quarters and two per cent recorded expenditure on durables in all four quarters.

The measure of expenditures over the survey year as a whole given in Table 4.7 was obtained by summing the expenditures over the four quarters. As will already have become apparent from the discussion of the number of items purchased by the members of the survey panel, only a minority failed to make any outlays on the purchase of consumer durables at some time during the survey year. The average expenditure was £458 and twenty-five per cent spent £758 or more. The highest recorded expenditure by any informant was £3495.

In the final questionnaire respondents were asked to indicate how much they thought they had spent on durables over the survey year. There was a reasonably close correlation between this value and the figure derived from the summation of the quarterly expenditures ($r = .797$). However, as Table 4.8 indicates there were some cases where there was quite a wide divergence between the two figures. If it can be assumed that the quarterly figures are likely to be the more accurate

TABLE 4.8 Alternative measures of individual expenditures on consumer durables numbers

Estimate based on the sum of four quarters' expenditure figures. £	Respondent estimates of outlay over the whole year: £								
	0	1-200	201-400	401-600	601-800	801-1000	1001-1400	1401 and over	Total
0	50	4	0	0	0	0	0	0	54
1-200	21	70	13	2	2	0	1	0	109
201-400	4	6	42	6	2	0	1	0	61
401-600	0	7	8	14	9	1	0	2	41
601-800	2	1	2	1	13	5	1	3	28
801-1000	0	2	0	1	6	10	3	0	22
1001-1400	3	1	1	2	0	1	7	4	19
1401 & over	0	1	1	0	0	2	6	16	26
Total	80	92	67	26	32	19	19	25	360

since they were collected nearer to the time of the actual outlay, this gives some indication of the extent of the error likely to occur if reliance is placed on respondent recollections over a whole year.

Associations between household characteristics and durable purchasing

In Chapter 6 we shall report the results of some multivariate statistical investigations of the extent to which household characteristics and circumstances help to explain variations in expenditure on consumer durables. Here, we shall consider the extent to which individual characteristics or circumstances are associated with durable purchasing. In Table 4.9 details are set out of the way in which durable purchasing was related to the basic socio-economic characteristics of the members of the sample. [Due to computing limitations all mean expenditure values in the remainder of this chapter are based on the average values of grouped data rather than the means of actual values.] Care should be taken in drawing inferences from this table, especially where the number of observations of people with a particular socio-economic characteristic is small, but several interesting pointers emerge.

Those in the highest social class and income groups tended to be more likely to buy a larger number of items, to have larger total outlays and a higher average outlay per item bought. The poorer members of the sample tended to buy fewer items and to spend much smaller amounts on durables. Younger people and those married less long also tended to buy more items, to have higher outlays in total and per item purchased. The unmarried members of the sample were less likely to buy durables at all and spent less on average on those items that were purchased. Larger families tended to make more purchases and to spend larger sums of money in total on consumer durables.

Looked at the other way, the most frequent purchases and largest expenditures in total were most likely to be made by those in the highest social class groups, with the largest incomes, married for less than ten years and with five or more people in the household. The largest outlays per item were made by those in the highest social class and income groups and those married for less than five years. Older, poorer, unmarried people and single person households were less likely to buy durables and had lower average expenditures. Average outlays per item purchased were lowest in the case of those in the lower social class and income groups, amongst older people, those married longest and in single person households.

It is also interesting to investigate the extent to which variations in expenditure were associated with changes in the household's

TABLE 4. 9 Durable purchasing behaviour over the survey year
analysed by the socio-economic characteristics of the
sample

Socio-economic characteristic	Average number of items purchased per household	Per-centage not buying any items	Average expenditure on durables over the year per household: £	Average outlay per item purchased (see note): £	Number
Social Class					
A	2. 51	17	611	243	70
B	2. 21	8	577	261	119
C1	1. 75	10	336	192	87
C2	2. 10	16	281	134	58
DE	1. 28	28	152	119	25
Age					
16-24	3. 00	0	683	228	12
25-34	2. 16	5	511	237	85
35-44	2. 11	17	472	224	107
45-54	2. 03	15	389	192	95
55-64	1. 77	18	305	172	60
Duration of Marriage					
Not married	1. 57	34	334	213	35
0-4 years	2. 11	13	542	257	38
5-9 years	2. 33	7	505	217	58
10-20 years	2. 03	17	474	233	116
20 +	2. 11	11	396	188	111
Household Size					
1 person	2. 23	46	362	162	13
2	1. 78	15	428	240	88
3	2. 08	15	413	199	79
4	2. 08	15	429	206	116
5 +	2. 49	8	533	214	63
Household Income £					
0- 999	1. 10	40	100	91	10
1000-1499	1. 17	39	94	80	18
1500-1999	1. 78	20	307	172	55
2000-2499	2. 09	9	410	196	67
2500-2999	2. 41	17	543	225	46
3000-3999	2. 03	10	483	238	69
4000-5999	2. 48	14	674	272	42
6000 +	2. 86	0	857	300	14

Note This value is obtained by dividing the average expenditure on
durables by the average number of items purchased for each
row in the table.

TABLE 4.10 Average expenditures in £ on consumer durables over the survey year analysed by changes in the household's financial circumstances

Change over the survey year in:	Direction of changes: Less and considerably less	The same	More and considerably more
Income of the HoH	423	392	472
Income of the household	386	459	456
Savings of the household	514	396	442
Real financial position	398	409	570
Use of HP and credit	358	383	667
Level of shareholdings	458	421	620

TABLE 4.11 Average expenditure in £ on consumer durables over the survey year analysed by changes in other household circumstances

Whether during the survey year the informant:	YES	NO
Moved house	785	422
Bought a second car for the first time	580	441
Bought a third car for the first time	591	444
Retired	529	445
Increased the size of the family	417	451
Took an overseas holiday	546	417
Redecorated or improved the house	521	391
Installed central heating	822	419
Entered into new financial commitments	671	361
Incurred heavy expenses	608	416
Received large unexpected payments	320	456
Received a credit card for the first time	455	447

circumstances over the survey year. We have already discussed in this chapter the nature of the changes in the financial and other circumstances of the households in the sample. Table 4.10 shows how average annual expenditure levels varied according to changes in that household's financial circumstances and Table 4.11 deals with the relation between expenditure and other changes in the circumstances of the household.

Table 4.10 shows that the average level of expenditure on durables was highest in the case of those who had increased their use of credit, had extended their shareholdings, whose real financial position had improved and where the level of savings over the survey year had declined. The association between higher levels of expenditure on consumer durables and a decline in the recorded level of savings held not only over the year as a whole but also applied in relation to individual quarters where households reporting a decline in their savings also recorded higher average levels of expenditure on durables. This suggests therefore that durable purchases are a major cause of declining savings and lends further support to the view that saving and durable purchasing are often competitive activities, or at least that durable purchases are frequently financed from accumulated savings.

Increased incomes alone do not seem to be a major determinant of higher expenditures, though this is perhaps not unduly surprising since two-thirds of the sample reported an increase in incomes over the survey year. However when the much smaller number of cases is considered where the informant reported that the income of the HoH or household had increased substantially, the average expenditure was above £690, thereby suggesting that, where the household received what was perceived to be a substantial increase in income, durable expenditures were also likely to be much higher. While this association held on the annual data we did not find much evidence that income increases in one quarter were associated with higher outlays in subsequent quarters.

Below average expenditures were most likely to have been reported where the household did not increase its usage of hire purchase or other credit facilities and where the income of the household had actually fallen. Those informants who said they had not anticipated the changes that had actually occurred spent less than those who had anticipated the changes and those who had experienced changes that were less favourable than they had anticipated spent considerably less (£371) than the average of £458. Even those whose unexpected changes had been more favourable than they had anticipated spent slightly less (£432) than the average for the sample as a whole.

Turning to Table 4.11 we find that heavy expenditure on consumer durables was strongly associated with the installation of central heating, moving house, buying a second car for the first time and entering into new financial commitments. Most of these are not unexpected since some are durable purchases anyway and it is generally accepted that house moves involve a commitment to purchase other items for the home. The association between increased financial commitments and higher expenditure on consumer durables is perhaps more surprising. As examples of the sort of increased financial commitments that we were interested in, the questionnaire referred to increased mortgage re-payments and new commitments for the education of children. Those who moved house and so increased their mortgage liabilities would be likely also to have spent heavily on durables but it seems that others in this group also recorded above average expenditures. However, it is relevant to point out that expectations of increased financial com-mitments in the future were found in an earlier investigation to be a predictor of higher expenditure on consumer durables (Pickering and Isherwood 1975) and the present findings are not inconsistent with this.

Of the other results here, it is interesting that the receipt of large unexpected payments (windfall gains) and having the use of a credit card for the first time did not give rise to heavy expenditures on consumer durables, contrary to the relationships that had been hypothesised in these cases. Having two members of the household rather than one at work during the survey year did not appear to add much to the average level of expenditure since those households with one person working (forty-four per cent of the sample) averaged £429 expenditure on durables, the average for households where two people worked – not necessarily full time – (also forty-four per cent of the sample) was £452. However, in eight per cent of the households three or more people worked and there the average was much higher at £614, while in the four per cent of households where no-one was working the average expenditure was £300.

In response to an invitation in the final questionnaire to add other comments related to the subject matter of the research, several informants stressed the importance of family circumstances in influencing their purchasing behaviour. The effect of a wife starting to go out to work or stopping work was clearly important in individual cases even though, as we have just observed the impact over the sample as whole of a second person working does not seem to have been very noticeable. Three members of the panel reported that over the survey year they had become redundant and consequently their incomes and expenditures had been severely hit. Others referred generally to the effects of rising prices in adversely affecting their financial well being and so forcing them to cut back on their expenditures, although others said that inflation had encouraged them to spend money rather than to save. It is to the effects of inflation on buyer behaviour that we now turn.

Attitudes and responses to inflation

The survey year was a time when the inflationary process was gaining rapidly in force although the rate of inflation was still well below that experienced more recently in Britain. We have already seen that considerably fewer people considered themselves to have become better off in real terms over the survey year than reported increases in their income levels. In order to investigate further the impact of rising prices on consumer behaviour we asked informants in the final postal questionnaire how they found the level of prices (for food and durable goods separately) compared with what they would have expected a year before, and whether the level of prices and the changes in the price level had caused them either not to buy an item they would otherwise have acquired or to bring forward a purchase that they would have made later. [Lesley Cook and Guy Routh made helpful suggestions regarding this aspect of the investigation.]

Table 4.12 indicates that people were much more surprised at the level of food prices than at the level of durable prices. This is not to be wondered at since, as we have already noted, food prices rose much faster than durable prices over the survey year. People of all socio-economic groups tended to give similar patterns of answers to these questions, though those married less long were less likely to comment that they found prices substantially higher than they had expected. To some extent it would appear that there is a learning process about the level of prices and older people tend to have a different and

TABLE 4.12 Opinions on the level of prices and average expenditure levels on consumer durables

	Food Prices		Durable Prices	
	per cent	£	per cent	£
Substantially higher than expected	43	424	10	392
Higher than expected	50	462	46	460
About the same	7	} 496	42	} 450
Lower than expected	0		3	

normally lower benchmark of prices to serve as a frame of reference in assessing actual prices than younger people whose shopping experience is more recent (see also Behrend 1966 on this question). It is perhaps plausible to suggest that, since it is marriage and the setting up of a home that marks for many people the start of major shopping and household budgeting activities, it may well be that it is the duration of marriage rather than the age of the informant that actually influences the point of reference that the individual adopts in assessing prices.

In Table 4.12 we also tabulated the mean expenditures on consumer durables over the survey year by those giving different answers to the questions about prices. This shows that expenditures were slightly lower the more adversely surprised people reported themselves to be at the level of prices. However, these differences are quite small and tests of the rank ordering of these answers and the expenditure levels indicate that there is no statistically significant difference between the various answer categories.

Rising prices may have two quite different effects on consumer durable purchases. Rising prices for food or other necessities may cause people to postpone or abandon purchases of durables because they are less well off in real terms and need to devote higher proportions of their incomes to purchases of essentials. Higher prices of durables would also tend to reduce the number of people who felt they could afford such a purchase. Alternatively, awareness and expectations of rising prices either generally or on specific commodities may encourage the bringing forward of purchases that would otherwise have been made later. This may be associated with a 'flight from money' with consumers preferring to purchase goods rather than hold rapidly depreciating savings.

Table 4.13 indicates that about forty per cent of the sample reported that they had taken one or other of these actions. There is little evidence that socio-economic status influenced the answers, except that those

TABLE 4.13 Effects of prices on purchase decisions and expenditure levels on consumer durables

	YES		NO	
	Per cent	£	Per cent	£
Level of prices stopped an acquisition	22	359	78	465
Expectations of rising prices caused an earlier purchase than planned	19	504	81	436

married fewer than five years were much less likely to have reported that they had abandoned a purchase because of the level of prices and it was in the larger households that purchases were most likely to have been brought forward. Average expenditures on consumer durables were somewhat lower for those people who reported that the level of prices had prevented them making a purchase and rather higher where informants said that an item had been bought earlier than planned.

The items most frequently mentioned that people said they had been unable to buy because of the level of prices were cars (mentioned sixteen times), carpets (ten), furniture (nine), deep freeze (eight), colour television (eight), cooker (five), vacuum cleaner (five), record player (four), central heating (four), washing machine (four). The items most frequently mentioned as having been bought early were furniture (eleven), deep freeze (nine), car (seven), carpets (seven), clothing (seven), home and garden improvements (seven), cooker (six), caravan/dormobile (four).

Although the general tenor of the questionnaire was concerned with consumer durables, there was no particular constraint on informants to refer only to consumer durables when giving details of the products whose purchases had been affected one way or the other by inflation. The references to clothing and home improvements suggest that informants did not generally assume that only consumer durables should be listed in their answers. Consequently, the much greater overall emphasis on durables as items where purchases might both be abandoned and speeded up (even though durable prices themselves were not considered by most of the sample to have risen unexpectedly rapidly) does suggest that durables are a particular type of commodity where the nature and timing of the purchase decision are more clearly at the discretion of the consumer. It appears that inflation has a dual effect on purchase decisions, causing some consumers to speed up purchases and others to abandon a proposed acquisition. It is interesting that some of the major consumer durables featured strongly both in the lists of products not purchased and of those bought earlier than planned, thereby giving further support to the notion that different consumers will respond to the same situation in quite different ways even where the same product is involved.

5 *The structure of consumer confidence*

Indicators of consumer confidence

As we saw in Chapter 1, a major element in the psychological or behavioural economic approach to the analysis of the demand for consumer durables is the view that variations in purchases through time are associated with measurable ebbs and flows in consumer confidence. There is also some evidence of a cross-sectional nature that, at a given point in time, purchasers of consumer durables tend to be more confident than non-purchasers. In this Chapter our task is therefore to describe the indicators of consumer confidence used in this investigation and to report the ways in which consumer confidence changed over the survey year.

This chapter largely follows the approach of an earlier paper based on previous survey data (Pickering et al 1973a), however, the material is different since in the light of the analysis of the earlier data it proved possible to omit some variables that were highly correlated with others and/or appeared to make little independent predictive contribution. In the present investigation some new variables were added and in all twenty-nine variables were used as the main group of consumer confidence indicators.

Each variable was expressed as a seven-point semantic differential scale with opposing statements at each end of the scale. The battery of scales was set out for self-completion by the informants and the identical battery was used in each of the five surveys conducted with the panel, thereby allowing the collection of considerable information about changes in consumer confidence over the survey year. A summary description of each of the scales is provided in Table 5.1 and the actual scales are set out in the Appendix to this study.

While we shall have occasion to consider the inter-relationships between these variables later in this Chapter, we might note here that three broad types of variable may intuitively be identified. These are:

TABLE 5.1 Variables used as indicators of consumer confidence

Variable	Summary Description of Variables
AS 1	Personal financial position compared with previous year.
AS 2	Personal financial expectations for next year.
AS 3	Personal employment prospects for next year.
AS 4	Expectations regarding economic development for next year.
AS 5	Expectations regarding change in sums of money available to spend next year.
AS 6	Prospects for economic progress.
AS 7	Effect of economic policy on personal financial position.
AS 8	Effect of economic policy on personal buying of durables.
AS 9	Good time to buy durables.
AS 10	Good time to save.
AS 11	Good time to buy stocks and shares.
AS 12	Confidence in economic policy.
AS 13	Price expectations.
AS 14	Car buying expectations.
AS 15	Intentions to acquire an additional durable.
AS 16	Durable replacement expectations.
AS 17	Effect of temporary income increase on durable purchasing.
AS 18	Whether saving up to buy a durable.
AS 19	Unemployment expectations.
AS 20	Perceptions of price trends.
AS 21	Effect of temporary income decrease on durable purchasing.
AS 22	Effect of durable price changes on durable purchasing.
AS 23	Effect of prices of necessities on ability to buy durables.
AS 24	Durable buying expectations compared with previous year.
AS 25	Ability to finance durable purchases from savings.
AS 26	Ability to finance durable purchases on credit.
AS 27	Expectations regarding future financial commitments.
AS 28	General assessment of country's performance.
AS 29	Whether increasing discretionary income.

variables dealing with the personal, financial and employment expectations of the informant (AS 1, 2, 3, 5, 27, 29); variables reflecting the attitude of the informant to general economic conditions in the country (AS 4, 6, 7, 12, 13, 19, 20, 22, 23, 28); and variables relating to the personal discretionary activities of the informant (AS 8, 9, 10, 11, 14, 15, 16, 17, 18, 21, 24, 25, 26). The variables were selected for inclusion following depth interviews, consideration of other studies and our own earlier surveys, as likely to exercise an influence on the level of durable purchasing activity. The number of variables is in excess of that used in the construction of other indices of consumer confidence, though not necessarily in other surveys of consumer confidence (Survey Research Center, Michigan, for example, uses for purposes of index construction, only a small proportion of the questions in its regular surveys). More important, it is considered that the additional variables extend considerably the psychological 'field' that is relevant to the consumer's durable purchasing decision process.

If changes in confidence are to be quantified, some basis of measurement has to be adopted and we have previously argued that the three-point response schedule normally used is insufficiently incisive (Pickering *et al* 1973a). The seven-point semantic differential scale therefore allows seven response categories and for analysis it was assumed that the scale was a linear equal interval scale. Other research indicates that this is a reasonable assumption (Lemon 1973). All answers at the extreme left hand end of the scale were scored one and all answers at the extreme right hand end were scored seven and so on. However, the direction of the scales was varied with some having the more favourable statement at the left hand of the scale and in others the right hand statement was the more favourable. This was done to try to avoid the danger of response sets in the recording of answers, though this had to some extent to be tempered by the need to ensure that respondents felt the questionnaire had a logical structure.

The interpretation of statistical results has to be made in the light of knowledge of the direction in which individual variables were coded. This is not easy where the scale ends were deliberately varied so that there was not in every case one end at which more confident answers were always coded. Some consideration was therefore given to the question of the desirability of adjusting the variables throughout this study so that a common direction of coding was reflected in the tabulations of empirical results. While this had attractions and might have been possible with the attitude variables discussed in this chapter, it would not have been as easy with other sorts of variables introduced in other chapters. Even with the attitude scales discussed here, it is not easy to say with certainty in every case just which scale end represents greater respondent confidence. Consequently the results set out through the book (with the single exception of Table 5.3 where certain alterations to the direction of the scales were made for ease of exposition for that Table and the related section of text only) relate to the actual direction of coding reflected in the original questionnaire design. The meaning of a particular result can be readily established by reference to the coding of the individual variables set out in the Appendix to the book and is clearly described in the text. In general, it can be said that the statistical results indicate throughout that larger expenditures were associated with higher levels of consumer confidence.

A summary description of the actual semantic differential scales used in this analysis is given in Table 5.1. It may be noted that even here it is not always clear which of the polar opposite statements in each scale is the more confident. It may be there is a possible conflict between an expression of economic confidence and a commitment to the purchase of consumer durables. Thus, for example, a view that it is a good time to save or buy shares (AS 10, 11) may indicate confidence in the stability of the economy but may imply a lower level of expenditure on consumer durables, at least at the level of the individual consumer. Again, awareness of rising prices of consumer durables (AS 22) may reflect a lack of economic confidence but a stronger commitment to the purchase of consumer durables.

The relation between confidence and socio-economic status

It is sometimes argued that attitudes are closely associated with the socio-economic status of informants. To test this, the correlation between the individual attitude scales from the first survey and certain socio-economic characteristics of the panel was investigated. The socio-economic variables used were:

social class (SOCL), age of the HoH (AGE), duration of marriage (TMRD), number of people in the household (PPL), income of the head of the household (YHOH), total household income (YHH), savings level (STOT), and the amount of credit outstanding (TOTCRDT).

The results of this investigation are set out in Table 5.2 in which all instances where the correlation coefficient was significant at the one per cent level are tabulated. [It might be argued that granted the nature of the data, a correlation coefficient is not the ideal indicator of association. However, it is unlikely that it would give seriously misleading results, it is more readily interpreted and it offers a more expeditious way of dealing with a large number of variables than the available alternatives.]

With such a large number of observations a correlation coefficient as low as .11 may be highly significant although a correlation as low as this is not likely to be particularly meaningful.

The Table indicates that greater confidence was more likely to be expressed by people in higher social class and income groups, with larger savings and by those who were younger or married less long. The highest correlations were recorded with AS 23 and AS 25 which indicated that those who were better off economically were more likely to believe that the rising prices of necessities would not affect their

TABLE 5.2 Correlations between attitude scales and certain socio-economic variables; cases where coefficient is significant at the 1% level

Variables	SOCL	AGE	TMRD	PPL	YHOH	YHH	STOT	TOTCRDT
AS 1	.168	.175	.159		−.260	−.296	−.133	−.116
AS 2	.120	.268	.190		−.174	−.174		−.115
AS 3	.250	.200	.147		−.308	−.294		
AS 4	.113				−.198	−.188		
AS 5	.122	.194			−.193	−.180		
AS 6					−.122			
AS 7								
AS 8								
AS 9	.181				−.165	−.169		
AS 10							−.158	
AS 11	.157				−.163	−.154		
AS 12	.186				−.142	−.111		
AS 13								
AS 14	.152	.195	.138		−.146	−.154		
AS 15		.287	.262					
AS 16	.136			−.108	−.131	−.149		−.121
AS 17	.151		−.131		−.175	−.197	−.238	.118
AS 18		.195	.130					
AS 19	−.175				.129	.121	.138	
AS 20								
AS 21	−.217				.257	.244	.199	−.107
AS 22						.127		
AS 23	−.265				.336	.318	.319	
AS 24		.109						
AS 25	.247			.121	−.314	−.326	−.432	.149
AS 26		.188	.194	−.112	−.157	−.171		−.138
AS 27		.172	.182					
AS 28	.161				−.111	−.124		
AS 29		.167	.125			−.121		−.179

buying of consumer durables and that they could afford to finance any durable purchases from their savings. However, even here one variable only explains a small amount of the variance in the other. Although the direction of association between consumer confidence and socio-economic status is as would be expected, there is support for the view that the formation of attitudes and expectations is quite largely independent of the age and socio-economic status of the informant.

Changes in consumer confidence

By collecting information about consumer confidence, using the same questionnaire, at regular intervals it is possible to observe changes in the degree of consumer confidence and, where the series is long enough, to construct from this an index which may be useful in short-term forecasting. In the case of this study it was possible to collect five sets of observations from the panel during the survey year and in this sub-section we shall consider the nature of the changes in consumer confidence that these surveys indicated. For this purpose we shall use information provided by all respondents to each survey and consequently the number of observations was much larger for the first survey than for subsequent surveys. The possibility has therefore to be considered that any changes in attitudes between the first two surveys may be due to non-response bias. As we saw in Chapter 2 there were four attitude variables on which non-response bias seemed to affect the results in the second survey and in those cases answers to the first two surveys were also compared for just those who completed both stages. The discussion in the text for those four variables is based on the observations for the identical group of respondents only.

Table 5.3 sets out details of the answers obtained for each of the twenty-nine attitude scales. The distribution of the answers on the first survey is tabulated with each scale having the least confident answer at the left hand end and mean values for that variable are shown for each of the five surveys. It is also helpful to be able to identify significant differences between mean values. To do this it is possible to apply standard tests of the significance of the differences of means between two samples if they are independent of each other and are drawn at random from the same population. In our case this does not apply since the same panel of informants was used throughout the survey year. However, it is extremely unlikely that respondents would have remembered the answers they gave three months previously and although continued participation may have produced some conditioning this may well have been compensated by an improvement in the quality of the data obtained. It is therefore arguable that we might be justified in treating our panel at each survey as the equivalent of a new, random sample. On this assumption, Student's t test can be applied to identify which movements in the mean values of a particular attitude scale between surveys can be considered to be statistically significant and not the result of random influences. Strictly speaking, separate calculations need to be made for each pair of values being considered. However, with the standard deviations on many variables in the range 1.4–1.9 we can note as a rough rule of thumb that a difference of about .150 between mean values would be significant at the ten per cent level, a difference of about .180 would be significant at the five per cent level and a difference of about .235 would be significant at the one per cent level. Where the standard deviation was higher a larger difference would be required to be significant.

It will be observed that while some of the response patterns shown in Table 5.3 tend to a normal distribution, many do not. Some are heavily skewed towards one or other of the poles while others are almost bimodal, indicating wide differences of opinion among informants on some issues. Granted the nature of the questions, such disparity in the distributions is to be expected. Indeed, a normal distribution on most questions would give rise to some concern since a concentration of answers about the mid-point of such scales would suggest that the question was not relevant or that the informants found difficulty in expressing an opinion. Since major changes in the strength of consumer confidence would not be expected to be occuring all the time it is encouraging to be able to report that not only did the mean values remain within reasonable bounds but that other measures of the distribution – the mode, standard deviation and skewness also exhibited considerable stability through the five surveys.

The most substantial changes in consumer confidence during the survey year occurred between the first and second surveys, that is between March and July 1972 (it should again be emphasised that these were not the result of non-response bias). As can be seen in Table 5.3 not only were there a large number of variables on which a fall in consumer confidence was recorded at this time, the magnitude of some of the reductions in mean scale values was very considerable indeed. It seems that people realised that the reflationary action taken early in 1972 was not going to solve the country's economic difficulties. By July people were more pessimistic about their financial position and prospects and their employment prospects, they expected to have less money available to spend than in the previous year, that they would be less able to finance durable purchases from their savings, a temporary reduction in their incomes was now more likely to affect their durable purchasing and they expected their financial commitments to increase. There was less

TABLE 5.3 Distribution of responses and mean values on twenty-nine attitude scales

Variable	Variable Description	Distribution of Responses, per cent Survey I on the seven-point scale							Mean Values				
		Least Confident						Most Confident	Survey I	Survey II	Survey III	Survey IV	Survey V
AS 1	Personal financial position compared with previous year	9.5	6.6	8.9	16.9	17.9	25.4	14.9	4.63	4.44	4.41	4.20	4.06
AS 2	Personal financial expectations for next year	4.4	5.1	6.7	19.7	23.4	26.2	14.4	4.89	4.31	4.33	4.10	4.32
AS 3	Personal employment prospects for next year	4.1	2.5	3.0	20.7	10.3	33.3	26.2	5.35	5.05	5.08	5.08	5.00
AS 4	Expectations regarding economic development for next year	9.8	7.9	9.2	25.7	21.8	17.4	8.2	4.27	3.31	3.32	3.21	3.54
AS 5	Expectations regarding sums of money available to spend next year	7.2	8.0	8.7	20.0	21.1	21.8	13.1	4.58	4.00	3.99	3.82	3.92
AS 6	Prospects for economic progress	10.8	9.3	12.8	22.6	20.5	18.4	5.6	4.10	3.05	3.13	3.67	3.94
AS 7	Effect of economic policy on personal financial position	21.8	23.9	16.4	20.0	7.5	6.6	3.8	3.02	3.01	2.94	2.93	2.99
AS 8	Effect of economic policy on personal buying of durables	14.1	14.3	11.3	16.9	12.1	19.8	11.5	4.04	3.70	3.76	3.78	3.89
AS 9	Good time to buy durables	8.5	5.9	6.1	28.9	14.4	19.5	16.7	4.60	4.71	4.70	4.82	4.31
AS 10	Good time to save	12.3	23.8	17.2	16.7	8.5	10.5	11.0	3.61	4.54	4.27	4.11	4.05
AS 11	Good time to buy stocks and shares	10.5	18.7	14.9	37.9	5.7	6.1	6.2	3.53	3.81	3.76	3.67	3.68
AS 12	Confidence in economic policy	16.6	7.7	10.7	19.8	19.3	19.0	6.9	4.02	3.34	3.30	3.49	3.74
AS 13	Price expectations	48.2	30.2	11.3	5.1	2.0	1.8	1.5	1.94	1.57	1.77	1.66	1.93

AS 14	Car buying expectations	46.6	10.0	3.8	13.4	5.2	8.2	12.8	2.97	3.19	3.01	3.07	3.17
AS 15	Intentions to acquire an additional durable	31.0	13.6	4.9	13.9	9.8	11.6	15.1	3.53	4.05	4.12	4.17	4.19
AS 16	Durable replacement expectations	28.5	12.3	5.1	13.0	11.6	14.8	14.8	3.70	4.04	4.25	4.16	4.19
AS 17	Effect of temporary income increase on durable purchasing	10.5	15.2	13.3	16.2	5.2	15.6	23.9	3.67	3.70	3.79	3.76	3.78
AS 18	Whether saving up to buy a durable	42.1	13.1	4.1	16.6	3.4	10.2	10.5	2.98	3.14	3.24	3.26	3.20
AS 19	Unemployment expectations	11.5	11.3	11.6	17.5	17.9	19.0	11.1	4.21	4.05	3.34	3.39	4.64
AS 20	Perceptions of price trends	42.3	31.3	13.3	4.6	3.0	4.4	1.1	2.13	1.75	1.82	2.20	2.14
AS 21	Effect of temporary income decrease on durable purchasing	21.3	15.1	13.8	19.2	6.1	9.5	15.1	3.63	3.45	3.36	3.47	3.60
AS 22	Effect of durable price changes on durable purchasing	16.2	15.6	8.5	31.5	11.0	7.9	9.3	3.66	4.05	4.29	4.46	3.78
AS 23	Effect of prices of necessities on ability to buy durables	18.4	19.8	14.6	17.9	7.4	10.0	12.0	3.54	3.21	3.22	3.07	3.33
AS 24	Durable buying expectations compared with previous year	26.1	16.2	6.9	28.9	6.7	8.5	6.7	3.26	3.37	3.34	3.44	3.24
AS 25	Ability to finance durable purchases from savings	9.8	5.9	3.8	14.8	14.8	24.9	26.1	4.98	4.67	4.77	4.71	4.86
AS 26	Ability to finance durable purchases on credit	5.9	3.8	2.5	24.6	8.0	27.0	28.2	5.19	5.24	5.17	5.15	5.04
AS 27	Expectations regarding future financial commitments	15.9	23.4	14.9	27.0	4.9	6.9	6.9	3.30	3.06	3.26	3.27	3.50
AS 28	General assessment of country's performance	17.4	16.7	10.8	17.9	19.7	13.6	3.9	3.62	2.54	2.68	2.95	3.27
AS 29	Whether increasing discretionary income	32.0	15.9	2.5	17.0	7.9	12.8	12.0	3.39	3.30	3.19	3.04	3.37

Note Increasing mean values, in this Table only, indicate increasing confidence on all variables and vice versa. In order to achieve a consistent direction of scaling in this Table, compared with the layout of the semantic differential scales in the Appendix, the direction of coding has been changed here for the following variables: AS1, 2, 3, 4, 5, 6, 8, 9, 12, 14, 15, 16, 17, 18, 22, 24, 25, 26, 28, 29.

agreement that it was a good time to save or buy stocks and shares. There was less confidence about the economic policy in force at the time and in the prospects for economic progress. There was a strong feeling that the country was not doing well. Probably at the heart of this fall in confidence was increasing concern about prices since there was greater awareness of rising prices, an expectation of further price increases and a stronger feeling that the rising price of necessities would weaken the ability to buy durables.

Despite the declining level of general confidence, there appears to have been some increase in expectations of buying consumer durables. Car purchasing expectations were higher and expectations of buying a new durable and replacing an existing item also increased. This seemed to be associated with a feeling that rising durable prices would make it desirable to bring forward durable purchases. The notion that durable purchasing might increase at a time of generally falling confidence is unusual but is not altogether surprising in a time of rapid inflation. The possibility also has to be recognised that durable purchasing expectations may be subject to seasonal variation. With just one year's observations it is not possible to test this.

Fewer significant changes in consumer confidence became apparent between the second and third surveys, that is between July and October 1972. Unemployment expectations worsened but price expectations improved slightly and informants were less likely to anticipate increasing financial commitments. There was more confidence about saving, and while durable replacement expectations rose and informants were inclined to agree that it was desirable to bring forward durable purchases, car buying expectations fell.

Between October 1972 and January 1973 there was an improvement in confidence about economic policy, in the prospects for economic progress and in the assessment of the country's performance. Respondents were somewhat less conscious of rising prices. On the other hand, informants were slightly less confident on average in their answers about the changes in their own financial position over the past year and in their personal financial expectations for the next twelve months. All these changes in confidence are plausible responses to the imposition of the pay and prices freeze during the autumn of 1972, with the incomes restraint affecting personal financial well-being, but the policy generally gaining public approval.

This improvement in confidence continued between January and April 1973. Personal financial expectations were stronger, informants were less aware of future increases in their likely financial commitments and were more likely to be increasing their discretionary incomes. They continued to show increasing confidence in economic policy, in the country's performance and in the prospects for economic progress. There was a small improvement in price expectations and less concern about the effects of rising prices of necessities on the ability to buy consumer durables. However, as general confidence increased so it seems that once again durable purchasing expectations moved in the opposite direction with less agreement that it was a good time to buy durables, lower durable purchasing expectations and less emphasis on bringing forward purchases to beat rising prices.

The general picture that Table 5.4 offers is that between Surveys I and III confidence about the economy and the way it was being managed declined but rose between Surveys III and V when government pay and price control policies were in force. Informants' confidence in their own circumstances and prospects largely fell between Surveys I and II but rose between Surveys IV and V. On the other hand, durable purchasing expectations were higher between Surveys I and II during the time of low general economic confidence but fell between Surveys IV and V when general confidence seemed to be recovering. As we have already commented, this is perhaps somewhat surprising but it is quite possible that in major inflationary conditions the relationship between consumer economic confidence and durable purchasing expectations may be different from that which exists in more stable conditions. This does not necessarily mean that durable purchases would inevitably be higher. The achieved level of purchases will be dependent upon other influences as well – real disposable incomes, credit conditions etc. All we are observing is that the willingness to buy durables appears to have been higher under such circumstances. It is quite plausible that a high level of inflation may encourage people to take the view that purchases should be brought forward to beat further price rises or in order to use savings whose real value is rapidly depreciating.

The structure of consumer confidence

While each variable is of interest in its own right, there are also two reasons for investigating the inter-relationships between the variables. First, by so doing it may be possible to clarify the psychological 'field' of consumer confidence. Secondly, it may offer ways of combining the variables so that a composite index may be constructed to report changes in the strength of consumer confidence through time.

The basis of the approach adopted here is a principal components analysis based on the correlation matrix of the twenty-nine attitude scales. (The correlation matrix was used in preference to the covariance matrix since it was more appropriate to deal with the possibility that different informants would have had different perceptual views of the

TABLE 5.4 Loadings of each variable on the first three principal components averaged across five surveys

| | | Average loading on: | | |
Variable	Variable Description	First Principal Component	Second Principal Component	Third Principal Component
AS 1	Personal financial position compared with previous year	.256	.067	.225
AS 2	Personal financial expectations for next year	.281	.098	.169
AS 3	Personal employment prospects for next year	.210	.086	.183
AS 4	Expectations regarding economic development for next year	.318	−.044	−.078
AS 5	Expectations regarding sums of money available to spend next year	.289	.107	.178
AS 6	Prospects for economic progress	.302	−.075	−.257
AS 7	Effect of economic policy on personal financial position	−.123	.119	.005
AS 8	Effect of economic policy on personal buying of durables	.219	−.092	.119
AS 9	Good time to buy durables	.124	.076	.037
AS 10	Good time to save	.150	−.057	−.045
AS 11	Good time to buy stocks and shares	.155	.008	−.139
AS 12	Confidence in economic policy	.295	−.111	−.296
AS 13	Price expectations	−.073	.125	.193
AS 14	Car buying expectations	.096	.232	.018

AS 15	Intentions to acquire an additional durable	.128	.324	.065
AS 16	Durable replacement expectations	.094	.308	−.004
AS 17	Effect of temporary income increase on durable purchasing	−.023	.337	−.265
AS 18	Whether saving up to buy a durable	.052	.339	−.165
AS 19	Unemployment expectations	−.179	.138	.208
AS 20	Perceptions of price trends	−.162	.142	.183
AS 21	Effect of temporary income decrease on durable purchasing	−.078	.282	−.262
AS 22	Effect of durable price changes on durable purchasing	−.055	.248	−.065
AS 23	Effect of prices of necessities on ability to buy durables	−.215	.218	−.273
AS 24	Durable buying expectations compared with previous year	.152	.282	.019
AS 25	Ability to finance durable purchases from savings	.137	.000	.215
AS 26	Ability to finance durable purchases on credit	.136	.092	.262
AS 27	Expectations regarding future financial commitments	−.010	.148	.017
AS 28	General assessment of country's performance	.281	−.083	−.282
AS 29	Whether increasing discretionary income	.077	.175	.041
	per cent of variance explained	18.0	10.1	7.1

actual location of the scales.) This produces a loading for each variable on each principal component. Higher loadings indicate that a variable is more important in establishing the structure of that particular component. It is of the nature of principal components analysis that there are as many principal components, each orthogonal to all others, as there are variables included in the analysis. (A factor analysis was carried out on the data but failed to produce a clear factor structure. This is not unduly surprising granted the non-normal distribution of many of the variables.)

While, strictly speaking, it is statistically correct to include all principal components in any analysis, the large number of components and the instability of many of them across the five surveys renders this impracticable in a situation where the same exercise is likely to be undertaken on a number of occasions at different times and where replicability of the component structure is important.

Consequently, a detailed analysis was carried out of the structure of the first eight principal components for all five surveys. These accounted for just under sixty per cent of the variance. Using a measure of the correlation of the loadings of each of the variables on each component between the five surveys, it was found that the first three principal components had stable structures but the others did not. The average correlations of the component structures across the five surveys for the first eight principal components were as follows:

1st principal component = .970	5th principal component = .000
2nd principal component = .915	6th principal component = .140
3rd principal component = .882	7th principal component = .027
4th principal component = .435	8th principal component = .118

Attention in this and the next chapter will therefore focus upon the first three principal components.

The actual structure of these components is indicated by the pattern of loadings of each variable on each principal component in Table 5.4. They are averages of the loadings across all five surveys and it will be observed that these three components accounted, on average, for about thirty-five per cent of the variance in the data. In each survey the actual amount of the variance explained was close to the average since the range on the first principal component was 16.7 per cent – 18.6 per cent, the range for the second principal component was 9.7 per cent – 10.7 per cent and that for the third principal component was 6.6 per cent – 7.8 per cent.

The first principal component has high positive loadings on those variables dealing with the performance and prospects of the economy, the informant's response to the economic policy being adopted, and his view of his personal financial and employment position and expectations. Price and unemployment expectations have negative loadings and so appear to exercise a countervailing influence to general economic considerations. [The program used for this analysis normalised the scales so the direction of coding does not influence the signs on the principal component loadings.] This seems therefore to be a component reflecting general economic confidence. It indicates that worries about rising prices and unemployment may weaken the confidence that individuals otherwise feel about the prospects for economic growth and in their own personal economic situations.

The second principal component has highest positive loadings on variables relating specifically to durable purchasing expectations and the effect of temporary income changes on durable purchasing. This is therefore a component with a specific durable purchasing orientation. The third principal component is more bipolar in structure with the highest positive loadings on variables reflecting the ability to finance durable purchases and the informant's present financial position. High negative loadings apply to variables dealing with general economic performance considerations, the effects of rising prices of necessities, and of temporary income changes. This seems to indicate a conflict between assessments of the ability to make durable purchases on the one hand and a degree of caution arising out of uncertainties about the state of the economy and the consequences of money and real income changes which are not under the control of the individual. We might describe this as an 'economic uncertainty' component.

It will be observed that the first two principal components have the same description as that given to the first two principal components in our earlier work (Pickering *et al* 1973a) and where the same variables have been used in both surveys they tend to have largely similar loadings, although the signs of the loadings on the key variables in the second principal component have now been reversed.

There are, of course, a number of procedures available for establishing attitude structure (see Lemon 1973, Chapter 8) but if the principal component loadings are plotted in two-dimensional space this will offer a clearer indication of the psychological field which they help to define. The plots for pairs of the first three components are shown in Figures 5.1 to 5.3. The values for each variable are the average loadings from all five surveys as in Table 5.4. The clusters of variables were established taking into account also the individual loadings from each of the five surveys separately.

Figure 5.1 is based upon the loadings from the first two principal components. Five groups of variables are distinguishable. Group A contains variables relating to informant perceptions of general economic conditions and in Group B are the variables dealing with the informant's

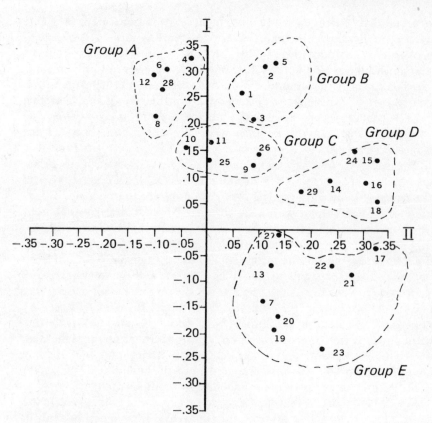

Fig.5.1 Plots of 29 Attitude Scales in Principal Components Space
Components I and II

own financial and employment position and expectations. These two
groups are inter-related on the first component but are clearly distinct on
the second. This suggests that while both general economic conditions
and personal circumstances are relevant to a reflection of general
economic confidence (Component I), the influence they exert on
durable purchasing decisions (Component II) is conflicting, with
considerations of economic circumstances acting to restrain (though
weakly) purchases that consideration of personal well-being might
encourage. Group C relates to the timing of discretionary activities –
saving, buying shares or durables and also includes considerations of the
ability to finance durable acquisitions, which presumably is a further
influence on the timing of such purchases. Group D consists of variables
that emphasise durable purchasing expectations. The location of AS 29

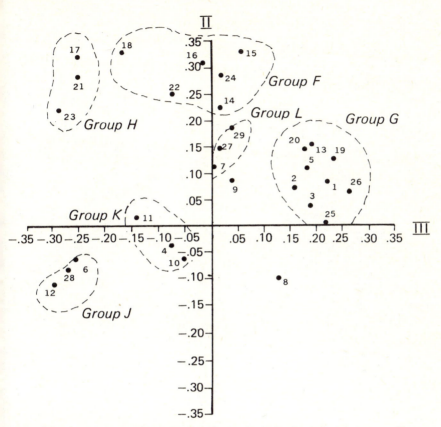

Fig. 5.2   Plots of 29 Attitude Scales in Principal Components Space
Components II and III

(whether the household was increasing its discretionary income) is interesting and supports the evidence from our original depth interviews that there was a close association between increasing discretionary income and durable purchasing. Group E consists of variables dealing with the financial aspects of the purchase decision. While they seem to be positively associated with durable purchasing confidence (Component II), they have a weak negative association with general economic confidence (Component I) and are, for this reason, distinct from Group D.

Figure 5.2 contains plots of loadings from the second and third principal components. There seem to be two main groups and several small clusters. Group F relates to durable purchasing expectations. Group G contains variables dealing with confidence over financial and

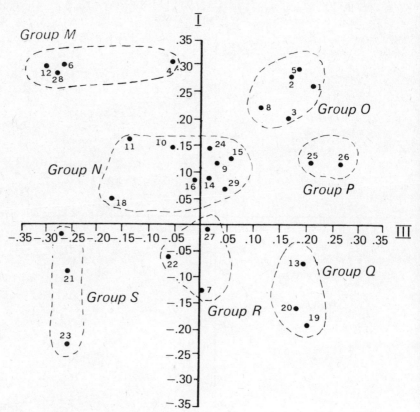

Fig.5.3 Plots of 29 Attitude Scales in Principal Components Space
Components I and III

employment circumstances. Group L also contains variables dealing
with aspects of the household's financial circumstances but this group is
distinct from Group G. Group H deals with the impact of permanent and
real income considerations on the purchase of consumer durables.
Groups J and K both deal with aspects of general economic confidence
with Group J, which deals explicitly with the state of the economy,
having the greater significance in relation to the economic uncertainty
considerations implicit in Component III.

Figure 5.3 deals with the first and third principal components. The
largest cluster, Group N, relates specifically to discretionary activities,
particularly durable purchasing but the loadings on the variables in this
group are low. Since the two principal components involved here are not
primarily concerned with durable purchasing as such it is not surprising

that such variables appear to have little association with either component. Of the other clusters, Groups M and S have the same membership as Groups J and H in Figure 5.2. It is, however, interesting that while economic performance considerations (Groups J and M) are positively associated with general economic confidence (Component I) but negatively associated with durable purchasing expectations (Component II), the situation is reversed for the influence of real and permanent income influences which are negatively associated with Component I and positively associated with Component II. Group O consists of variables reflecting personal financial well-being and is largely similar to Group B in Figure 5.1. Group P is concerned with the means of financing durable purchases, Group Q deals with price and unemployment considerations and Group R also includes variables that reflect aspects of the individual's financial position, though not in a way that has much bearing on either of these components.

From this, admittedly exploratory, investigation of the two-dimensional structure of the psychological field represented by these twenty-nine attitudinal variables, certain comments do appear to be justified. The clusters identified are all readily interpretable and consist of variables which it is intuitively acceptable to see as being related to each other. Some clusters appear in more than one figure and by ignoring the duplications we can reduce the seventeen groups plotted in the figures to eight. Of these, four appear to be major clusters, normally standing on their own, while the other four are sometimes distinct and sometimes part of another cluster.

The clusters identified are as follows.

1. A personal financial expectations cluster (AS 1, 2, 3, 5 and possibly 8).
2. An economic performance cluster (AS 4, 6, 12, 28 and possibly 8).
3. A durable purchasing expectations cluster, also including discretionary income considerations (AS 14, 15, 16, 18, 24, 29).
   In some cases this cluster also appears to contain
   3a. Indicators of the timing of discretionary activities (AS 9, 10, 11) and
   3b. The financing of consumer durable purchases (AS 25, 26).
4. A prices and unemployment expectations cluster (AS 13, 19, 20).
   In some cases this also includes
   4a. Permanent and real income considerations (AS 17, 21, 23) and
   4b. Financial commitments (AS 7, 22, 27).

These clusters expand considerably on the three broad categories into which the variables were placed at the beginning of this chapter. Not only are the perceptual considerations made more explicit but in some cases individual variables have been shown to have a different informational content from that intuitively anticipated. This particularly applies to variables AS 8, 17, 21, 27 and 29.

Indices of consumer confidence

The primary purpose of this particular study is to investigate cross-sectional influences upon the purchase of consumer durables. However, it will be remembered that an important reason for undertaking research in this area was the view that indices of consumer confidence made a predictive contribution in short-term forecasting of the demand for consumer durables, but that there was scope to refine the indices normally constructed for this purpose. The basic ideas on this question were set out in an earlier paper (Pickering *et al* 1973a) and in particular it was argued that in comparison with the procedures normally adopted a larger number of variables covering the relevant psychological field would be desirable; a longer rating scale than the three point scales normally adopted would provide more incisive information on changes in confidence; it was not necessarily correct to assume that all variables were of equal importance and should have equal weight in the construction of an index.

That earlier study indicated how – using more variables, a seven-point rating scale, and a weighting procedure using loadings derived from a principal components analysis as weights for the individual variables – an alternative form of index could be constructed. It was further argued that in order to allow for possible changes in the relative importance of individual variables it would be appropriate to adopt a Fisher Ideal Index, which is the geometric mean of the product of the Laspeyres and Paasche indices, namely:

$$I = 100 \times \sqrt{\frac{\Sigma\, p_1 q_0}{\Sigma\, p_0 q_0} \times \frac{\Sigma\, p_1 q_1}{\Sigma\, p_0 q_1}}$$

where p_0 and p_1 are, respectively, the mean scale values in the base periods and at subsequent points in time, and q_0 and q_1 are the weights for each variable, derived from the loadings in a principal components analysis.

In fact, in view of the stability, interpretability and relevance of the first two components in the earlier study, it was argued that two indices could usefully be produced. These would be an index of general economic confidence using the loadings on the first principal component as weights, and an index of durable purchasing confidence and intentions using the loadings on the second principal component as weights. In the present study, using a greater number of attitude variables we found that the first three principal components were stable and interpretable. However, there does not appear to be a case for constructing an index based on the third component since in view of its greater bipolarity there was a possibility that the positive and negative values might cancel each other out, or at least that small movements in the net value would cause wide swings in the index. However, it seems much more appropriate to continue to construct two indices – of general economic confidence and of durable purchasing confidence – based on the loadings from the first and second principal components respectively. These have considerable similarity to the two indices reported in our previous work.

The values of the indices constructed for the survey year March 1972 – April 1973 are set out in Table 5.5, with March 1972 = 100. This indicates that there was a marked fall in consumer confidence after March 1972. The decline appears to have been more substantial in the case of the indicator of general economic confidence (Index I) which did not improve until January 1973 and in April 1973 was still well below the level of March 1972. In the case of durable purchasing confidence (Index II) the decline in confidence appears to have been less substantial and in 1973 the level was perhaps slightly in excess of that prevailing at the beginning of the survey year.

By combining all variables into composite indices, we are therefore able to offer a succinct summary of the changes in attitudes that were noted individually in Table 5.3 and discussed under 'Changes in consumer confidence' (p.70 above). As would be expected, the movements in the index values largely reflect the individual changes noted in that section. It should, however, be pointed out that in the earlier section it was shown that variables dealing specifically with durable purchasing expectations showed an increase in confidence in the

TABLE 5.5 Values of indices of consumer confidence: March 1972- April 1973

	Time of Survey				
	March 1972	*July 1972*	*October 1972*	*January 1973*	*April 1973*
Index I (general economic confidence)	100	89.0	85.0	89.2	92.6
Index II (durable purchasing confidence)	100	96.8	99.5	101.0	101.3

TABLE 5.6 Linked series of index values of consumer confidence

		Feb 1971	May 1971	June 1971	Sept 1971	Nov 1971	Feb 1972	March 1972	July 1972	Oct 1972	Jan 1973	April 1973
Index I (general economic confidence)	1st surveys Feb 1971=100	100	99.8	103.8	105.7							
	2nd surveys March 1972=100							100	89.0	85.8	89.2	92.6
	Linked series Feb 1971=100	100	99.8	103.8	105.7			108.1	96.2	92.7	96.4	100.1
Index II (durable purchasing confidence)	1st surveys Feb 1971=100	100	92.4	115.8	128.9							
	2nd surveys March 1972=100							100	96.8	99.5	101.0	101.3
	Linked series Feb 1971=100	100	92.4	115.8	128.9			119.7	115.9	119.1	120.9	121.3
Gallup index (adjusted)		76	70	70	83	89	94	104	104	112	115	130

early part of the survey year and then a decline. The values for Index II do not support this, because the index is a weighted average of the movements in attitudes on twenty-nine variables whereas the earlier section described changes in just a few individual variables. This serves to emphasise that even though a summary index has many advantages it is also necessary to investigate the nature of the changes in the individual variables that cause the index value to alter, or even, by balancing each other out, to remain unchanged.

As both the present and the earlier investigations were regarded as experimental, no priority was given to using the same battery of attitude scales in both sets of survey work. The objective in the present study has been to extend and improve upon the earlier work. Consequently, it is difficult to compare directly the index values from the first set of four surveys reported in our earlier paper (Pickering *et al* 1973a) with those reported here. However, there might be some interest in attempting to unite the two series. Seventeen of the variables were used in both sets of surveys and it is possible to calculate an index value for March 1972 based on February 1971 = 100 for just those seventeen scales. If, then, we can assume that these seventeen variables moved compositely in a way that was not markedly different from the full batteries of twenty-three and twenty-nine scales used in the two sets of surveys, the index value for March 1972 for seventeen variables only can be used to link the two series. The results of this exercise are shown in Table 5.6, the values of the Gallup Poll Consumer Confidence Index (1960 = 100) are also included for comparison.

The effect of linking the two series suggests that the level of consumer confidence on both indices was higher in March 1972 than in September 1971, the time of the ending of the previous surveys. This is also confirmed by the Gallup index. There is a fair degree of similarity in the direction, if not the magnitude of changes in consumer confidence recorded by the linked indices on the one hand and the Gallup index on the other.

The test of the value of one or more indices of consumer confidence is in their ability to improve the short – term forecasting of shifts in the demand for consumer durables. With so few observations it is unfortunately not meaningful to attempt such a test with the present data. The general position remains, however, that other indicators of consumer sentiment have been found to have predictive power. If, as has been suggested here, the approach advocated in this chapter has certain advantages over the methods hitherto adopted, it is likely that this sort of index would prove of even greater value for forecasting purposes.

6 *The determinants of expenditure on consumer durables*

In the previous chapters we have investigated certain characteristics of the sample, noted the way in which their circumstances and confidence changed during the survey year and recorded the pattern of their reported expenditures aggregated over a number of major consumer durables. The durables concerned were black and white televisions, central heating, carpets, colour television, cooker, deep freeze, dishwasher, major furniture, new car, used car, record player, refrigerator, tape recorder, vacuum cleaner and washing machine. All expenditures were reported gross except that outlays on cars were reported net of trade-in allowances.

In this chapter we shall investigate by means of multiple regression analysis the extent to which the levels of recorded expenditure of different households can be explained and the type of variables that appear to have a major role in influencing variations in such expenditure. This is based upon those respondents completing the postal follow-ups and for whom we therefore have information about expenditures over the survey year.

The primary attention will be on the attempt to explain variations in expenditure levels over the survey year as a whole but some consideration will also be given to quarterly expenditures. Table 6.1 sets out the actual distribution of expenditure levels of those households providing information on their durable purchasing throughout the survey year. (The annual expenditure figure used here was that derived by the summation of the recorded expenditures over the four quarters.) As was to be expected, the dispersion of expenditures was much greater over the whole year than within a particular quarter. In each of the four quarters more than fifty per cent of the sample did not buy any consumer durables, but over the year as a whole only fifteen per cent had zero expenditures on these items. Table 6.2 provides details of the relationship between expenditure in the different quarters. None of the correlation coefficients there are significant and this suggests that expenditure in one quarter is independent of expenditure in the preceding or succeeding quarter. This is not surprising since consumer durables are expensive items, infrequently purchased and consequently recorded patterns of expenditure for most households are likely to be lumpy rather than continuous.

The annual and quarterly expenditures constitute the dependent variables for the analysis in this chapter. Some consideration was given to the exact form in which the dependent variable might be specified. In an earlier paper on a similar question (Pickering and Isherwood 1975)

TABLE 6.1 Distribution of annual and quarterly expenditures (*percentages*)

	Expenditure over:				
£	Whole Year	First Quarter	Second Quarter	Third Quarter	Fourth Quarter
0	15	54	67	63	61
1-200	30	28	17	25	25
201-400	16	8	7	5	5
401-600	12	4	3	3	4
601-800	9	3	3	2	1
801-1000	6	1	2	1	1
1001-1200	2				
1201-1400	3				
1401-1600	4	}3	}2	}2	}2
1601 and over	4				
Mean values	£458	£138	£115	£101	£103

TABLE 6.2 Correlation between recorded expenditures in each quarter

	1st Quarter	2nd Quarter	3rd Quarter	4th Quarter
1st Quarter		.038	−.050	.050
2nd Quarter			−.014	−.050
3rd Quarter				−.021

we had argued that variations of a few pounds one way or the other were not likely to be particularly important in consumer durable purchasing, the crucial decision was whether to make a purchase or not. We chose in that case to take the log of the dependent variable as a way of giving effect to this view and reported that compared with a linear regression, the log form of the dependent variable gave a slightly better fit without materially influencing the selection of significant variables in the regression equations. In the case of the present data, further consideration was given to the appropriate form of the dependent variable. Various tests were run to try to establish which form was likely to give the best fit. It was found that this was given by a cube root transformation which is not unlike the log of the dependent variable. Linear regression equations were also run for comparative purposes. These showed, on average, a slightly reduced coefficient of multiple determination and no substantial difference in the variables selected as significant. Accordingly therefore the discussion in this chapter will be based upon results using as the dependent variable the cube root of the recorded expenditure. However, since the use of a linear dependent variable allows a more ready interpretation of the parameter estimates, the results obtained from the linear analysis are set out in Tables 6.7 – 6.10 in the Appendix to this chapter.

Annual expenditures

The method of analysis

Economists normally assume that the household's ability to finance purchases is the main type of influence on variations in expenditure levels. The hypothesis underlying this work and that of other investigations in the area of behavioural economics is that it is not only *ability* but also *willingness* to purchase that determines behaviour. Consequently, different sorts of variables that fall within each of these broad categories were used as independent variables in the regressions to explain variations in observed annual expenditure levels. Regressions were run initially using the different types of independent variable separately and then composite equations investigated the overall explanatory power of the data. While most studies are solely concerned with the testing of a static model – that *ex ante* circumstances influence subsequent behaviour, the availability of panel data from which observations were taken at a number of different points in time meant that it was also possible to introduce dynamic considerations into the model and in particular to investigate the extent to which changes over the survey year in consumer confidence and changes in the household's economic circumstances during that year helped to explain consumer behaviour.

The basic data used in this analysis has been described in earlier chapters (though see also Chapter 7 for details of ownership of consumer durables) and details of the coding etc, are set out in the Appendix to the study (p.235). Summary descriptions of the independent variables used in each stage of the analysis are as follows.

1. Socio-economic status of the household – social class (SOCL), age of HoH (AGE), length of time married (TMRD), number of people in the household (PPL), household income (YHH).

2. Durable goods ownership – number of cars owned by the household (CARS), total number of durable goods owned (TOTG), whether the household owned central heating (CH), whether there was a colour television in the home (CTV).

3. Financial circumstances of the household – whether the household had any outstanding HP commitments (HP), whether any hire purchase agreements were due to terminate in the following three months (HPEND), the total amount of credit outstanding in the household – excluding mortgages (TOTCRDT), total savings of the household (STOT), how the household's savings had changed over the previous twelve months (DS), how the savings level was expected to change in the following twelve months (EXPDS).

4. Expectational variables – whether the household expected to move house in the following twelve months (MOVE), whether the household could increase its income temporarily (INCY), whether the household expected to use more or less bank credit in the following three months (MRLSCR), whether any hire purchase agreements were expected to be ended early (HPEARLY), whether the household expected to use more or less hire purchase over the next three months (HPEXP), the amount of money the household expected to spend on consumer durables in the following three months (EXPSP3), the amount of money the household expected to spend on durables in the following twelve months (EXPSP12).

5. Consumer confidence: Survey I – levels of confidence recorded on twenty-nine attitude scales at the start of the survey year, see Chapter 5 for a description (AS 1_1 . . . . . AS 29_1)

6. Respondent scores on the principal component combinations: Survey I – of the twenty-nine attitude scales used in equation 5

(OPT1$_1$ . . . . OPT3$_1$). The first three principal components only were used as they were found to be stable in structure throughout the five surveys (see Chapter 5).

7. *Composite equation* of variables used in equations *1, 2, 3, 4, 5.*

8. *Composite equation* of variables used in equations *1, 2, 3, 4, 6.*

Dynamic Equations

9. *Changes in consumer confidence* between surveys I and V. The differences between the level of confidence recorded by each respondent on each of the twenty-nine attitude scales between the surveys marking the beginning and the end of the survey year were used as the regressors (DAS1$_{1-5}$ . . . . . DAS29$_{1-5}$)

10. *Changes in respondent scores on the principal component combinations* between surveys I and V. The differences between respondent scores on the first three principal components of the twenty-nine attitude scales for surveys I and V were used (DOPT1$_{1-5}$ . . . . . DOPT3$_{1-5}$)

11. *Composite equation* of variables used in equations *1, 2, 3, 4, 9.*

12. *Composite equation* of variables used in equations *1, 2, 3, 4, 10.*

In addition, while regular surveys made it possible to investigate the relation between expenditure and changes in consumer confidence over the survey year, it was also possible to investigate the extent to which the household's circumstances had changed in that time and the likely effect of such changes on expenditure. In Chapter 4 we saw the way in which average expenditures varied according to information about different facets of the household's activities and changes in circumstances over the survey year. In particular, we collected information on the amount spent over the year compared with what the respondent had expected to spend during that time (EXPCFD); changes in income of the HoH (DYHoHYR) and household (DYHHYR); changes in levels of savings (DSYR), hire purchase commitments (DHPYR) and shareholdings (DSHYR) all compared to the previous year; whether the changes just listed were anticipated (ANTD) and favourable (DFAV); whether during the past year the respondent had moved house (WMOVD), bought a second car or a third car for the first time (WBCAR2 and WBCAR3), retired from work (WRETD), increased the size of his

family (WINCHH), taken an overseas holiday (WHOLS), spent sums of
£100 or more on house decorations or improvements (WDEC), installed
central heating (WCH), entered into new and substantial financial
commitments (WFIN), incurred heavy expenses (WHXP), received
large unexpected payments (WGN), received a credit card for the first
time (WCC); how the household's financial position in real terms
compared with the position a year earlier (FPCFD); opinions on the
prices of food (OPF) and durable goods (OPDG) – whether they were
higher or lower than had been expected; whether the level of prices had
stopped a purchase that had otherwise been anticipated (PNB) or
whether items had been bought earlier because of anticipated price
increases (PERL); the number of people in the household working, full
time or part time, over the previous year (NOWK).

Some of these circumstances were expected to have had an influence
on durable purchases, indeed some of them related directly to
expenditure on consumer durables. Since they occurred after the time at
which the *ex ante* observations were taken, for predictive purposes there
was little point in trying to incorporate them into a model to forecast the
level of expenditure as such. However, it was considered that such
events might have had some effect in causing actual levels of
expenditure to deviate from those predicted for individual households
from the *ex ante* data alone. In other words, it was hypothesised that at
least some of these variables dealt with changes in circumstances which
would have caused actual expenditures to be either higher or lower than
had initially been predicted. In order to test this, it was considered more
appropriate to regress these variables not on the actual expenditure
levels used as the dependent variables but on the *residuals* from the
composite equations used in the previous analysis. Consequently further
analyses were run regressing the variables dealing with the change in the
household's circumstances on the residuals (that is the unexplained
variance from the initial predictive equations) from equation 7.

Correlations of Predictive Variables with Expenditure

It is desirable to be aware of the extent to which variables that are
assumed to be independent are in fact collinear with each other. Where
such multicollinearity does exist it does not necessarily follow that a
variable that is not selected in a multiple regression analysis is not in fact
significant, it may simply be the case that another variable with which
this variable is collinear has accounted for all the variance which the
other could have explained.

In order to meet this problem it is helpful to consider the extent to
which each variable is individually correlated with the expenditure
dependent variable and to identify those variables that are also

significantly correlated with other independent variables. In this way the reader can, if he is surprised at the omission of a particular variable from the optimum set in a regression equation, establish whether or not this may be due to multicollinearity amongst the independent variables.

Table 6.3 sets out the variables which are significantly correlated with the cube root of the recorded expenditure level, their zero order correlation coefficients, the other variables with which they are substantially correlated ($r \geqslant .4$) and the size of those correlation coefficients. It will be observed that while there is some ·multicollinearity between variables of the same type, there is little evidence of multicollinearity between different types of variables.

The signs on the coefficients have to be interpreted in the light of the direction of the coding of each variable (set out in the Appendix at the end of the book). Using this we find, for example, that higher expenditure was associated with both higher social class status (SOCL) and higher household income (YHH). There is a negative correlation between SOCL and YHH because the coding of SOCL rises as social class status falls but the coding of YHH rises as income rises. In all cases, the signs on the AS and OPT variables indicate that higher expenditure was correlated with higher levels of confidence.

Table 6.3 indicates that larger expenditures on consumer durables were associated with households in higher social class and income groups. They already owned more cars and a larger number of consumer durables in aggregate, had experienced an increase in their savings over the twelve months preceding the first survey, reported expectations of moving house and spending larger sums of money in the following three and twelve months. The heads of heavier spending households were younger. The households who subsequently spent the largest amounts on durables were those who in the first survey had indicated greater confidence about their financial position and expectations. They were also more likely to have considered it was a good time to buy durables, expected to buy a car in the next twelve months, expected to buy a new durable item they did not own at that time and to replace an existing durable, expected to buy more durables in the following twelve months than in the last year, said they were saving up to buy a particular durable, and expected to be able to finance any durable purchase from their savings. The coefficients on the first two principal components of the attitude scales also indicate that heavier spenders were more confident in respect of both their general economic confidence and their durable purchasing expectations. This is a consistent and plausible picture of the durable purchaser as financially more confident, better able to afford and more willing to finance durable purchases, and having stronger expectations of making durable acquisitions in the following year.

TABLE 6.3 Zero-order correlations between variables and with the cube root of the recorded expenditure level

Variable	*Correlation with Cube Root of Expenditure*	*Other significant variables with which the variable is correlated and size of correlation coefficient (in brackets)*
SOCL	$-.271$	YHH $(-.45)$, CARS $(-.41)$, TOTG $(-.43)$
AGE	$-.163$	
YHH	$.224$	SOCL $(-.45)$
CARS	$.262$	SOCL $(-.41)$, TOTG $(.65)$
TOTG	$.209$	SOCL $(-.43)$ CARS $(.65)$
DS	$.134$	
MOVE	$-.199$	
EXPSP 3	$.300$	EXPSP 12 $(.46)$
EXPSP 12	$.340$	EXPSP 3 $(.46)$, AS 14_1 $(.45)$
AS 1_1	$-.141$	AS 2_1 $(.54)$
AS 2_1	$-.123$	AS 1_1 $(.54)$
AS 9_1	$-.123$	
AS 14_1	$-.339$	EXPSP 12 $(.45)$
AS 15_1	$-.199$	AS 24_1 $(.40)$
AS 16_1	$-.113$	
AS 18_1	$-.179$	
AS 24_1	$-.156$	AS 15_1 $(.40)$
AS 25_1	$-.126$	
OPT 1_1	$-.184$	
OPT 2_1	$-.188$	
DAS 14_{1-5}	$-.306$	
DAS 15_{1-5}	$-.107$	DAS 24_{1-5} $(.41)$
DAS 16_{1-5}	$-.132$	
DAS 18_{1-5}	$-.159$	
DAS 24_{1-5}	$-.252$	DAS 15_{1-5} $(.41)$
DOPT 2_{1-5}	$-.186$	

Notes Only variables with correlations with the expenditure level significant at the five per cent level were recorded here. Correlations between variables are noted only where the correlation coefficient was at least .4, and where both variables were significantly correlated with the expenditure variable.

The description of the variables is available in the text of this chapter. The Appendix at the end of the book contains descriptions of all variables together with details of their coding.

Some OPT and DAS variables are of course correlated with the AS variables. Since they are never combined in the same multiple regression analysis the problem of multicollinearity does not arise and such cases are therefore not recorded in the table.

The variables reflecting changes in consumer confidence over the survey year (DAS_{1-5}; $DOPT_{1-5}$) are interesting. They indicate that larger outlays were made by households who, at the end of the survey year compared with the beginning, had lower expectations of buying a car or a new durable or of replacing an existing item, were less likely to be saving up to buy a durable and expected to buy fewer durables in the following twelve months. This is also reflected in a decline in durable purchasing expectations as indicated by the second principal component combination of the attitudinal variables.

Since we have already observed that greater confidence in these respects at the start of the survey year was associated with larger expenditures on consumer durables during that year, it is quite reasonable that a cross-sectional investigation should find that larger outlays were associated with those who, by the end of the year, had reduced expectations of making durable purchases. This also serves to emphasise that, for most individual households, durable purchases are discrete activities and a high level of purchasing in one period is unlikely to be associated with an equally high level of expenditure in the next.

Static multiple regression analysis

The results for those multiple regression equations that we have described as static are set out in Table 6.4. Of the equations using single types of variable, those using the expectational, confidence and socio-economic variables have the largest corrected coefficients of multiple determination. The equations using principal component combinations of the confidence data need not necessarily be considered unsuccessful, especially when it is remembered that the first three principal components accounted for only thirty-five per cent of the variance in the attitude scales. The composite equations have a higher overall predictive success rate which, with up to twenty-three per cent of the variance explained, is not high but is certainly not worse than that obtained for many cross-sectional studies.

Rather fewer variables were selected by the composite equations, but it is encouraging that the choice was, in every case but one, from among the variables that had been found to be significant in the equations based on a single type of variable only. The one exception, AS 18_1, was also shown in Table 6.3 to be significantly correlated with expenditure. The results of equations 7 and 8 suggest that higher expenditures on consumer durables were more likely to have been made by households in the higher social class groups, those who owned more cars, expected to spend larger sums of money on consumer durables, thought they were more likely to move house, had a higher level of consumer durable purchasing confidence especially in their expectations of buying a car, and were more likely to be saving up to buy a particular durable. (Car ownership is closely correlated with the total number of consumer durables owned and may be considered to be a proxy for this variable.) These results are meaningful and indicate that consumer expectations do make an important independent predictive contribution. This therefore supports the underlying hypothesis that the demand for consumer durables is a function of both the household's ability and its willingness to buy.

There are, however, some interesting aspects which are worthy of further comment. The regression coefficients on the expected levels of expenditure on consumer durables (EXPSP3 and EXPSP12) in Table 6.4 are not very informative because of the use of the cube root form of the dependent variable. Referring however to the linear regressions where these variables were again significant (Table 6.8) we find that the regression coefficients on these variables in the composite equations were of the order of 0.3. This indicates that for every extra £1 that a household reported expecting to spend over the following three or twelve months it actually spent about thirty pence over the ensuing year.

Since car purchases represent an important element in total household outlays on consumer durables, the significance of the car purchasing expectations variable (AS 14_1) is encouraging. It might be that this not only helps to predict car purchases but possibly non-car durable expenditures as well. Our data does not readily allow us to test this hypothesis. Heavier expenditures were also associated with households that thought they were more likely to move house in the following twelve months (MOVE). As we observed in Chapter 4 these were also the households who were in fact proportionately more likely to have moved during the survey year.

As in our previous investigation, the results indicate that the households that already owned more consumer durables were also most likely to be heavy spenders on such items. While there is some positive association between socio-economic status and durable ownership, other influences seem also to be at work here. Perhaps those who own several cars or large numbers of durables are more oriented to the acquisition of durables rather than to other discretionary activities. If so, then such variables may be as much a measure of willingness to buy durables as an indication of socio-economic status. An alternative explanation may be that higher existing durable ownership levels increase the chances that one or more items will need replacement during a particular period and so in this way durable ownership tends to beget durable replacement demand.

The results involving respondent scores on the principal component combinations of the confidence variables are of interest. Both the first two principal components, reflecting respectively general economic confidence and durable purchasing expectations ($OPT1_1$ and $OPT2_1$), were significant when just the first three principal components were used to predict expenditures in equation 6. The signs on the regression coefficients indicate that higher expenditures were recorded by those

TABLE 6.4 Multiple regressions of cube root expenditures on socio-economic, durable goods ownership, financial expectations and confidence variables

| | $N = 361$ | | | | | | | |
| | *Equation* | | | | | | | |
Variables	1	2	3	4	5	6	7	8
Constant	7.970	4.607	4.780	7.712	9.290	6.140	9.525	7.335
SOCL	-.559 (.163)	—	—	—	—	—	-.333 (.152)	-.381 (.153)
AGE	-.719 (.182)	—	—	—	—	—		
TMRD	.344 (.158)	—	—	—	—	—		
YHH	.218 (.094)	—	—	—	—	—		
CARS	—	1.458 (.284)					.998 (.284)	1.036 (.287)
DS	—	—	.459 (.179)	—	—	—		
MOVE	—	—	—	-.841 (.318)	—	—	-.749 (.304)	-.694 (.308)
EXPSP 3	—	—	—	.003 (.001)	—	—	.001 (.001)	.002 (.001)
EXPSP 12	—	—	—	.002 (.000)	—	—	.001 (.000)	.002 (.000)
$AS\ 14_1$	—	—	—	—	-.469 (.077)	—	-.218 (.083)	—
$AS\ 15_1$	—	—	—	—	-.176 (.080)	—		—
$AS\ 18_1$	—	—	—	—		—	-.191 (.076)	—
$AS\ 21_1$	—	—	—	—	.165 (.085)	—		—
$AS\ 27_1$	—	—	—	—	-.196 (.107)	—		—
$OPT\ 1_1$	—	—	—	—	—	-.299 (.084)	—	
$OPT\ 2_1$	—	—	—	—	—	-.392 (.107)	—	-.310 (.103)
$\bar{R}^2$	.113	.063	.012	.149	.131	.061	.234	.218

Notes All regression coefficients are significant at the ten per cent level. Figures in brackets are standard errors of the parameter estimates
— indicates that a variable was not included in that particular equation.

who were more confident and had stronger purchasing expectations. When considered in combination with other types of variable the durable purchasing expectations component remained highly significant.

The variables that were significant in the earlier equations but not in the composite equations also support the general picture already described. Higher expenditures were associated with households with higher incomes, where savings over the preceding year had increased, where there was anticipation of buying a new durable the following year, and greater confidence that durable purchases would not be affected by a temporary fall in the household's income but there was an expectation of increased future financial commitments. In addition, higher outlays were made by households where the HoH was younger but higher expenditures seem also to be related to a longer duration of marriage in a household. The positive relation between the duration of marriage and recorded expenditure on durables seems only to hold where the cube root form of the dependent variable is used (the zero order correlation between these two variables was also positive). The relation between duration of marriage and expenditure recorded on a linear scale was negative though in this case the duration of marriage was not significant in any of the linear expenditure regression equations.

In general, if we compare the results in Table 6.4 with those for the linear regressions in Table 6.8, we find a considerable similarity in the significant variables in the two cases. The overall explanatory power is also extremely close in both analyses.

Dynamic multiple regression analysis – changes in consumer confidence

The equations incorporating measures of the change in consumer confidence between the beginning and the end of the survey year are set out in Table 6.5. As we have already noted when considering the zero order correlations, higher expenditures were associated with those who, at the end of the survey year, had lower durable purchasing expectations. This is again reflected in Table 6.5 where, at the end of the survey year compared with the first survey, lower car purchase expectations, less responsiveness of durable purchases to a temporary income increase and an expectation of buying fewer durables in the following year were all associated with greater expenditures on consumer durables over the survey year (DAS14, 17, 24 and DOPT2). However, the signs on DAS27 and 28 indicate that heavier expenditures were also associated with those who, between the beginning and the end of the survey year, became less likely to anticipate a future increase in

TABLE 6.5 Multiple regressions of cube root expenditure on variables incorporating measures of the change in consumer confidence

	Equation			
Variable	9	10	11	12
Constant	6.185	6.169	7.633	7.532
SOCL	—	—	-.402 (.147)	-.383 (.152)
AGE	—	—	-.409 (.167)	
TMRD	—	—	.270 (.142)	
CARS	—	—	1.181 (.277)	1.061 (.284)
MOVE	—	—	-.530 (.295)	-.782 (.304)
EXPSP 3	—	—		.002 (.001)
EXPSP 12	—	—	.002 (.000)	.002 (.000)
DAS 14_{1-5}	-.322 (.063)	—	-.242 (.059)	—
DAS 17_{1-5}		—	-.112 (.066)	—
DAS 24_{1-5}	-.269 (.073)	—	-.285 (.067)	—
DAS 27_{1-5}		—	-.224 (.088)	—
DAS 28_{1-5}		—	.211 (.087)	—
DOPT 2_{1-5}	—	-.334 (.093)	—	-.338 (.084)
$\overline{R}^2$	.119	.029	.300	.233

Notes All regression coefficients are significant at the 10% level. Figures in brackets are standard errors of the parameter estimates.
— indicates that a variable was not included in that particular equation.

their financial commitments and showed greater confidence in the state of the country.

This pattern of higher expenditure where buying expectations had, by the end of the survey year, declined because they had already been fulfilled but where, in some measure, personal and general economic confidence had improved is again entirely plausible. In the composite equations 11 and 12 we again find that larger expenditures were also associated with households in the higher social classes, with younger HoH's but also those that had been married longer, that owned more cars and had stronger expectations of moving and of spending larger sums of money on consumer durables. These results are again largely confirmed by the linear regressions (Table 6.9).

While changes in consumer confidence, in some of its different facets, between the beginning and the end of the survey year seem to be associated with durable expenditures, other influences may have been at work during the survey year in influencing the actual purchase behaviour of individual households. It is therefore to the influence of changed household circumstances that we now turn.

Dynamic analysis: the effect of changed household circumstances

The extent to which different types of change in household circumstances were associated with varying levels of expenditure on consumer durables over the survey year was investigated for each variable separately in Chapter 4. It was found there that substantially higher expenditures were recorded in cases where the household subsequently reported that it had improved its real financial position, had increased its usage of hire purchase and other credit facilities, had increased its share holding, had moved house, had purchased a second and/or a third car for the first time, had installed central heating, had entered into substantial new financial commitments, and had incurred heavy unexpected expenses.

While these results are reassuring in that they are plausible in their patterns of association, they are not particularly surprising. Our interest here, however, is not so much in the way in which total expenditures were influenced by such circumstances and actions but in the extent to which changes in household circumstances may have caused the actual level of expenditure to be different from that which the initial information about each of the respondents would have predicted. Consequently, as we have already described in the earlier part of this chapter, we took the residuals from the composite predictive equation 7 and regressed them on the variables relating to changes in the household's circumstances during the survey year. The results obtained, standard errors in brackets, were as follows:

13.   *Expenditure Regression Residuals*= $-4.793 + .909$ EXPCFD
$$(.140)$$
$+ .461$ DHPYR $+ 1.267$ WCH $- .645$ WCC
$$(.185) \qquad (.550) \qquad (.332)$$
$$\bar{R}^2 = .147$$

In the light of this result it would appear that changes in household circumstances explained about fifteen per cent of the residual variance after the initial predictive equation had been estimated. As regards the particular respects in which the change in household circumstances appeared to have a significant influence on unpredicted levels of expenditure, we find that four variables were significant in the multiple regression analysis. These indicate that higher levels of the initially unexplained expenditure occurred where respondents reported that over the survey year as a whole they had spent more on consumer durables than they initially anticipated, they had increased their usage of hire purchase and other credit, were more likely to have installed central heating, but were less likely to have received a credit card for the first time.

The results based upon the regression of the residuals from the original multiple regression analysis using a linear dependent variable (see equation 13 in Table 6.9) are similar in that they also indicate higher unexplained variance where households reported at the end of that year that they had spent more than they had initially anticipated and where they had also undertaken other discretionary activities by increasing their shareholdings, spending more than £100 on home decorations or improvements and entering into substantial new financial commitments. They were also more likely to have experienced a reduction in their savings over the previous year, presumably as a result of these outlays.

Once again, the explanatory power is not high and it might justifiably be pointed out that, with the exception of the most significant variable (EXPCFD) which is common to both analyses, the selection of significant variables in the two alternative forms of the analysis, based respectively on the residuals from the cube root and linear forms of the dependent variable, are not stable, though they do both reflect the influence of similar sorts of activity. Nevertheless there are some noteworthy implications from the results. It is interesting that where consumers made outlays above the level which our initial information about them would have led us to predict, they were likely to report at the end of the survey year that they had spent more on consumer durables than they had initially expected. This gives grounds for confidence in the internal consistency of the data and suggests that it is meaningful to ask consumers about their own expectations, even if, subsequently there is some divergence between the anticipation and the actual outcome. That higher unexplained expenditures were associated with particular forms of discretionary spending and with increased usage of hire purchase indicates the desirability of improving still further the *ex ante* prediction of the level of such activities.

It had been hypothesised that some association would be found between the unexplained variance in expenditure levels and windfall gains or losses, with windfall gains leading to expenditures in excess of those initially predicted on the basis of the *ex ante* information and windfall losses leading to expenditures below the predicted level. The results gave no support to this hypothesis, although the proportions reporting either a windfall gain or heavy unexpected expenses were so small that such an effect may have been difficult to detect. However, it is relevant to recall the finding reported in Chapter 4 that the actual expenditure levels of such households also did not appear to support this hypothesis.

Analysis of quarterly expenditures

Because there are higher levels of expenditure, and a much greater proportion of the sample recording purchases over the year as a whole than in any single quarter, it is appropriate to pay most attention to explaining variations in the expenditures recorded by the panel aggregated across the whole survey year. However, there is also potential interest in exploring the influences upon the expenditures recorded for each quarter. In particular, the availability of data on quarterly expenditures and on the nature of consumer attitudes at quarterly intervals allows us to investigate the temporal duration of the relationship between consumer confidence and consumer purchasing behaviour. Time series analysis has frequently suggested that changes in consumer confidence lead changes in expenditure by a period of six to nine months. While the number of observations is too small to test this effectively it is possible at least to investigate the extent to which attitudes expressed at one moment are related to behaviour over subsequent periods.

The data for this investigation are therefore the indications of the level of consumer confidence in each of the first four surveys (AS 1_1 . . . . . AS 29_1; . . . ; AS 1_4 . . . . AS 29_4) and details of expenditure by each informant over each of the four quarters making up the survey year (see

Table 6.1). The first survey was carried out at the beginning of the first quarter and the second survey was carried out at the end of the first quarter/beginning of the second quarter and so on. Thus the fifth survey and set of attitudinal scales relates to the end of the fourth quarter and consequently does not make a predictive contribution to forecasting expenditure in any quarter of the survey year. The average expenditure levels per respondent in each quarter are also set out in Table 6.1. The method of analysis is again stepwise multiple regression. There are in fact ten analyses possible since the predictive power of the first set of attitude scales can be investigated for each of the four quarters' expenditures separately, the consumer confidence measures from the second survey have a possible predictive relation with expenditure in three quarters, and so on.

The comments about the possibility of multicollinearity that were made in the discussion of the determinants of annual expenditures also apply to the quarterly expenditure analysis. In fact for the present analysis it appears that quite strong multicollinearity ($r \geqslant \cdot 4$) between AS 15 and AS 24 may have had some influence on the selection of either as significant variables in the regressions and there is a slight possibility that in a single analysis multicollinearity between AS 1 and AS 2, AS 1 and AS 5, AS 3 and AS 5, AS 4 and AS 5 may be a reason why one variable was selected rather than the other in the pair. With these minor exceptions the influence of multicollinearity can be discounted.

The main results of this analysis are set out in Table 6.6. In that table, in the top left hand corner of each cell where appropriate, a $+$ or $-$ indicates cases where the zero order correlation of that variable with the relevant quarterly expenditure was significant at the five per cent level and the direction of association. The lower right hand segment indicates the sign and size of the regression coefficient for each variable where significant at the ten per cent level. Five attitude variables (AS 2, 10, 11, 13, 28) are omitted in the table since they were not significant in any of the analyses.

At the most, it appears that the attitude scales explain about twelve per cent of the variance in expenditures in an individual quarter, with greater explanatory power for expenditures made in the following three months than for longer predictive time horizons. The failure to find any significant variables for two analyses based on expenditure recorded in the fourth survey is disappointing, though there were some individual variables that would have been significant if a slightly less stringent selection criterion had been adopted.

While quite a high proportion of the twenty-nine attitudinal variables were found to be significantly associated with expenditure in one or other of the 10 analyses, there were fewer which were found to be

TABLE 6.6 Results of correlation and multiple regression analyses of cube root of quarterly expenditures on attitude scales from successive surveys

| Variable | Predictive Time Horizon | | | | | | | | | |
| | 3 months | | | | 6 months | | | 9 months | | 12 months |
	I v 1	II v 2	III v 3	IV v 4	I v 2	II v 3	III v 4	I v 3	II v 4	I v 4
Constant	5.184	2.800	3.878	4.325	3.553		3.212		2.361	3.719
AS 1					—					
AS 3	−.228			+.192						
AS 4			+.207				+.255			
AS 5							—			
AS 6		+.287								
AS 7				+.204						
AS 8				+.149						
AS 9	—									
AS 12									+.241	+.176
AS 14	−.398	−.297		−.346	−.129		−.314			−.123
AS 15				−.205						
AS 16		−.171								

	1	2	3	4	5	6	7	8	9	10
AS 17					− .204		− .273			
AS 18		− .258	− .221	− .164						− .234
AS 19							+ .188			
AS 20	+ .139									
AS 21			− .178							
AS 22		+ .336	+ .179		+ .238		+ .280			
AS 23			− .367		− .177					
AS 24									− .284	
AS 25	− .186									
AS 26				− .222						
AS 27							− .184			
AS 29										− .190
R^2	.119	.116	.098	.123	.043	.000	.099	.000	.027	.042

Notes   The signs in the upper left hand segments identify those cases where a variable had a zero order correlation with the relevant expenditure significant at the five per cent level and of the direction indicated. The values in the lower, right hand, segments indicate regression coefficients significant at the ten per cent level.

The sets of attitude scales are shown as follows: first survey March 1972 = I, second survey July 1972 = II, third survey October 1972 = III, fourth survey January 1973 = IV. The expenditure quarters April–June 1972, July–September 1972, October–December 1972, January–March 1973 are shown as 1, 2, 3, 4 respectively. Thus analysis of I v 1 means that the indicators of consumer confidence recorded in March 1972 were used to predict expenditures over the period April–June 1972.

Variables that were not significant at any stage of this analysis are not included in this table.

significant in several different analyses. The expectation of buying a car (AS 14) was the most frequently selected predictor. The common significant variables and their signs indicate that higher quarterly expenditures were recorded by respondents who had previously indicated that they had stronger expectations of buying a car, were more likely to be saving up to buy a consumer durable, would not be put off by the rising prices of necessities and anticipated buying more durables than in the previous twelve months (AS 14, 18, 23, 24). Heavier spenders were also more likely to be those who had indicated that their durable purchases would be responsive to a temporary income increase and who expected their future financial commitments to increase (AS 17, 27). Higher quarterly expenditures were also significantly correlated with the view that it was a good time to buy consumer durables, that the informant anticipated buying a new durable and/or replacing an existing one, and that it was as well to buy quickly because of the perceived rising prices of durables (AS 9, 15, 16, 22) but these variables were not also significant in the multiple regression analyses. The results of the quarterly expenditure analyses based upon a linear dependent variable are set out in Table 6.10. They give a very similar picture to those in Table 6.6 with even greater proportionate emphasis on the predictive power of the car purchase expectations variable.

There is no obvious evidence to suggest that some variables have different predictive time horizons than others, the inevitably smaller number of opportunities to analyse the determinants of expenditure over nine and twelve month time periods, however, precludes detailed analysis of this. As is to be expected, in most cases the significant variables in the quarterly expenditure analyses were also significant in the analysis of expenditures over the year as a whole. A major exception to this seems to be price attitudes – whether it is desirable to buy quickly because of perceptions of rising durable prices and whether the effects of rising prices of necessities would lessen the ability to buy durables (AS 22, 23). These variables were significant in the analysis of quarterly expenditures but not of annual expenditures. The influence of price attitudes on buyer behaviour is something that seems to require further investigation. Our earlier research and the present results suggest that where price attitudes are significant they are more likely to be so in influencing short period expenditures rather than expenditures aggregated over a whole year.

Appendix to Chapter 6

Results of analyses using a linear measure of expenditure on consumer durables

TABLE 6.7 Zero order correlation of variables with expenditure

Variable	correlation coefficient
SOCL	$-.284$
AGE	$-.170$
YHH	$.211$
CARS	$.225$
TOTG	$.199$
DS	$.119$
MOVE	$-.163$
EXPSP 3	$.314$
EXPSP 12	$.373$
AS 1_1	$-.143$
AS 2_1	$-.151$
AS 14_1	$-.343$
AS 15_1	$-.127$
AS 24_1	$-.140$
AS 25_1	$-.125$
AS 29_1	$-.132$
OPT 1_1	$-.192$
OPT 2_1	$-.130$
DAS 5_{1-5}	$-.120$
DAS 14_{1-5}	$-.320$
DAS 16_{1-5}	$-.144$
DAS 18_{1-5}	$-.125$
DAS 24_{1-5}	$-.209$
DOPT 2_{1-5}	$-.166$

Notes See Notes to Table 6.3

TABLE 6.8 Results of multiple regression analyses of the determinants of aggregate expenditure on durables, using a linear dependent variable.

Variable	Equation							
	1	2	3	4	5	6	7	8
Constant	827.81	251.19	267.07	553.63	945.06	450.43	617.12	570.90
SOCL	-100.22 (24.67)	—	—	—	—	—	-64.40 (23.18)	-71.38 (23.14)
AGE	-81.87 (24.11)	—	—	—	—	—	—	-45.30 (23.19)
YHH	30.45 (14.22)	—	—	—	—	—	—	—
CARS	—	189.28 (43.34)	—	—	—	—	80.45 (42.73)	92.25 (43.30)
DS	—	—	61.69 (27.11)	—	—	—	—	—
INCY	—	—	—	—	—	—	90.41 (53.48)	—
MOVE	—	—	—	-84.89 (47.70)	—	—	—	—

EXPSP 3	.326 (.118)	.265 (.118)	—	—	.383 (.121)	—	—	—
EXPSP 12	.308 (.069)	.248 (.072)	—	—	.358 (.070)	—	—	—
AS 2_1	—	—	—	-32.77 (17.24)	—	—	—	—
AS 14_1	—	-38.26 (12.13)	—	-75.48 (11.28)	—	—	—	—
AS 21_1	—	—	—	23.91 (12.75)	—	—	—	—
AS 29_1	—	-30.48 (11.62)	—	-23.24 (12.03)	—	—	—	—
OPT 1_1	—	—	-47.40 (12.78)	—	—	—	—	—
OPT 2_1	—	—	-40.70 (16.38)	—	—	—	—	—
$\bar{R}^2$	.208	.235	.045	.135	.163	.009	.045	.108

Notes   See notes to Table 6.4

TABLE 6.9 Multiple regression of linear expenditure on variables incorporating measures of the change in consumer confidence

	Equation			
Variable	9	10	11	12
CONSTANT	430.50	453.83	554.74	559.33
SOCL	—	—	-70.94 (22.32)	-75.80 (22.85)
AGE	—	—	-43.33 (22.27)	-42.53 (22.88)
CARS	—	—	132.05 (42.31)	108.51 (42.96)
EXPSP 3	—	—	.212 (.116)	.306 (.117)
EXPSP 12	—	—	.238 (.068)	.288 (.069)
DAS 5_{1-5}	-30.64 (13.86)	—		—
DAS 14_{1-5}	-57.67 (9.63)	—	-35.97 (9.21)	—
DAS 15_{1-5}	19.08 (11.17)	—		—
DAS 17_{1-5}	-21.77 (11.64)	—		—
DAS 21_{1-5}	24.11 (11.20)	—		—
DAS 24_{1-5}	-28.64 (12.07)	—	-32.86 (10.30)	—
DAS 28_{1-5}		—	22.26 (13.24)	—
DOPT 2_{1-5}	—	-45.11 (14.11)	—	-42.65 (12.76)
$\bar{R}^2$	.134	.022	.270	.230

Equation *13* Expenditure Regression Residuals (from Equation *7*) =
$-696.59 + 108.93$ EXPCFD -50.99 DSYR $+ 75.74$ DSHYR
$\quad\quad$ (21.44) $\quad\quad$ (25.24) $\quad\quad$ (42.01)
$+ 83.34$ WDEC $+ 125.74$ WFIN $\quad \bar{R}^2 = .110$
(47.04) $\quad\quad$ (50.88)

Notes See notes to Table 6.5

TABLE 6.10 Results of correlation and multiple regression analyses of linear quarterly expenditures on attitude scales from successive surveys

Predictive Time Horizon

Variable	3 months	6 months			9 months			12 months		
	I v 1	II v 2	III v 3	IV v 4	I v 2	II v 3	III v 4	I v 3	II v 4	I v 4
Constant	321.68	176.61	245.88	267.34	252.63		180.33		95.64	116.56
AS 1	—	—			-16.56					
AS 2		—	+23.22		—					
AS 3		—								
AS 4				—	—					
AS 6					—					
AS 8		+18.50								
AS 9			—							
AS 11	+18.52				—					
AS 12									+13.08	+16.17
AS 13									+23.88	
AS 14	-38.26	-33.74	-20.08	-34.37	-15.99		-27.87		-18.46	-12.82
AS 15		—	—	—	—					
AS 16	—		—							
AS 17		-19.47	-14.86	—	-15.63		—			
AS 18			—	—						
AS 19							+18.20			
AS 20										+17.02
AS 22			—							
AS 23		+33.13	+16.65		+17.45					
AS 24			-25.30							
AS 25	-22.22									
AS 27										-16.05
$\bar{R}^2$	.107	.128	.109	.096	.054	.000	.071	.000	.021	.031

Notes The signs in the upper left hand segments identify those cases where a variable had a zero order correlation with the relevant expenditure significant at the five per cent level and of the direction indicated. The values in the lower, right hand, segments indicate regression coefficients significant at the ten per cent level.

The sets of attitude scales are shown as follows: first survey March 1972 = I, second survey July 1972 = II, third survey October 1972 = III, fourth survey January 1973 = IV. The expenditure quarters April–June 1972, July–September 1972, October–December 1972, January–March 1973 are shown as 1, 2, 3, 4 respectively. Thus analysis of I v 1 means that the indicators of consumer confidence recorded in March 1972 were used to predict expenditures over the period April–June 1972.

Variables that were not significant at any stage of this analysis are not included in this table.

7 The ownership of consumer durables

In this chapter we shall deal with the reported levels of ownership of the eleven consumer durables that are the subject of our interest: black and white television, car, colour television, cooker, deep freeze, dishwasher, record player, refrigerator, tape recorder, vacuum cleaner and washing machine; the way in which they were acquired; and respondent perceptions of the general state of the stock of durables they owned. Compared with the chapters on purchase behaviour, this excludes carpets and furniture because it is difficult to compare ownership levels. Central heating is also excluded, and new and used cars are not distinguished.

From this we shall be able to build up a general picture of the way in which socio-economic status influences ownership levels and methods of acquisition. Information on the state of the stock of consumer durables, and attitudes towards their replacement will throw light on expected product lives and will be useful subsequently in dealing with the nature of the influences upon decisions to purchase replacements. This chapter is therefore an introduction to the subsequent chapters that deal with different ways of handling the interpretation and prediction of buyer behaviour for individual consumer durables. Since it does not utilise reinterview information it is possible to base this discussion on information derived from the full panel. It is not possible to reproduce more than a small proportion of the main tables relating to the subject matter of this chapter. Consequently the text refers to the results of further analyses which are not tabulated here.

The overall pattern of durable ownership

From the information collected, we can identify the total number of units of the eleven durables owned by each household in the sample. The influence of socio-economic status upon the accumulation of durables is of interest in its own right. There is also evidence, as we observed in the last chapter and in an earlier paper (Pickering and Isherwood 1975), that ownership of a large number of durables tends to be associated with higher subsequent levels of expenditure on consumer durables. Since there is some incidence of ownership of more than one unit of a particular durable (see Table 7.4) the distribution of units owned set out in Table 7.1 does not necessarily indicate the number of different durables owned. It also follows that the number of units owned may be in excess of the number of durable goods under consideration.

The number of units owned by members of the sample ranged between one and twenty-one. Over four-fifths of the sample owned between five and nine units. Half the sample owned either seven or eight units. The mean was 7.4 units. There was a strong association between the number of units owned and both the household income and social class of the respondent (Table 7.2). There was also a significant tendency for the number of units owned to increase as family size increased. The average for one-person households was 5.0; for two-person households 6.9; for three-person households 7.3; for four-person households 7.7 and for households with between five and

TABLE 7.1 Ownership of consumer durables

Number of units owned	% of respondents
1-3	2.5
4	3.8
5	8.0
6	13.1
7	26.7
8	23.9
9	11.5
10	5.1
11	3.4
12 & over	2.1

Note Ownership figures are based on the eleven consumer durables noted at the beginning of this chapter. The number of units owned may exceed the number of durables under investigation as a result of multiple ownership.

TABLE 7.2 Mean ownership of consumer durables analysed
              by social class and household income

Social Class	Mean number of units owned	Household Income: £	Mean number of units owned
A	8.4	Less than 1000	5.0
B	8.0	1000-1499	6.2
C1	7.0	1500-1999	6.8
C2	6.5	2000-2499	7.1
DE	5.6	2500-2999	7.6
		3000-3999	7.7
		4000-5999	9.1
		6000+	10.2

Note Ownership figures are based on the eleven consumer durables
        noted at the beginning of this chapter. The number of units
        owned may exceed the number of durables under investigation
        as a result of multiple ownership.

TABLE 7.3 Mean ownership of consumer durables analysed
              by life cycle indicators

Age of HoH	Mean number of units owned	Length of time married	Mean number of units owned
16-24	6.1	0-4 years	6.9
25-34	7.2	5-9	7.3
35-44	7.9	10-20	7.8
45-54	7.7	Over 20	7.5
55-64	6.7		

seven people the average was 8.2. When the life cycle variables, of age
of HoH and duration of marriage, were considered (Table 7.3) we found
some evidence that ownership was lower at both ends of the life cycle.

Ownership levels for individual items

Table 7.4 indicates the distribution of ownership of each individual item
and the proportion of households owning more than one unit of each

TABLE 7.4 Ownership of individual consumer durables percentage of sample owning:

	Number of units owned				
	0	*1*	*2*	*3 or more*	*Total*
Cooker	1	99	0	0	100
Vacuum cleaner	5	88	6	1	100
Refrigerator	8	92	0	0	100
Black and white television	15	80	5	0	100
Washing machine	17	83	1	0	100
Car	17	62	19	2	100
Record player	20	72	6	1	100
Tape recorder	61	37	2	0	100
Colour television	84	16	0	0	100
Deep freeze	88	12	0	0	100
Dishwasher	97	3	0	0	100

item. Seven of the items were owned (which here really means 'having the use of' and therefore includes cases where television sets were being rented) by more than three-quarters of the households in the sample. Tape recorders were owned by just over one-third of the sample while colour televisions, deep freezes and dishwashers were owned by only a small minority of the sample. Multiple ownership was important in the case of cars where twenty-one per cent of the sample (which it will be recollected was skewed towards the higher income groups) and twenty-five per cent of car owners in the sample owned more than one car. There was also a small amount of multiple ownership of vacuum cleaners, black and white televisions and record players.

In general, higher income and higher social class were associated with greater proportions of the sample owning an item, (Tables 7.5 and 7.6). Washing machines however, represent an exception to this principle since the proportion owning washing machines appears to remain more or less constant at above eighty per cent for all those with household incomes of £1500 or more. This indicates that washing machines have penetrated to quite a considerable extent in most socio-economic groups but further suggests that market saturation may be achieved at less than one hundred per cent penetration. Demand for a washing machine is perhaps as likely to be dependent upon family structure as on economic well-being.

There was also no linear relationship between income or social class and possession of a black and white television. In this case at least eighty per cent of members of all social class groups and over seventy-five per cent of members of all income groups had the use of a set but there was, if anything, a tendency for the proportion to be greater in the lower social class and income groups. Possession of black and white sets was relatively low in the household income range £2500–3999. This appears to be attributable to an increased probability that these income groups would have a colour television set rather than a black and white set. Households with incomes of £6000 or more tended to have on average a greater number of television sets in the household, thirty-five per cent of the sample in that income category possessed both black and white and colour televisions. In all, four per cent of the sample had both a colour and black and white set, twelve per cent owned a colour set only, eighty-one per cent owned a black and white set only and three per cent did not possess a television set at all.

TABLE 7.5 Percentages owning different consumer durables analysed by social class

| Item | Social Class | | | | |
	A	B	C1	C2	DE
Black and white television	80	81	86	93	94
Car	97	96	76	73	43
Colour television	26	20	12	7	4
Cooker	100	100	99	99	98
Deep freeze	24	15	5	5	6
Dishwasher	11	4	0	0	0
Record player	89	82	80	73	63
Refrigerator	97	99	94	86	69
Tape Recorder	52	45	33	32	22
Vacuum Cleaner	99	98	97	90	81
Washing Machine	90	89	83	78	61
Number in sample	116	186	157	97	54

TABLE 7.6 Percentages owning different consumer durables analysed by household income

Item	Household Income Group £							
	less than 1000	1000- 1499	1500- 1999	2000- 2499	2500- 2999	3000- 3999	4000- 5999	6000+
Black and white television	90	95	91	89	79	76	89	83
Car	29	46	77	84	92	95	100	100
Colour television	3	5	5	11	21	25	16	52
Cooker	100	97	98	100	100	100	100	100
Deep freeze	3	3	10	8	10	14	23	35
Dishwasher	0	0	0	1	1	1	10	26
Record player	58	67	76	78	88	84	87	91
Refrigerator	58	82	89	95	99	97	98	100
Tape recorder	13	36	28	34	39	47	61	65
Vacuum cleaner	77	90	96	93	97	99	100	100
Washing machine	58	72	87	83	90	84	90	87
Number in sample	31	39	92	104	77	109	62	23

Of the two life cycle variables used for analysis – age of HoH and length of time married – there was a clearer pattern of association between age and ownership than between time married and ownership. Generally speaking, where there were differences between HoH age groups in the proportions owning a particular item, the proportions owning tended to be lowest in the youngest and/or the oldest age group, (Table 7.7). An inverted U-shaped relationship between age of the HoH and ownership existed most clearly in the case of cars, deep freezes, refrigerators, tape recorders and washing machines. The observed pattern of ownership levels for washing machines gives support to the view that life cycle influences are particularly relevant to the demand for this item.

Peaking of ownership levels in the middle age range is not inconsistent with evidence that household income also tends slightly to peak in the middle age ranges, for this sample at least. It is also possibly indicative of a life cycle influence that younger people are still in the process of making acquisitions; older people may have had different tastes or faced different purchasing opportunities when they were

TABLE 7.7 Percentages owning different consumer durables analysed by age of head of household

	Age of HoH, years				
Item	16-24	25-34	35-44	45-54	55-64
Black and white television	100	82	86	86	85
Car	59	87	90	83	70
Colour television	0	13	18	16	17
Cooker	100	100	100	98	99
Deep freeze	0	9	19	12	4
Dishwasher	0	2	5	3	4
Record player	86	80	84	83	64
Refrigerator	77	94	98	91	86
Tape recorder	18	36	41	45	34
Vacuum cleaner	68	94	98	96	96
Washing machine	64	83	88	87	73
Number in sample	22	138	186	159	105

younger, and now find that some items are not as necessary or desirable as to younger consumers.

Multiple ownership was important with cars and, to a lesser extent, black and white television, record players and vacuum cleaners. Multiple ownership of cars was positively associated with higher social class and income groups and was particularly high where household incomes were in excess of £4000 and where the occupation of the HoH placed him in social class A. Multiple car ownership was slightly more likely to be found where the HoH was in the age range thirty-five–fifty-four. Multiple ownership of black and white televisions tended to be largest in social classes A, B, C_1, and where incomes were in the range £3000–£6000. Ownership of more than one record player was concentrated in social class B and in age groups sixteen–twenty-four and thirty-five–fifty-four. It rose as household income increased. Multiple ownership of vacuum cleaners also tended to have its greatest incidence amongst the higher social class and income groups and in cases where the HoH was aged thirty-five–fifty-four.

Method of acquisition of durables

Table 7.8 shows that the vast majority of acquisitions of all items except colour television and, to some extent, black and white television, were through the personal purchase of the item. Television sets were likely to be rented, especially by lower income households. A small minority of cars used by the sample was provided by an employer and this was most likely to be found amongst A and B social class groups and those with household incomes in excess of £2500.

A small proportion of most items had been provided as gifts, with record players and vacuum cleaners the most likely to have been obtained in this way. Recipients of gifts were more likely to be found in the lower social class and household income groups, and to be younger or married for a shorter length of time.

We did not ask whether an item had initially been obtained on hire purchase. We did, however, investigate the extent to which there was, at the time of the survey, credit outstanding on each particular item (Table 7.9). In absolute terms there were substantially more households with credit outstanding on cars than on any other item. As a proportion of the number of people owning each particular item, we found that credit was most likely to be outstanding on deep freezes, cars and colour televisions. The small number of people with credit outstanding rather precludes extensive analysis of the socio-economic characteristics of credit users. There seems, however, to be little evidence that social class

TABLE 7.8 Method of acquisition of consumer durables per cent of households

	Bought personally	Gift	Rented, hired	Provided by employer	Other	Total	Number of cases
Black and white television	53	3	43	1	1	100	520
Car	85	2	1	12	1	100	505
Colour television	27	0	72	1	0	100	95
Cooker	90	4	3	2	2	100	606
Deep freeze	92	4	4	0	0	100	72
Dishwasher	86	9	0	6	0	100	21
Record player	85	12	0	1	2	100	485
Refrigerator	90	7	2	0	1	100	563
Tape recorder	89	9	1	1	1	100	238
Vacuum cleaner	86	11	1	1	1	100	581
Washing machine	93	6	1	0	1	100	509

Note: The percentages in this table are based on those respondents having the use of an item and therefore exclude non-owners. Where more than one unit of an item was owned by a household, the answers related to the main one.

TABLE 7.9 Instances of credit outstanding

Item	Per cent of owners with credit outstanding	Per cent of total sample with credit outstanding
Black and white television	6	5
Car	18	15
Colour television	13	2
Cooker	7	7
Deep freeze	19	2
Dishwasher	9	*
Record player	3	3
Refrigerator	4	4
Tape recorder	1	1
Vacuum cleaner	2	1
Washing machine	3	2

* less than one half per cent of the sample

or household income influenced variations in the use of credit but it does appear that younger people and those married less long were more likely to be using credit, especially on cars, cookers, and black and white televisions. These were the items on which the greatest number of people had a credit commitment and, as Chapter 8 will indicate, they tended to be acquired early on in the process of acquisition.

The state of the stock of consumer durables

If we view consumer durables as capital assets in the household (just as production plant is a capital asset in the firm) it becomes apparent that they are also subject to depreciation and that the state of each durable will influence the chance that it will be replaced within a specified period of time. For prediction it is therefore desirable to have some indication of the state of the stock of durables in each household. We attempted to investigate this by collecting information on the age of each item and the length of time it had been in the possession of the household (there would be a difference between the two where an item had been acquired second-hand), the respondent's assessment of the chances that the item owned would require 'major attention' during the following twelve months (it was left to the respondent to decide what would be 'major' in the light of his own circumstances) and the strategy that would be adopted if major attention was in fact required – whether the item would be repaired, replaced or abandoned.

Information on the age of the item and the length of time it had been in the household's possession is set out in Table 7.10. (The median value was used in preference to the mean in view of the use of grouped age categories rather than actual ages.) While there was some divergence between age and duration of ownership in almost all cases, only in respect of cars was the difference substantial. This clearly reflects the particular importance of the secondhand market for cars. The extreme right hand column in Table 7.10 indicates the estimated proportion of owners who acquired each item secondhand. Because the age groups in the questionnaire were grouped, this is, if anything an underestimate of the proportion that acquired secondhand durables.

When the age of the stock of each item is considered, using the first three columns in Table 7.10 we find that, on average, the oldest items tended to be cookers, vacuum cleaners, washing machines, refrigerators, tape recorders and record players. This probably reflects both the relatively high market penetration of these items (other than tape recorders) and the durability of the products.

Black and white televisions and cars also have high market penetration but the lower average age of the stock suggests they are more frequently purchased, perhaps because they are less durable or subject to more frequent changes in style or improvements in performance which encourage a faster rate of replacement. Low ownership items would be expected to be relatively new and this is confirmed by the low average age of colour televisions and deep freezes. The relatively high average age of dishwashers is an indication that they had failed to make much improvement in their market penetration in the years immediately preceding the survey.

As might be expected, older people normally had older durables. However, as an exception to this, older people tended to own newer cars, this suggests that older people were more likely to buy new cars while younger people tended to buy secondhand vehicles. Higher income households were also more likely to own newer cars, though there was no significant difference between income groups in the length of time they had owned their existing cars. This indicates that lower income households, though perhaps buying a car as frequently as those in higher income groups, were also more likely to buy secondhand. With this important exception there was little evidence that the

TABLE 7.10 Age of durable and length of time in possession of household

	median age of durable years	per cent less than one year old	per cent five or more years old	median length of time in possession of household years	Estimated proportion who acquired secondhand, per cent
Black and white television	3.7	16.7	36.6	3.1	11
Car	3.4	18.7	31.3	1.6	45
Colour television	0.9	55.0	1.3	0.9	0
Cooker	6.2	11.1	57.9	5.6	9
Deep freeze	1.2	46.4	4.5	1.1	1
Record player	4.8	13.1	49.2	4.5	7
Dishwasher	3.8	15.6	34.4	3.5	10
Refrigerator	5.3	11.6	51.8	4.9	5
Tape recorder	4.8	13.2	48.2	4.6	6
Vacuum cleaner	5.8	9.7	55.4	5.4	6
Washing machine	5.5	10.9	53.8	4.8	9

socio-economic position of the household was associated with the age of a durable or the length of time it had been owned.

It is likely that for most durables, other than those where there is an effective secondhand market or where major quality improvements have occurred, households mainly make replacement purchases when products have incurred faults that would involve the household in heavy expense on repairs. We therefore asked respondents to assess on a 0–10 probability scale the chances that each of the items they owned would require major attention during the next twelve months and to indicate whether, if this happened, they would repair, replace or abandon the item. From this information we might assume we have some indication of the relative rates of depreciation of different products.

For purposes of analysis the probabilities were converted from 0–10 to 0–1.0 and the mean probabilities of major attention for each item are set out in Table 7.11. A mean probability of 0.5 would, if accurate, indicate that on average half the units of that consumer durable owned by the sample would be likely to require major attention over the following year. The products which, on this basis, were considered most likely to require major attention were cars, washing machines and black and white televisions, of which it was predicted that at least thirty per cent would require major attention during the following year. For all other items, with the exception of deep freezes, the implication was that at least one in six would require major attention in the following twelve months.

In Table 7.11 we have also set out the mean probabilities of major attention when analysed by the age of the item. It will be observed that the probability of major attention rises consistently as the age of the product increases. It is also apparent that certain products were rated as much more likely to require major attention than others at all product age levels. Products which had high mean probability values were televisions (colour and black and white), cars, and washing machines.

All owners were then asked whether, if major attention was required on a product, they would repair, replace or abandon it. The distribution of answers is shown in Table 7.12. It will be observed that in the majority of instances for all products the choice would be to repair. Replacement purchases would be made relatively more frequently on black and white televisions, vacuum cleaners, cookers, refrigerators and washing machines. Considering the distribution of answers by those in different socio-economic groups, replacements were relatively more likely to be chosen by older and higher income and social class respondents. This suggests that the ability to finance the acquisition of a

TABLE 7.11 Probability of major attention during the next twelve months

	Mean probability, all respondents owning an item	Mean probability by age of product				
		less than 1 year	1-2 years	3-4 years	5-9 years	10+ years
Black and white television	.30	.15 (81)	.21 (125)	.32 (102)	.46 (130)	.54 (48)
Car	.33	.14 (93)	.23 (135)	.32 (113)	.39 (113)	.66 (42)
Colour television	.20	.17 (50)	.23 (33)	.36 (7)	.20 (1)	—
Cooker	.17	.06 (63)	.11 (77)	.11 (98)	.18 (186)	.24 (141)
Deep freeze	.05	.02 (32)	.02 (27)	.06 (7)	.30 (3)	—
Dishwasher	.21	.03 (3)	.02 (5)	.22 (5)	.30 (5)	.45 (2)
Record player	.21	.07 (59)	.11 (97)	.17 (74)	.28 (118)	.34 (105)
Refrigerator	.17	.06 (63)	.07 (89)	.15 (108)	.18 (152)	.28 (128)
Tape recorder	.22	.02 (29)	.13 (37)	.21 (48)	.24 (72)	.42 (35)
Vacuum cleaner	.27	.09 (53)	.17 (83)	.23 (108)	.31 (168)	.36 (136)
Washing machine	.32	.07 (53)	.20 (79)	.30 (94)	.39 (164)	.41 (99)

Note: The numbers in brackets indicate the number of respondents with durables in each age group.

— indicates no observations

new item is a relevant consideration, as is the age of the product concerned.

When the replacement strategy selected was standardised for the effect of the age of the product, as in the second part of Table 7.12, the proportion saying they would replace is shown to increase as the age of the product increases. People do seem, therefore, to have some sort of view regarding the appropriate life of a product and, in choosing between repairing and replacing, seem implicitly to adopt a view about the extent to which the item is fully depreciated and due for replacement. After standardising for differences in the age of the durables, the different proportions saying they would replace offer some indication of the variation in the implicit rate of depreciation assumed by households. This interpretation must be tentative since, especially for older units, the number of observations was often small. However, bearing this in mind, it would appear that at least over the first four or so years of a product's life, televisions (black and white and colour) and cars are subject to the highest rates of implied depreciation in the consumer's mind.

If we combine the mean probability of major attention and the proportion of respondents indicating that they would choose to replace rather than repair, we obtain some indication of the proportion of owners of each item in the sample who might be expected to make a replacement purchase over the following twelve months.

These values are set out in Table 7.13. On this basis it would seem that ten per cent of black and white television sets, nine per cent of washing machines, nearly nine per cent of vacuum cleaners and so on would be replaced over the following twelve months because they needed major attention. This would not necessarily give a prediction of total replacement demand since not all replacements occur for reasons associated with product failure. It would also not provide a forecast of total demand since initial purchases and purchases of second or subsequent units for multiple ownership would not be predicted by this method. Nevertheless it does seem to be a way of estimating a major element of replacement demand and in so doing points to a way in which survey data may be introduced into stock adjustment estimates.

A small minority of respondents stated that if major attention was required they would abandon the product altogether. As a proportion of owners of each item, this applied most strongly to tape recorders and then to record players and dishwashers. In absolute terms, forty-two people said they would probably abandon their tape recorders and not buy a replacement, thirty-nine would abandon a record player and sixteen would abandon a black and white television set. These are all 'leisure' items on the basis of our previous grouping of products by their perceived characteristics (Pickering *et al* 1973b). As it was people in the

TABLE 7.12 Replacement strategy if durables required major attention

Item	Replacement strategy per cent			Percentage who would replace by age of durable				
	Repair	Replace	Abandon	less than 1 yr	1-2 yrs	3-4 yrs	5-9 yrs	10+
Black and white television	61	35	3	19	25	33	46	60
Car	76	22	1	8	26	21	29	31
Colour television	82	17	1	12	19	29	100	—
Cooker	68	32	0	3	12	19	35	58
Deep freeze	94	6	0	0	4	14	33	—
Dishwasher	82	9	9	0	0	0	33	50
Record player	73	19	8	3	7	15	20	38
Refrigerator	68	31	1	5	15	20	35	56
Tape recorder	72	11	18	7	8	13	13	12
Vacuum cleaner	66	33	2	4	17	23	33	63
Washing machine	70	28	2	4	10	14	39	54

TABLE 7.13 Estimated percentage of owners likely to make a replacement purchase

Black and white television	11
Car	8
Colour television	3
Cooker	5
Deep freeze	0
Dishwasher	2
Record player	4
Refrigerator	5
Tape recorder	2
Vacuum cleaner	9
Washing machine	9

higher social class groups who said they would abandon their black and white televisions, the inference is probably that they would use this as an opportunity to obtain a colour television. The reported likelihood of abandoning either a tape recorder or record player was higher where the existing items were older.

8 *Orders of acquisition of consumer durables*

In the previous chapter we observed the patterns of ownership of each of the durables under consideration. However, the observation of market penetration does not necessarily indicate the likely order in which the different items would be, or have been, acquired and hence the relative priorities that households appear to place upon the various consumer durables. In this chapter we shall, therefore, investigate various aspects of the order in which the durables were purchased and are thought likely to be acquired in the future as implicit indications of consumer priorities for different durables. We shall consider cross-sectional information on the existing patterns of ownership and also data relating to the historic order in which the sample stated they had first acquired each of the items. We shall also report on the choice by respondents of the durable they would be most likely to acquire next. Where appropriate, the effects of differing income, social class and life cycle influences will be indicated.

Cross-sectional analysis of ownership patterns

Earlier studies have tended to concentrate mainly upon cross-sectional comparisons of ownership patterns using either the Guttman coefficient of reproducibility or the point correlation method. However, Pyatt pioneered a technique which allowed the probability to be calculated that a particular item would be owned at each point in the accumulation of a specified set of durables (Pyatt 1964). We have discussed these studies in an earlier paper (Hebden and Pickering 1974) and have referred briefly to their findings in Chapter 1 of this study. The reader is referred to that paper for a more detailed consideration of the implications and value of this technique.

The information on which this section is based is a matrix of the actual items owned by each individual member of the original panel of 610. Because of the computational and significance problems involved in handling a large number of items, and questions regarding the desirability of including less homogeneous goods in a set (see Pyatt 1964; Hebden and Pickering 1974 on this question) a number of smaller sets were specified for analysis. Following our earlier investigations of the groupings of durables (Pickering *et al* 1973b; Hebden and Pickering 1974), the sets used for analysis were:

Leisure items – black and white television, colour television, record player, tape recorder.

Kitchen items – cooker, deep freeze, dishwasher, refrigerator, washing machine.

Diverse items – first car, second car, colour television, deep freeze, vacuum cleaner.

Low ownership items – second car, third car, colour television, deep freeze, dishwasher.

The question we are really seeking to answer is whether the order in which durable items are acquired tends to be consistent (unique) for all households or whether it is subject to variations in individual choice. It may be that even if there is consistency in the order of acquisition for particular types of people, variations in income, geographical location, availability of physical facilities etc. may affect the order of acquisition for different groups of consumers. Some investigation of this possibility has been made in respect of social class (Pyatt 1964); social class, income and life cycle (Hebden and Pickering 1974); life cycle, location and income (McFall 1969); and income, geographical origin and location (Paroush 1965, 1973). Where appropriate, we shall investigate the extent of socio-economic and life cycle influences upon the order of acquisition, contrasting: those in social class A and B against the C1, C2, DEs; those with total household incomes above and below £2500 p.a; those married less than ten years and those married ten years or more. These distinctions have to be somewhat arbitrary granted the relatively small number in the total sample. Nevertheless they do allow the testing of hypotheses about the influences of such factors on the order of acquisition.

The basic output used in this analysis is the calculation of the conditional probability that at each stage 1 . . . . . n of the accumulation process (where n is the number of items in the set that might be owned) a specific item is owned, and of its average position in the accumulation pattern. The lower the average position, the more likely it is the items will be acquired early on in the accumulation process (before others in the set). This procedure deals only with the order of acquisition, not the speed of accumulation.

These values will be shown in a composite table for each set of durables. This includes the conditional probability of owning a particular item given that a specified number of items are owned, a measure of the probabilistic order of acquisition and the average position for each item. The probabilistic order of acquisition is derived directly from the conditional probability of ownership. If, for example, the conditional probability of owning item A as the first item in a set is 0.6 and the conditional probability that it is owned when two items in the set are owned is 0.8 then the probability that A is the second item to be acquired is $0.8 - 0.6 = 0.2$.

There are two ways of testing for uniqueness in the order of acquisition. First we can investigate whether the average position for each product differs significantly from its integer. If it does not then for that product the average order of acquisition is unique. However, this is a very strict test of uniqueness and a less severe but still informative approach is to test whether the average positions between adjoining items in the order of acquisition are significantly different from each other. If they are, it is reasonable to assume that the order of acquisition is approximately unique. The statistical procedures are described in the Appendix to this Chapter.

Results for leisure items

Table 8.1 provides information on the conditional probabilities of ownership, probabilities of acquisition, average position in the set and tests of significance of the uniqueness of the order of acquisition for the four items: black and white television, colour television, record player and tape recorder. In this set a black and white television was the first to be acquired, followed by a record player as the second purchase, tape recorder as the third purchase and colour television was the last item in the set to be acquired. Although only the average position for record player is not significantly different from its appropriate integer, the last column in the table indicates that the differences between the adjacent average positions are all statistically significant and suggests that a unique order of acquisition of these items does exist. As in our earlier investigation, there are negative 'probabilities' of acquisition of black and white televisions at one stage in the accumulation process. Although the negative 'probability' concerned was low and may have a statistical explanation, the results were repeated when the sample was subdivided by socio-economic and life cycle variables. It is consistent with our earlier explanation that for some people a black and white television can

TABLE 8.1 Conditional probabilities of ownership and probabilities of acquisition: 4 leisure items

Item		Number of items owned				Average position	Deviation from unique pattern	Differences between average positions
		1	2	3	4			
		Number of purchases made						
		1st	2nd	3rd	4th	(x)	(y)	(z)
Black and white television	a	.854	.861	.859	1	1.425 (0.048)		⎫ *
	b	.854	.007	-.002	.141			⎬
Record player	a	.073	.909	.995	1	2.024 (0.032)	*	⎫ *
	b	.073	.836	.086	.005			⎬
Tape recorder	a	.000	.105	.979	1	2.916 (0.021)		⎫ *
	b	.000	.105	.874	.021			⎬
Colour television	a	.073	.126	.167	.833	3.635 (0.042)		
	b	.073	.053	.041	.833			

Notes: In each case row (a) represents the conditional probability that each item is owned when the number of goods owned from the set is given (1...4); row (b) represents the probability that, as the household adds one extra item from the set to the range already owned, it will be the product specified. Thus the conditional probability of ownership where one item is owned plus the probability of purchase when the second purchase is made will give the conditional probability of ownership when two items are owned.

Column (x): figures in brackets are standard errors.

Column (y): an asterisk opposite an item indicates that its estimated average position in the acquisition pattern does not differ significantly from the corresponding integer. Asterisked results therefore support the hypothesis of a unique pattern.

Column (z): an asterisk opposite a particular pair of durables indicates that the difference between the estimated average positions of those items with adjacent positions is statistically significant. Asterisked results therefore again favour the hypothesis of a distinct ordering.

become an inferior product when the opportunity arises to acquire a colour television.

This analysis was also run for the same set of durables but distinguishing higher and lower social class and income households and those married for shorter or longer periods of time. The average positions for the different products from this analysis are set out in Table 8.2. The results here are very similar to those obtained for the whole sample and the order of acquisition is the same for all groups of respondents. All the differences between average positions are significant but only record players tend to have an average position that is not significantly different from the appropriate integer. The average position for black and white televisions is significantly lower for the lower income group than for higher income households, while the average position for colour televisions is significantly lower (i.e. on average it would be purchased earlier) for those households with a higher social class status and higher income. A larger proportion of higher income and social class families would make their first purchase in this set a colour television rather than a black and white television. The detailed probabilities, (not reproduced here), indicate, for example, that seventeen per cent of those with incomes of £2500 and over would buy a colour television first, against a proportion of three per cent for those with incomes of less than £2500.

TABLE 8.2 Average positions analysed for sample sub-groups: 4 leisure items

	Social Class		Household Income £		Duration of Marriage	
	A, B,	$C_1, C_2,$ DE	0-2499	2500+	0-9 yrs	10+ yrs
Black and white television	1.586	1.300	1.237	1.679*	1.434	1.393
Record player	2.007	2.030	2.048	1.983	1.967	2.074
Tape recorder	2.898	2.938	2.932	2.900	2.851	2.941
Colour television	3.509	3.732*	3.783	3.439*	3.748	3.592

Note *An asterisk indicates that the difference between the average positions for the same items when compared between the two sample sub-groups in each pair is statistically significant at the one per cent confidence level.

The analysis by life cycle influence is of potential interest since it may indicate the extent to which different age groups reveal different preferences. However, the differences between the average positions for those households married fewer than ten years as compared with those for households married more than ten years are not statistically significant.

We may conclude, therefore, on the basis of our less stringent test of the significance of differences between the average positions of adjacent items, that there is a unique pattern of acquisition. But it would appear that amongst higher income and social class households there is some evidence that colour televisions are likely to be purchased sooner and in preference to black and white televisions. At the moment, however, the proportions behaving in this way are not sufficient to affect the overall rank ordering. They are, however, an indication that a change in tastes and in priorities may be in progress for the items in this set.

Results for kitchen items

Table 8.3 indicates that there is an equally well defined order of acquisition for the set of five kitchen goods – cooker, refrigerator, washing machine, deep freeze and dishwasher, which were likely to be acquired in that order. The majority of purchases of each item were predicted to occur at the stage in the accumulation process closest to its average position. Thus ninety-two per cent of first purchases would be cookers, seventy-seven per cent of second purchases would be refrigerators, seventy-four per cent of third purchases would be washing machines, eighty-seven per cent of fourth purchases would be deep freezes and eighty-eight per cent of fifth purchases would be dishwashers. Virtually no purchases of either deep freezes or dishwashers would be expected until a household owned a cooker, a refrigerator and a washing machine. This is consistent with the suggestion in our earlier paper that dishwashers and deep freezes may, on the basis of respondent perceptions of their characteristics, be classed as household luxuries, whereas cookers, refrigerators and washing machines are perceived as basic utilities or necessities (see Pickering *et al* 1973b).

In Table 8.4 we find that the same orders of acquisition remain when variations in social class, income and duration of marriage are taken into account. It would, however, appear that on average, the higher income and social class groups were slightly more likely to acquire a refrigerator a little earlier and a washing machine a little later than households with lower incomes or occupational status.

TABLE 8.3 Conditional probabilities of ownership and probabilities of acquisition: 5 kitchen items

Item		number of items owned					Average position	Deviation from unique pattern	Difference between average position
	a	1	2	3	4	5			
	b number of purchases made						(x)	(y)	(z)
		1	2	3	4	5			
Cooker	a	.917	.980	1	1	1	1.104	*	
	b	.917	.063	.020	.000	.000	(0.058)		} *
Refrigerator	a	.000	.773	.997	1	1	2.229		
	b	.000	.773	.224	.002	.000	(0.043)		} *
Washing machine	a	.083	.247	.985	1	1	2.684		
	b	.083	.164	.738	.014	.000	(0.072)		} *
Deep Freeze	a	.000	.000	.014	.883	1	4.102		
	b	.000	.000	.014	.869	.117	(0.042)		} *
Dishwasher	a	.000	.000	.002	.116	1	4.881		
	b	.000	.000	.002	.114	.883	(0.042)		

Notes In each case row (*a*) represents the conditional probability that each item is owned when the number of goods owned from the set is given (1 ... 4); row (*b*) represents the probability that, as the household adds one extra item from the set to the range already owned, it will be the product specified. Thus the conditional probability of ownership where one item is owned plus the probability of purchase when the second purchase is made will give the conditional probability of ownership when 2 items are owned.

Column (*x*): figures in brackets are standard errors.

Column (*y*): an asterisk opposite an item indicates that its estimated average position in the acquisition pattern does not differ significantly from the corresponding integer. Asterisked results therefore support the hypothesis of a unique pattern.

Column (*z*): an asterisk opposite a particular pair of durables indicates that the difference between the estimated average positions of those items with adjacent positions is statistically significant. Asterisked results therefore again favour the hypothesis of a distinct ordering.

TABLE 8.4 Average positions analysed for sample sub-groups: 5 kitchen items

	Social Class		Household Income £		Duration of Marriage	
	A, B	C_1, C_2, DE	0-2499	2500+	0-9 yrs	10+ yrs
Cooker	1.000	1.121	1.095	1.000	1.000	1.189
Refrigerator	2.105	2.284*	2.321	2.070*	2.197	2.289
Washing machine	2.919	2.605*	2.596	2.956*	2.831	2.529
Deep freeze	4.133	3.990*	4.044	4.090	4.065	4.123
Dishwasher	4.843	5.000*	4.944	4.884	4.908	4.870

Note *An asterisk indicates that the difference between the average positions for the same items when compared between the two sample sub-groups in each pair is statistically significant at the one per cent confidence level.

Results for diverse goods

The two previous sets were selected as being more likely to meet Pyatt's condition that sets selected for analysis should be homogeneous (Pyatt 1964), although, in the kitchen items set just discussed, our previous analysis of the characteristics of durables indicated that dishwashers and deep freezes seemed to have different strengths of characteristic from other kitchen items included in the analysis (Pickering *et al* 1973b); so even there, in a perceptual sense, the items in the set could not necessarily be assumed to be homogeneous. We are not, however, convinced that it is necessary to select sets of items for analysis that are more likely to be homogeneous and our earlier investigation has shown that a unique pattern may still be identified with less homogeneous goods. In this section we shall consider the order of acquisition of colour television, first and second cars, deep freeze and vacuum cleaner, items which clearly have quite different types of function in the home and so may be classed as heterogeneous. It is, however, quite likely that these items may be seen within the household as competing for limited discretionary spending power and so indications of consumer preferences through the order in which they are obtained are of interest.

As Table 8.5 indicates, the order of acquisition is vacuum cleaner → first car → second car → colour television → deep freeze. All differences between adjacent positions are significant and the value of

TABLE 8.5 Conditional probabilities of ownership and probabilities of acquisition: 5 diverse items

Item		Number of items owned 1	2	3	4	5	Average position (x)	Deviation from unique pattern (y)	Difference between average position (z)
		Number of purchases made b 1	2	3	4	5			
Vacuum cleaner	a	.839	1	1	1	1	1.161		
	b	.839	.161	.000	.000	.000	(0.038)		*
First car	a	.151	.964	.993	1	1	1.894		
	b	.151	.813	.029	.008	.000	(0.039)		*
Second car	a	.000	.000	.512	.834	1	3.655		
	b	.000	.000	.512	.322	.167	(0.065)		*
Colour television	a	.011	.020	.283	.684	1	4.004	*	
	b	.011	.009	.263	.401	.317	(0.073)		*
Deep freeze	a	.000	.017	.214	.484	1	4.286		
	b	.000	.017	.197	.270	.517	(0.074)		

Notes   In each case row (*a*) represents the conditional probability that each item is owned when the number of goods owned from the set is given (1...4); row (*b*) represents the probability that, as the household adds one extra item from the set to the range already owned, it will be the product specified. Thus the conditional probability of ownership where one item is owned plus the probability of purchase when the second purchase is made will give the conditional probability of ownership when **2** items are owned.

Column (*x*): figures in brackets are standard errors.

Column (*y*): an asterisk opposite an item indicates that its estimated average position in the acquisition pattern does not differ significantly from the corresponding integer. Asterisked results therefore support the hypothesis of a unique pattern.

Column (*z*): an asterisk opposite a particular pair of durables indicates that the difference between the estimated average positions of those items with adjacent positions is statistically significant. Asterisked results therefore again favour the hypothesis of a distinct ordering.

the average position for colour television is not significantly different from its appropriate integer. If, however, we look more closely at the results for the last three items in this set – second car, colour television and deep freeze – we find that the numerical values of the average positions are quite close together and there is some overlap in the estimated distribution of the third, fourth and fifth purchases between these three durables.

When the results for different sub-samples are considered in Table 8.6, the average position of second car is interesting. It indicates that those married more recently were likely to buy a second car significantly sooner than those married for ten or more years. There is also some variation between the average positions of second car and colour television when analysed by social class. Although overall and for most sample sub-groups the average position for second car is lower (that is it is bought sooner) than for colour television and the two are often significantly different from each other, in the case of those in social class groups C_1, C_2, DE the rank orderings are reversed so that colour television has a lower average position than second car. Although this difference between adjacent positions is not significant, the average position for second car, which for the sample as a whole is 3.655, is for the lower social class sub-group not significantly different from 4.

TABLE 8.6 Average positions analysed for sample sub-groups: 5 diverse items

	Social Class		Household Income £		Duration of Marriage	
	A, B	C_1, C_2 DE	0-2499	£2500+	0-9 yrs	10+ yrs
Vacuum cleaner	1.364	1.134	1.157	1.231	1.261	1.087
First car	1.658	1.951	1.948	1.777	1.846	1.950
Second car	3.598	3.905	3.722	3.609	3.378	3.735*
Colour television	4.094	3.725	4.013	4.023	4.127	3.946
Deep freeze	4.287	4.285	4.160	4.361	4.388	4.283

Note *An asterisk indicates that the difference between the average positions for the same items when compared between the two sample sub-groups in each pair is statistically significant at the one per cent confidence level.

This does not imply that lower social class groups will obtain a colour television before those in higher social class groups since it makes no allowance for the *speed* with which the item in the set will be acquired. Since the analysis was based on information as to whether an item was 'in the home' rather than 'owned' and colour televisions are frequently rented rather than purchased it does not even necessarily imply that lower social class households would prefer to *purchase* a colour television before they bought a second car. Nevertheless, the apparent difference in the preferences of different social class groups between a colour television and a second car is worthy of note.

Results for low ownership items

The possibility of using the approach adopted here for predicting likely relative rates of market penetration for new items is attractive. It is, however, inevitably subject to statistical difficulties since the number of owners of items with low market penetration is, by definition, likely to be small, even in a sample skewed towards the higher income groups. Taking as a set second and third car, colour television, deep freeze and dishwasher, we found that the predicted order of acquisition (with average positions in parentheses) was second car (1.87) → colour television (2.44) → deep freeze (2.64) → dishwasher (3.42) → third car (4.64). Although the differences between the adjacent positions (except that between colour television and deep freeze) are significant, there cannot be said to be a unique pattern of acquisition. The average position for second car, which is shown to be on average the most likely to be purchased first is much nearer two than one. In this set colour television and deep freeze are almost as likely to be acquired first as a second car. In view of the relatively small number of observations, it would be unrealistic to discuss any observed differences in the patterns for different types of household.

It is not unduly surprising that the order of acquisition of low ownership and recently introduced durables should appear to be more randomly distributed than those of more established products. We are, of course, comparing once again items that are not necessarily homogeneous, though it is likely that they are all competing for limited consumer discretionary spending power. However, there seems no reason why this technique should not be used to monitor changes in the relative consumer acceptability of these items. A further way would be to build in to the analysis an indication of the item which the consumer would wish to acquire next as a way of extending the information available. This is therefore the next possibility that we shall consider.

Extension to include information on preferences for next acquisition

In his analysis Pyatt included not only the existing ownership pattern but also statements of household intentions to purchase other items. In this section we shall describe the effect of adding similar information to data on existing ownership levels. This is derived from our final postal questionnaire and relates to 329 respondents. Respondents were asked to indicate which one of the items they did not already own that they would wish to acquire next. As they were asked only to specify one item rather than one for each set of durables used in the analysis there is less scope to conduct a detailed analysis on the individual sets.

The distribution of answers indicating the one item that is not currently owned that people would most wish to buy next is shown in Table 8.7.

TABLE 8.7 Items the sample would most like to acquire next

Item	Number mentioning item	Per cent of those replying to this question	Per cent of those not owning each item
Black and white television	3	0.9	7.0
Colour television	86	26.1	36.1
Cooker	2	0.6	33.3
Deep freeze	77	23.4	28.7
Dishwasher	12	3.6	3.8
First car	6	1.8	18.8
Second car	28	8.5	14.6
Third car	5	1.5	1.8
Record player	25	7.6	38.5
Refrigerator	4	1.2	36.4
Tape recorder	16	4.9	9.2
Vacuum cleaner	1	0.3	20.0
Washing machine	8	2.4	21.6
Don't wish to own any more	56	17.0	
Total	329	100	

TABLE 8.8 Items the sample would most like to acquire next,
analysed by number of items already owned

Would like to acquire next:	Number of items already owned								Total
	1-4	5	6	7	8	9	10	11-12	
Black and white television	0	1	1	0	0	1	0	0	3
Colour television	2	5	12	16	17	20	12	2	86
Cooker	0	0	0	2	0	0	0	0	2
Deep freeze	2	2	7	13	19	19	10	5	77
Dishwasher	0	1	2	0	2	4	2	1	12
First car	1	1	3	1	0	0	0	0	6
Second car	0	1	3	6	10	4	4	0	28
Third car	0	0	0	0	3	1	0	1	5
Record player	3	2	8	3	7	1	1	0	25
Refrigerator	1	0	1	2	0	0	0	0	4
Tape recorder	0	0	3	4	3	4	1	1	16
Vaccum cleaner	0	1	0	0	0	0	0	0	1
Washing machine	0	2	1	3	0	2	0	0	8
No more	1	3	4	5	16	7	15	0	56
Total	10	19	45	55	77	63	45	15	329

Colour televisions and deep freezes are easily the most likely next acquisitions in absolute terms. They also represent quite a high proportion of the number of households in the sample not currently owning those items. It is interesting that the next most frequent answer was that the household did not wish to acquire any further durables from amongst those used in this investigation.

Table 8.8 allows us to look at these indications of acquisition intentions when the answers have been standardised for the effects of varying levels of existing ownership of these durables overall.

In proportionate terms, it appears that preferences for acquiring a colour television next are independent of the number of durables already owned while the intention to acquire a deep freeze next appears mainly to increase as the number of items already owned increases. This suggests that colour televisions are more likely to cause a change in the ordering of preferences and hence in the future pattern of acquisition of consumer durables. The proportion of households saying they did not wish to own any more durables increases as the number of durables already owned increases but it is noteworthy that for a number of households satiation in the accumulation process seems to have been reached well before all the durables under investigation have been acquired. We did not find any evidence that lack of a desire to acquire more durables was significantly associated with income or social class phenomena but the proportion not wishing to acquire any more durables was markedly higher in the case of respondents married a longer time.

It is possible to combine information on the existing pattern of ownership of particular sets of durables with information on the items that respondents would like to acquire next. This procedure really needs larger numbers of observations for effective and complete analysis than we have at our disposal. However, we can identify the ownership situations for which there are a reasonably large number of observations and indicate the probabilities of different items being acquired next, based on respondent indications of the item they would most like to acquire next where that item was within the set specified for analysis. These results are set out in Table 8.9.

Considering the set of leisure items (black and white and colour television, record player and tape recorder) discussed earlier, we find two important combinations of goods owned on which further analysis to incorporate indications of the items to be acquired next can be carried out. Of the households only owning a black and white television at the time of the survey but with an intention to make their next acquisition another item from this set, fifty-six per cent would acquire a record player next and forty per cent a colour television. Of those already owning a black and white television and a record player and intending next to acquire a further item from this set, seventy-nine per cent would acquire a colour television and twenty-one per cent would acquire a tape recorder. Comparing these results with the estimated probabilities of ownership based on cross-sectional ownership levels alone shown in Table 8.1, we find that colour television has a relatively higher priority based on future preferences than was obtained using the cross-sectional observations of existing ownership.

In the set of five kitchen items, the ownership situation most frequently to be found where there was also a preference for acquiring next another item from the set is that where cooker, refrigerator and washing machine were already owned. In this case ninety-two per cent of the next purchases would be of a deep freeze and only eight per cent would be of a dishwasher. In this case, the result strongly confirms the

TABLE 8.9 Estimates of priority patterns using indications of durables to be acquired next, for selected combinations of products

Set of durables already owned

(i) Leisure Items

Item	Owned	Owned
Black and white television	Yes	Yes
Colour television	No	No
Record player	No	Yes
Tape recorder	No	No

(ii) Kitchen Items

Item	Owned
Cooker	Yes
Deep freeze	No
Dishwasher	No
Refrigerator	Yes
Washing machine	Yes

(iii) Diverse Items

Item	Owned	Owned
First car	Yes	Yes
Second car	No	Yes
Colour television	No	No
Deep freeze	No	No
Vacuum cleaner	Yes	Yes

(iv) Low ownership items

Item	Owned	Owned
Second car	No	Yes
Third car	No	No
Colour television	No	No
Deep freeze	No	No
Dishwasher	No	No

Durables to be acquired next, given the above ownership patterns, probability of acquiring:

(i) Leisure Items

Item	Prob	Prob
Black and white television	—	—
Colour television	.40	.79
Record player	.56	—
Tape recorder	.04	.21
Number of observations of this combination of durables owned and to be acquired next on which calculations were based	25	38

(ii) Kitchen Items

Item	Prob
Cooker	—
Deep freeze	.92
Dishwasher	.08
Refrigerator	—
Washing machine	—
Number of observations ...	76

(iii) Diverse Items

Item	Prob	Prob
First car	—	—
Second car	.20	—
Colour television	.49	.49
Deep freeze	.31	.51
Vacuum cleaner	—	—
Number of observations ...	70	43

(iv) Low ownership items

Item	Prob	Prob
Second car	.15	—
Third car	.00	.07
Colour television	.52	.31
Deep freeze	.29	.52
Dishwasher	.04	.10
Number of observations ...	86	29

cross-sectional evidence in Table 8.3 that a deep freeze is generally likely to be acquired before a dishwasher.

Of the various ownership combinations for the set of diverse items, the two most frequent ownership combinations occurred where a first car and vacuum cleaner were both owned and where a first and second car and vacuum cleaner were owned. Compared with the information set out in Table 8.5, that in Table 8.9 based on stated future buying preferences suggests that the third purchase in the set in future had a higher probability of being a colour television. Certainly considerably more respondents who currently owned just a first car and a vacuum cleaner said they would choose a colour television than would choose to buy a second car next. However, of those who owned two cars and a vacuum cleaner and would choose to buy either a colour television or a deep freeze next, the choice between the two was almost evenly distributed.

As would be expected, the most frequent ownership situation for the set of low ownership items was that where none of the items was owned. Rather more than fifty per cent of respondents in that ownership situation who would next buy a durable from this set said they would buy a colour television and only fifteen per cent would choose a second car. This is again contrary to the evidence from the cross-sectional pattern where a second car was found to have a significantly lower average position (and hence a higher priority) than a colour television.

If it can be assumed that indications of the item respondents would most like to buy next do have predictive validity, then comparison of the results obtained from the cross sectional approach estimating probabilities of ownership at different stages of the acquisition process with those based on respondent indications of the item they would like to purchase next, given their existing ownership patterns, may be quite informative. Where the results from the two approaches diverge it would suggest that there has been a change in tastes. Any item for which intentions to buy in the future are higher than the cross-sectional probability of ownership would have indicated is one which seems likely to increase its rate of market penetration in the future. In the light of the results obtained here it would appear that on this basis, the market prospects for colour televisions and perhaps also deep freezes were particularly favourable.

Historic orders of acquisition of consumer durables

Most investigations of the order of acquisition have concentrated upon cross-sectional comparisons of the pattern of ownership at a single point in time. From this inferences have been drawn about actual orders of acquisition, assuming that it is meaningful to make the transformation from cross-sectional into time-series predictions. In the final postal questionnaire to the sample of households participating in this investigation we also attempted to collect information about the actual historic order in which durables had been accumulated. The question asked respondents to indicate '. . . . for all the items that you now own, or have owned at some time in your life, the order in which you acquired them *in the first instance.*' The explanation emphasised that the answer should relate to the first unit obtained of a particular item.

The information collected on the historic order of acquisition is set out in Table 8.10, for 355 respondents. Since the number of owners varies from item to item this is not a complete matrix. In a number of cases, respondents said that they had initially acquired several items at the same time, so more first purchases were recorded than there were respondents answering the question. Ties were also recorded for a number of other positions in the order of acquisition.

For most durables there is a readily identifiable modal position with the frequency of purchases at other positions being more or less normally distributed. The exceptions to this occur in the case of first car and record player where purchases were more evenly distributed over several different positions and cooker and vacuum cleaner where the mode was respectively at the first and second position in the order. If we utilise just the modal values, a historic order of acquisition for all thirteen durables would be: 1=) cooker and first car; 3) vacuum cleaner; 4) washing machine; 5=) refrigerator and black and white television; 7) record player; 8) second car; 9=) tape recorder and colour television; 11=) deep freeze, dishwasher and third car. If we calculate the average position in the acquisition order based only on those cases where a purchase had been made, the order is: 1) cooker; 2) vacuum cleaner; 3) first car; 4) washing machine; 5) refrigerator; 6) black and white television; 7) record player; 8) tape recorder; 9) second car; 10) dishwasher; 11) colour television; 12) third car; 13) deep freeze.

The orderings obtained from these analyses of the mode and the mean are very similar. They do not, however, allow for variations in the number of households that had actually owned an item. The ranking for dishwasher, for example, is probably placed too high by this analysis because it takes no account of the fact that the proportion of households actually choosing to own it at all is very small. The positions of a first car and record player are perhaps less well defined since they are the items that are most likely to have been owned by some people before marriage and so their rank orderings here may be rather higher than their true position in the priority ordering of a household.

TABLE 8.10 Historic order of acquisition for thirteen durables

	Not owned	*Order of acquisition*												
		1st	2nd	3rd	4th	5th	6th	7th	8th	9th	10th	11th	12th	13th
Black and white television	47	9	21	40	65	74	57	25	12	5	0	0	0	0
Colour television	255	0	1	3	2	2	5	14	27	20	20	5	1	0
Cooker	4	207	62	32	25	14	4	3	0	4	0	0	0	0
Deep freeze	289	1	0	0	0	2	2	11	14	17	15	4	0	0
Dishwasher	337	1	0	2	0	0	3	2	3	4	1	1	1	0
First car	41	62	24	39	43	54	35	14	0	0	0	0	0	0
Second car	213	1	5	3	3	5	15	39	39	23	9	0	0	0
Third car	302	0	0	2	3	1	2	7	12	13	8	5	0	0
Record player	69	29	28	26	33	34	44	43	32	14	3	0	0	0
Refrigerator	15	13	28	53	68	71	63	29	7	5	3	0	0	0
Tape recorder	185	9	11	11	8	12	17	36	37	19	8	2	0	0
Vacuum cleaner	7	47	118	76	45	34	16	6	4	1	0	1	0	0
Washing machine	40	20	56	72	64	46	37	14	2	4	0	0	0	0

It is also possible to use the information reported by the individual households to calculate orders of acquisition for the sets of durables used earlier in this chapter for cross-sectional analysis. The method adopted was based on a reranking of the order of acquisition to take account only of the items in a particular set. Thus in a set of four items, the possible ranks of historic order of acquisition were in the range one to four. Where two or more items had an equal ranking reported, the normal procedure was adopted of giving each item a rank the sum of which would equal the sum of the ranks had the items been separately distinguishable. Thus if two items were ranked equal third in a set, a value of 3.5 was given to each. When an item in a set was not owned it was given a ranking equal to the empty element in a household row vector. Thus if one item in a set of four was not owned it was accorded the value four. If three items in a set of four were not owned each was given a rank value of three. The sums and average values of the ranks were then established and the coefficients of concordance calculated (Kendall 1955).

The rankings for the sets of four leisure items, five kitchen items and five diverse items are set out in Table 8.11. (A similar analysis was also carried out for the set of low ownership goods but was inevitably greatly affected by the need to insert interpolated values. This would make discussion of the results obtained unhelpful and not particularly meaningful.) For comparison, the figures in the last column are the average positions derived from the cross-sectional analysis of the probabilities of ownership reported earlier in this chapter. The values for the coefficient of concordance are all statistically significant at the one per cent level, thus confirming that there is a high degree of correspondence between the ranks or in other words a reasonably unique order in which these items were acquired.

There is a close similarity between the average rank positions established using the historic order of acquisition data and the average positions derived from the cross-sectional analysis. This is interesting since it suggests that for these items and for this sample a cross-section into time-series transformation could normally be assumed to have empirical validity. It should also be noted that the historic order of acquisition data were produced by only about sixty per cent of the sample from which the cross-sectional probability pattern was derived.

In the set of five kitchen items there is however a difference in the ordering established by the two procedures. The historic order of acquisition data suggests that the pattern was cooker → washing machine → refrigerator . . . whereas the cross-sectional analysis produced an ordering of cooker → refrigerator → washing machine . . . This is not altogether surprising since the market penetration of refrigerators has been quite rapid over recent years and it would be reasonable to interpret the discrepancy between the two results as indicating that it is only recently that refrigerators have become of greater relative importance to consumers than have washing machines.

TABLE 8.11 Historic orders of acquisition for sets of durables

(i) *Four leisure items*

	Total of rank positions historic order of acquisition	Average of rank positions historic order of acquisition	Average position in cross-sectional analysis of ownership probability
Black and white television	590.0	1.662	1.425
Record player	703.0	1.980	2.024
Tape recorder	1051.5	2.961	2.916
Colour television	1205.5	3.396	3.635

Coefficient of Concordance W = 0.40

(ii) *Five kitchen items*

Cooker	465.0	1.310	1.104
Washing machine	849.0	2.392	2.684
Refrigerator	905.0	2.549	2.229
Deep freeze	1535.0	4.324	4.102
Dishwasher	1571.0	4.425	4.881

Coefficient of Concordance W = 0.70

(iii) *Five diverse items*

Vacuum cleaner	499.5	1.407	1.161
First car	684.0	1.927	1.894
Second car	1279.5	3.604	3.655
Colour television	1385.0	3.901	4.004
Deep freeze	1477.0	4.161	4.286

Coefficient of Concordance W = 0.61

Table 8.4 gives some support to this interpretation since the difference in the average positions for refrigerators and washing machines in favour of refrigerators was considerably larger in the case of consumers more recently married than for those married longer.

Appendix to Chapter 8

Statistical procedures for calculation of a priority pattern

[This appendix is largely reproduced from an article in the *Oxford Bulletin of Economics and Statistics* (Hebden and Pickering 1974) and permission to reproduce this material here is gratefully acknowledged.]

There are several approaches to the estimation of a priority pattern, of varying degrees of complexity. The simplest, for a very small number of goods, is merely to construct an ownership matrix, by inspection to find the most likely pattern of accumulation, to impose this pattern and count the number of deviations from it. A refinement is to subject these deviations to a statistical test of significance, such as is provided by the Guttman Coefficient of Reproducibility (Guttman 1945; Goodman 1959; Sagi 1959). Another method is to study the matrix of point correlation coefficients between ownership of each pair of goods to see if it tends to have the particular structure associated with a unique order of acquisition (Guttman 1954). A third and more complex alternative is that reported by Pyatt which is based on the calculation of the probabilities of owning each product at each point in the accumulation of a specified set of goods. We favour Pyatt's approach since it provides more evidence on the structure of the ordering and the nature of any deviation from uniqueness. Consequently it offers greater insight into some aspects of durable acquisition behaviour. For the purposes of our analysis some modifications and extensions have been made to Pyatt's methodology and the calculation procedure is as follows.

Notation

$\wedge$ denotes sample estimate

$\sum_{i \in s}$ denotes the sum over all i such that i belongs to set s.

$n(i,j)$ $=$ no. of sample households owning goods i, j.

s = a certain set of goods.

$[s]$ = number of goods in set s.

n (s) = no. of sample households owning set s.

n $[s]$ = no. of sample households owning $[s]$ goods.

n $(i/ [s])$ = no. of sample households owning good i, given that they own $[s]$ goods.

Distribution of ownership of sets of goods

Once a particular set of goods has been selected for analysis, the basic input is information on the number of people owning each possible combination of the items in the set. For example, in a set consisting of five goods some households will own one item, some two . . . . some all five. From information on actual ownership of the different combinations of goods in the set we can calculate the conditional probability that a household owns a particular group of goods given that it owns a specified number of goods from the total set. Algebraically, this is given by:

$$\hat{Pr}(\text{owns set } s/\text{owns } [s] \text{ goods}) = \frac{n(s)}{n[s]}$$

for example, we could have $\hat{Pr}$(owns vacuum cleaner, colour television/owns [2] goods). These estimated conditional probabilities can each have a standard error attached to them, to indicate their reliability as estimates of values in the whole population.

Ownership probabilities for individual goods

The next step is to use the conditional probabilities found previously, to calculate the conditional probability of owning one particular good (rather than a particular combination), given that a certain number of goods is owned. For example, we have $\hat{Pr}$(owns vacuum cleaner/owns [4] goods). The rule for calculations is:

$$\hat{Pr}(\text{owns good } i/\text{owns } [s] \text{ goods}) = \sum_{i \in s} \hat{Pr}(\text{owns } s/\text{owns } [s])$$

$$[s] \text{ fixed}$$

Again, standard errors are calculated for each estimated probability. These probabilities are illuminating in the way that they show which goods are acquired early in the consumer's durable accumulation process, and how soon, relative to other items, the consumer is likely to acquire a certain item. So the beginnings of an acquisition pattern are emerging.

Order of acquisition

Finally we arrive at the acquisition pattern. At this stage we have to assume that it is valid to estimate a sequence of events occurring over time in one household, by studying the differences in ownership situations of various households at the same instant of time. We, therefore, have to assume that these various households are at different stages of a common time-path in acquiring durables, and it is the difference in their positions on the time-path, not differences in the time-paths (or the acquisition pattern itself) between households, that account for the differences in durable ownership between households at the same point of time.

Making this assumption, we estimate the probability that good i is the jth good bought by taking the difference between the probability of owning $[j]$ goods that include i and the probability of owning $[j-1]$ goods that also include i:

$$\hat{Pr} \ ([i] = j \equiv \hat{Pr} \ (j^{th} \text{ good bought is good } i)$$

$$= \hat{Pr}(\text{owns good } i/\text{owns } [j] \text{ goods})$$

$$- \hat{Pr} \ (\text{owns good } i/\text{owns } [j-1] \text{ goods}$$

For example, $\hat{Pr}$ (vacuum cleaner = 3rd good) = $\hat{Pr}$ (owns vacuum cleaner/owns three goods) $- \hat{Pr}$ (owns vacuum cleaner/owns two goods).

These probabilities are of interest in themselves because they show how likely it is that a certain good will feature at a certain position in the pattern of acquisition. If we tabulate the results with a row for each good and a column for each position in the accumulation process, we see that the entries (probabilities) in each row and each column must sum to unity: at each stage of accumulation, one or other of the goods *must* be bought, so the entries in a specific column show the relative chances of each good being bought at that stage; while each good must (we assume) be bought eventually, so the entries in a specific row show the relative chances of that good being bought at each stage of accumulation. Our final stage is to summarise these row entries, to give the expected, or average, position of each good in the accumulation pattern: this is our 'acquisition pattern' in its most concise form.

This summary measure, E ([*i*]) for good *i*, is given by:

E ([*i*]) = expected position of good *i* in the order of acquisition

$$= \sum_{j=1}^{[k]} j \cdot \hat{Pr}(\text{good } i \text{ is } j^{th} \text{ good bought})$$

and so it uses the results of the previous step. A check on the calculations is that the sum of the E's over all [*k*] goods in the set, should be [*k*]/2([*k*] + 1). The lower the value of E ([*i*]), the higher on the list of priorities is good *i* and hence the sooner it is acquired.

Statistical tests of the uniqueness of the acquisition pattern

Standard errors have been calculated for each of the 'average position' values, the E ([*j*]) – see Appendix to the original paper (Hebden and Pickering 1974) for the formulae – and with them statistical tests are made of the uniqueness of the underlying acquisition pattern for the population. Our hypothesis is that our sample was drawn at random from a population of households for which a unique order of acquisition exists. If the order were indeed unique, it would be identical for all members of the sample and so the 'average position' figures would be the set of integers 1, 2, 3 . . ., *k*. So one test of the approach to uniqueness is a Student's t-test of the deviation of each E ([*i*]) value from the corresponding integer, on the null hypothesis of no significant deviation. However, this is rather too strict a test for the uniqueness of the ordering, because the E ([*i*]) values are constrained to sum to [*k*] ([*k*] + 1)/2 and so any deviation of one figure from its corresponding integer will necessitate counter-balancing deviations in some of the others. A second test is, therefore, also used, of the statistical significance of the difference between adjacent 'average position' values, on the null hypothesis, in this case, that no such differences exist in the population and so there is no unique ordering. The test statistic is again Student's t, a test of the difference between two sample means. Since these means are not independent, strictly speaking such a test should take into account their covariance, but we have had to ignore this owing to the great difficulties of estimating covariance, given the varying sample sizes in each cell.

The results of these two tests, made at the ninety-five per cent level of confidence, are given in the final columns of the tables of results for each set of goods. In some cases, however, we found no instances where all goods in the set were owned by any respondents. Where this was so

Pyatt's methodology had to be extended by extrapolation or interpolation and in these instances it was impossible to calculate all the necessary standard errors. The Appendix to the original paper gives details of the actual modifications made to Pyatt's methodology in order to deal with this problem.

9 *Purchase probabilities and reported purchases*

The distribution of purchase probabilities

Chapter 7 described how information was collected on the state of the stock of consumer durables already owned by the panel at the time of the initial interview. At a later point in the interview, after dealing with other financial aspects all informants (whether or not they owned a particular consumer durable) were asked to assess, on a 0–10 probability scale, the chances that they would be making a purchase of each item at some stage within a specified period of time, in the foreseeable future.

A number of similar attempts have been made to use such expectational information in predicting the level of purchases of particular consumer durables. The evidence on this has been discussed in Chapter 1 and also in a previous paper (Pickering and Isherwood 1974). While early approaches to buying intentions were based on questions asking whether households intended to buy a particular item and were answered either 'yes' or 'no', more recent studies have tended to ask informants what they think the chances are that they will have made a purchase within the following *n* months and answers have been given on a more extended rating scale. Not only does this use of a multi-point scale increase the potential incisiveness of the information collected, the change in the emphasis of the question from an 'intention to buy' to an assessment of the 'chances that a purchase will be made' is perhaps more helpful, especially where the forecast of replacement demand is particularly dependent upon the previously assessed chances that the unit currently owned will break down. It is therefore possible that a forecast of sales based on purchase probability information would be in excess of a forecast based on reported buying intentions.

Each respondent was shown a card with all integers from 0–10 marked on it and was asked: (a) 'How likely is it that you/someone else in the household will have bought a [item specified] in three months from now – that is by the end of June 1972'; (b) 'and what is the probability of buying a [item] within the next six months, that is by the end of September 1972?'; (c) 'and what is the probability of buying a [item] within the next twelve months, that is by the end of March 1973?' This question, for each of the three different time periods, was asked in relation to fifteen different items: black and white television, central heating, carpets, colour television, cooker, deep freeze, dishwasher, a major item of furniture (costing £50 or more), new car, used car, record player, refrigerator, tape recorder, vacuum cleaner, washing machine. In an attempt to avoid any bias due to response sets the order of the products for which these questions were asked was rotated.

Our interest is in the extent to which this information can be used to predict the subsequent purchase behaviour of the members of the panel. We shall therefore concentrate in this chapter on those for whom full

TABLE 9.1 Distribution of twelve month purchase probabilities

Item	*Purchase probability value*										
	0	1	2	3	4	5	6	7	8	9	10
Black and white television	307	11	5	4	0	18	0	2	4	1	11
Central Heating	320	12	2	2	1	8	0	3	3	4	8
Carpets	250	10	8	7	2	21	2	4	10	18	31
Colour television	301	13	4	3	3	17	2	9	7	2	2
Cooker	293	16	8	2	2	12	4	2	5	5	14
Deep Freeze	300	13	7	5	2	16	3	5	4	4	4
Dishwasher	345	8	4	1	0	3	0	0	0	0	2
Furniture	233	7	10	7	7	35	6	8	9	11	30
New Car	290	9	1	2	2	18	3	3	9	4	22
Used Car	278	8	7	6	3	22	3	4	10	4	18
Record Player	310	9	11	3	0	11	2	6	3	0	8
Refrigerator	301	11	11	5	1	18	3	6	2	1	4
Tape Recorder	331	7	9	1	0	11	1	0	0	1	2
Vacuum Cleaner	271	14	9	8	3	32	2	2	5	6	11
Washing Machine	284	12	8	5	2	22	4	3	5	6	12

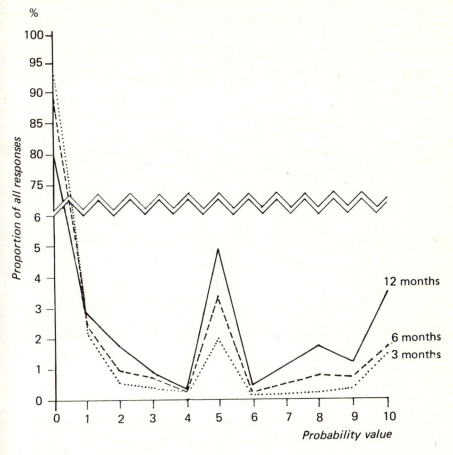

Fig.9.1 Distribution of purchase probabilities three, six, twelve months

information is available from the postal follow-ups during the survey year.

In Table 9.1 the distribution of recorded twelve month purchase probabilities is set out and this is summarised in Table 9.2 in terms of mean purchase probabilities and the predicted number of purchasers based on the 363 respondents completing the survey. Figure 9.1 shows the overall distribution of the purchase probabilities summed across all products. It will be observed that the vast majority of responses were at the zero purchase probability level for all three time horizons, three, six, and twelve months, but the longer the time horizon the greater was the proportion of the sample with some positive anticipation of purchasing a particular durable. However, the proportion of observations at all

TABLE 9.2 Mean purchase probabilities and predicted number of purchasers

Item	Mean purchase probabilities			Predicted number of purchasers		
	3 months	6 months	12 months	3 months	6 months	12 months
Black and white television	·026	·047	·079	9	17	29
Central Heating	·017	·034	·063	6	12	23
Carpets	·089	·140	·207	32	51	75
Colour television	·017	·041	·082	6	15	30
Cooker	·033	·043	·102	12	16	37
Deep Freeze	·013	·039	·080	5	14	29
Dishwasher	·010	·012	·015	4	4	5
Furniture	·090	·133	·224	33	48	81
New Car	·058	·070	·133	21	26	48
Used Car	·051	·075	·139	19	27	50
Record player	·015	·037	·070	6	13	25
Refrigerator	·025	·035	·074	9	13	27
Tape recorder	·009	·012	·033	3	4	12
Vacuum Cleaner	·051	·067	·126	19	24	46
Washing Machine	·045	·065	·116	16	24	42

non-zero probability values remained very small. There was a peaking at the mid-point of the scale and a tendency for the right hand end-point of the scale, representing absolute certainty, to turn upwards, thereby confirming earlier findings (Juster 1966; Gabor and Granger 1972; Pickering and Isherwood 1974).

The mean purchase probabilities and predicted numbers of purchasers in Table 9.2 are derived by summing the values in Table 9.1 after weighting each observation by the probability value on the assumption that the probability scale is linear from zero to 1.0. Thus a probability scale score of one is assumed to indicate a probability of .1, i.e. there is a one-in-ten chance that people stating this particular probability value will in fact make a puchase, and so on, with those giving a score of ten assumed to be absolutely certain they will purchase, that is a probability value of 1.0. Comparing the mean purchase probabilities on the individual items with those of our earlier study (Pickering and Isherwood 1974), it is encouraging to find that the probabilities were similar in the two surveys. (The overall distribution for all items aggregated together indicates higher purchase probabilities in the present study than in the earlier investigation. This is largely due to the introduction here of carpets, a high purchase probability item and the exclusion of certain low purchase probability items – caravan, floor polisher, fridge/deep freeze – that were included in the earlier survey.) The only substantial exceptions were central heating and colour televisions which had higher mean purchase probabilities here than in the previous investigation while the probability for record players was lower. The finding that the mean probability values are reasonably stable is reassuring. However, small variations in mean purchase probabilities would, if 'grossed up', imply quite substantial changes in the volume of total demand for a product within the economy. Clearly considerable care would be needed in using these figures alone as predictors of the likely level of demand.

The largest number of purchases in each time period were predicted to be of furnishings (furniture and carpets) and motor cars (new and used). In our previous study it was suggested that the varying ratios of twelve to three month purchase probability values offered some indication of the length of respondent time horizons in planning durable purchases. Low twelve to three month ratios were interpreted as indicating a short planning horizon and it was subsequently shown that purchases of such items were more likely to be underestimated using this procedure. In contrast, it was suggested that a high twelve to three month probability ratio indicated not so much a buying plan or intention but merely an expression of interest in making an acquisition at some time in the future. Purchases of such items appeared to be more likely to be over-predicted. On this basis, it appears that planning horizons for carpets, furniture, cars, vacuum cleaners and washing machines are subject to a short time horizon, while purchases of colour televisions, deep freezes and record players are subject to a long planning horizon. These are largely in line with the interpretations from our previous study though vacuum cleaner purchases now appear to involve a short rather than a long planning horizon and record players now appear to have a long horizon whereas previously it appeared to be neither unduly long nor short.

Observed purchase behaviour: the record for individual commodities

On each quarterly postal follow-up, the members of the panel were asked to indicate on a checklist which of the fifteen durables they, or members of their household, had purchased during the previous three months. It was hoped that relatively frequent recording of purchases would ensure the reliability of the data obtained. However, as has been explained in Chapter 4, difficulties arose due to the existence of a limited amount of double counting of the same purchases. Consequently, the most reliable basis for analysis is the information on the actual number of purchasers, taken over the year as a whole. While this effectively removes the influence of any erroneous double recording of the same purchase, it does also mean that the extent of multiple purchasing of particular items is not reflected in the details of actual purchases.

Table 9.3 indicates the number of households purchasing each item and contrasts this with the predicted number of purchasers. Most items were purchased by seven per cent or more of the sample. Furniture, carpets and cars (new and used) were bought by the largest numbers of households, and dishwashers and refrigerators had fewest recorded purchases. Levels of purchases seem to have been predicted with reasonable accuracy for most durables. However, refrigerator purchases were over-predicted while car (new and used), record player and tape recorder purchases were under-predicted. Over all the durables the predicted number of purchases was about sixteen per cent below the actual and this seemed also to apply to the relation between predicted and actual levels of purchase over the first three and six months of the survey year. Our earlier investigations during 1971 and the early part of 1972, had, however, found that taking all items together, actual purchases were slightly under-predicted by purchase probability information (Pickering and Isherwood 1974).

TABLE 9.3 Predicted and actual purchases of consumer durables

| Item | *Twelve months* | |
	Predicted	*Actual Purchasers*
Black and white television	29	21
Central heating	23	24
Carpets	75	85
Colour television	30	26
Cooker	37	37
Deep freeze	29	31
Dishwasher	5	6
Furniture	81	99
New car	48	66
Used car	50	94
Record player	25	54
Refrigerator	27	15
Tape recorder	12	33
Vacuum cleaner	46	37
Washing machine	42	42
Total	559	670

While a number of possible explanations may be offered for the difference in the two sets of results, it seems that the most likely interpretation is that during the period covered by the present investigation other forces were at work in the economy, encouraging a higher overall level of durable purchasing. (The variation in the durables included in the two studies does not appear to account for the difference.) This is consistent with the evidence, discussed in Chapters 4 and 5, of economic reflation during 1972 and a higher level of purchasing confidence in 1972 and early 1973 compared with at least the early part of 1971. This serves to emphasise that it cannot necessarily be assumed that a stable relationship between subjective purchase probabilities and subsequent purchases exists independently of other conditions in the economy. It might be appropriate to combine purchase probability data on specific durables with a general consumer confidence measure, this has been found to be useful in the USA (Juster and Wachtel 1972a) and to use either or both types of consumer expectations information within a fully specified forecasting model.

Observed purchase behaviour: the record for individual consumers

The concern in this study is as much with the micro-economic analysis of consumer behaviour as with the forecasting of sales. If we can explain individual behaviour with our models there is likely to be greater confidence in using them for forecasting purposes. The question therefore arises as to whether the purchase probabilities stated by individual informants do have predictive power for the way those particular informants subsequently acted. Now it is not possible for a consumer to purchase six-tenths or some other fraction of a car, although some people obviously come nearer to making a purchase than others. The dependent variable has therefore to be dichotomous – either the purchase was made within the time period specified or it was not. However, by observing the behaviour of groups of informants who had stated the same purchase probability value it is possible to establish whether, for each group as a whole, the probabilities stated *ex-ante* had any predictive power. Thus we wish to know whether informants stating a purchase probability of nine or ten on an item were proportionately more likely to have made that purchase than those stating a probability of five or six and so on. If the probability values were really very good predictors of behaviour of the groups of informants at each probability point and if the probability scale was indeed linear, then we might expect to find that ninety per cent of those stating a value of nine and fifty per cent of those stating a value of five actually reported a purchase, and so on.

The actual distribution of purchasers over the year analysed by their stated twelve month purchase probabilities for each item is set out in Table 9.4. It will be observed that slightly more than half of all purchasers of an item were respondents who had stated zero purchase probabilities and the proportion is not appreciably below forty per cent for any item. To this extent Juster's hopes that the use of a probability scale would substantially reduce the incidence of non-intenders who purchased have not been vindicated (Juster 1964) and our results are in keeping with other findings on this question (Gabor and Granger 1972/1973, Pickering and Isherwood 1974). However, there may be other respects in which the purchase probability approach does have predictive value. We have already seen that purchase probabilities predict reasonably well the actual number of purchases of an item. It may also be that individual buyer behaviour is systematically related to

TABLE 9.4 Distribution of twelve month purchasers analysed by twelve month purchase probability values

Item	Purchase probability value											Total
	0	1	2	3	4	5	6	7	8	9	10	
Black and white television	11	1	1	0	0	5	0	0	0	0	3	21
Central heating	15	1	0	1	0	1	0	0	2	2	2	24
Carpets	33	1	2	0	1	6	1	3	5	13	20	85
Colour television	16	1	0	0	0	3	1	3	2	0	0	26
Cooker	19	0	2	1	1	2	0	2	2	1	7	37
Deep freeze	18	1	1	1	1	1	2	2	2	1	1	31
Dishwasher	5	0	0	0	0	0	0	0	0	0	1	6
Furniture	51	1	2	1	1	14	1	4	4	4	16	99
New car	36	3	0	1	0	7	0	1	3	3	12	66
Used car	46	2	4	2	2	12	2	1	4	4	15	94
Record player	37	1	3	0	0	3	1	5	0	0	4	54
Refrigerator	6	0	1	0	0	5	2	0	0	0	1	15
Tape recorder	25	1	2	0	0	2	1	0	0	1	1	33
Vacuum cleaner	14	1	2	0	0	11	0	1	0	4	4	37
Washing machine	21	0	1	1	0	5	0	2	2	3	7	42
Percentage at each probability value reporting a purchase	8	9	20	13	21	29	31	42	34	54	53	

purchase probability levels. Table 9.5 sets out the mean subjective purchase probabilities, for each item, of buyers and non-buyers as separate groups. It will be observed that in all cases, except that for furniture, the ratio of mean purchase probabilities for buyers to that for non-buyers is in excess of three and for most of the items is in excess of four. This indicates that actual buyers as a group, were more likely to have anticipated making that particular purchase than non-buyers.

Because it is likely that the majority of informants will have no expectation of buying a particular durable over the following year and will not in fact do so it may be objected that this is an insufficiently stringent test of the performance of the purchase probability information. The next test is therefore to investigate how the objective purchase probabilities (that is the proportions actually making a purchase) relate to the subjective purchase probabilities. The ratio of purchasers over the survey year as a whole at each probability value is set out in Table 9.6, for three, six and twelve month subjective purchase probabilities respectively.

TABLE 9.5 Mean twelve month purchase probabilities of buyers and non-buyers

| Item | Mean probabilities | |
	Buyers	Non-buyers
Black and white television	.207	.069
Central heating	.263	.048
Carpets	.498	.118
Colour television	.227	.070
Cooker	.351	.073
Deep freeze	.245	.065
Dishwasher	.167	.012
Furniture	.347	.178
New car	.332	.089
Used car	.341	.068
Record player	.191	.049
Refrigerator	.327	.063
Tape recorder	.121	.024
Vacuum cleaner	.386	.097
Washing machine	.374	.082

TABLE 9.6 Proportions buying at each purchase probability value and linear regressions of the relation between subjective and objective purchase probabilities

	Probability Value										
	0	1	2	3	4	5	6	7	8	9	10
12 month probabilities and 12 month purchasers	.080	.088	.202	.131	.214	.291	.314	.421	.342	.537	.525
				$y = .05 + .47x$		$\overline{R}^2 = .90$					
6 month probabilities and 12 month purchasers	.092	.091	.177	.292	.400	.373	.435	.538	.556	.531	.622
				$y = .10 + .55x$		$\overline{R}^2 = .93$					
3 month probabilities and 12 month purchasers	.102	.113	.167	.350	.467	.420	.714	.750	.750	.619	.597
				$y = .13 + .66x$		$\overline{R}^2 = .74$					

Looking at the relationship between twelve month probabilities and twelve month purchasers, we find that the actual proportions buying tend to increase as the subjective purchase probability increases. Whereas eight per cent of those stating zero twelve month purchase probabilities actually made a purchase of that particular item in the twelve months, twenty-nine per cent of those stating a probability of five made a purchase and fifty-three per cent of those stating a probability of ten actually behaved as they had predicted. The proportions reporting a purchase at non-zero probability values tend to be below the proportion that it was assumed would make the purchase, purchases by zero probability respondents offset the shortfall at the other values. It seems therefore that the grouping of informants by their stated purchase probabilities does have some predictive power since higher subjective probabilities are associated with higher objective purchase probabilities. Although, as we had already noted, quite a high proportion of total purchases were made by respondents stating zero purchase probabilities, we can now recognise that the purchasers at the zero subjective probability level represented only a small proportion of those stating a zero probability.

When shorter (three and six month) subjective purchase probability time horizons are compared with twelve month purchaser behaviour, the proportions in each probability group who actually achieved a purchase increase and the same general tendency persists for the proportion purchasing to increase as the subjective probability value rises. This pattern is confirmed by the multiple regression equations also set out in Table 9.6 which were derived by regressing the proportions buying at each subjective probability level against the probability value itself. Figure 9.2 sets out graphically the actual and the estimated relationships between twelve month probabilities and twelve month purchasers. The low constant terms indicate that the proportion at the zero probability level making a purchase was small and the positive coefficient indicates that as the subjective probabilities rose so the proportions making a purchase also increased. It will be observed that where purchases are related to the shorter purchase probability time horizon of three and six months, so both the constant term and the regression coefficient increase in size. This is not unexpected. The larger constant term indicates that some people who had stated a zero probability of purchasing an item in the next three months, had stated a non-zero probability for a longer time period and had actually completed a purchase, although the proportions doing so remained small. The higher regression coefficient suggests that if allowed more time to achieve a purchase, a greater proportion of households at all probability levels would be expected to acquire the item concerned. This therefore indicates that the ability of subjective

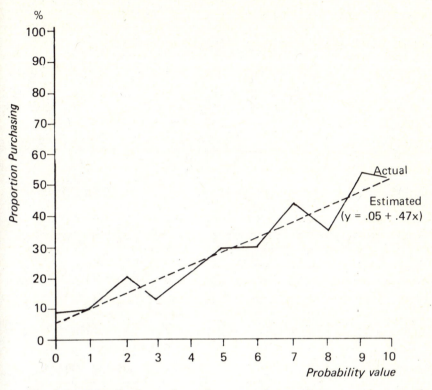

Fig.9.2 Distribution of twelve month purchases against twelve month Probabilities.

purchase probability information to distinguish between people who were more likely and those who were less likely to purchase a particular durable continues beyond the period of time to which the subjective purchase probability data nominally relates.

Detailed analysis of the proportions at each probability level buying individual items is hindered by the relatively small number of observations available, especially of those stating non-zero purchase probabilities. However, by grouping products it is possible to investigate the extent to which the proportions purchasing increase as the subjective purchase probability value rises. These are set out for certain groups of commodity in Table 9.7 and regressed values are tabulated in Table 9.8. Once again we find the proportions purchasing tend to increase as the subjective purchase probability value rises. This is particularly clearly established when purchase probability groups are also aggregated to some extent in order to reduce the problem of small numbers of observations in each cell. As we also found in our earlier

TABLE 9.7 Proportion buying different items at different probability values: twelve month purchasers and twelve month purchase probabilities

Item	Probability Value										
	0	1	2	3	4	5	6	7	8	9	10
Cars (new and used	14	29	50	38	40	48	33	29	37	88	68
				39			46			58	
Furnishings (carpets and furniture)	17	12	22	7	22	36	25	58	47	59	59
				17			34			57	
Furniture	22	14	20	14	14	40	17	50	44	36	53
				17			37			48	
Household durables	6	5	17	8	15	23	33	43	23	39	41
				14			25			40	
High ownership household durables	6	4	19	7	13	27	27	48	21	42	43
				14			27			42	
Low ownership household durables	5	7	13	10	20	13	67	36	36	29	30
				13			19			33	

Note: 'Low ownership household durables' were colour television, deep freeze, dishwasher and tape recorder. 'High ownership household durables' were black and white television, cooker, record player, refrigerator, vacuum cleaner and washing machine. 'Household durables' incorporated the 'Low ownership' and 'High ownership' household durables specified above.

study, the proportions actually achieving a purchase were consistently lower for household durables (and particularly those classed as low ownership durables – colour television, deep freeze, dishwasher and tape recorder) than for cars and furnishings. If different types of durables are found to have a consistently different pattern of relationship between subjective purchase probabilities and the proportions actually purchasing, then this would need to be taken into account in making predictions of the volume of sales of a particular durable.

The position of furniture is, as in our previous investigation, of particular interest as there is less evidence that the proportion actually reporting a purchase of furniture increases as the probability value rises. This is indicated in Table 9.8 where we find a higher constant term, lower regression coefficient and lower coefficient of multiple determination than for most other types of item. The result here for cars is disappointing since the value of the constant term is high, the slope of the regression line relatively flat and the $\bar{R}^2$ value low. Table 9.7 confirms that there was a less strong tendency for the car purchase rate to increase as subjective purchase probabilities also rose than for most other durables. The results from our earlier investigations were much more encouraging in this respect (Pickering and Isherwood 1974).

Characteristics of informants with purchasing patterns different from those predicted by the probability data

While the purchase probability data discussed so far in this chapter seem to have predictive validity both in terms of the proportion of people actually making purchases at each probability level and in terms of the

TABLE 9.8 Regression analyses of the proportions purchasing different items over twelve months
against twelve month subjective purchase
probability levels

Item	a	b	$\bar{R}^2$
Car	0.232	0.395	.36
Furnishings	0.070	0.524	.76
Furniture	0.117	0.357	.55
Household durables	0.041	0.378	.76
High ownership durables	0.035	0.400	.69
Low ownership durables	0.068	0.346	.33

relationship between predicted and actual purchases of particular durables, it is apparent that in quite a large number of individual cases anticipated purchases were not made and in other cases unanticipated purchases were made. Granted the degree of disaggregation of individuals and commodities it would be surprising if this were not the case. However, it did seem worthwhile to investigate whether such 'deviations' from predicted purchase behaviour were systematically associated with any particular respondent characteristics. For the purposes of this analysis the 363 informants were classified into three groups:

Group A. Strong intenders who did not purchase – that is informants with twelve month purchase probabilities of seven and above on a particular item who did not, during the survey year report a purchase of that particular consumer durable.

Group B. Non-intenders who did purchase – these were buyers of a particular durable on which their twelve month purchase probability had been in the range 0–2.

Group C. Non-deviants – respondents whose purchases were in line with that predicted by their subjective purchase probability statements.

Where an informant might have been classified into both groups *A* and *B* because an anticipated purchase on one item had not been made but an unanticipated purchase on another item had been made, this was classed as a group *C* case of non-deviation. Where an informant had more cases falling into group *A* than *B* he was classified into *A* and *vice versa*. In all, we classified sixty-eight informants to group *A*, 165 to group *B* and 130 to group *C*. Our hypothesis was that the three groups would differ significantly in respect of respondent characteristics relating to the socio-economic status of the members of those groups, their economic confidence and the nature of changes in their circumstances during the year. This investigation is therefore similar to that reported in Chapter 6 where the effect was investigated of changed household circumstances during the survey year in causing the level of expenditure on all durables taken together to deviate from that which had been predicted.

The members of group *A*, those who failed to make an anticipated purchase, tended to be younger and more likely to have reported an ability to achieve a temporary income increase. In terms of general economic confidence as indicated on the attitude variables described in Chapter 5, group *A* respondents were more confident at the start of the survey year than the sample as a whole. Their greater confidence was particularly marked in respect of their attitudes about their financial prospects and the sums of money they would have available to spend. Predictably, they were also more confident in reporting stronger intentions to buy a car and a new durable that they did not already own and also in their intentions to replace an existing durable. They were more likely to expect to buy more durables over the following twelve months. They considered themselves more directly affected by government economic policy than members of the other groups. Of the changes in circumstances during the survey year, group *A* members were more likely to have increased their family size during the year, presumably necessitating expenditure on other sorts of item than those durables on which this study is based and possibly reducing their ability to achieve temporary income increases, especially where this was based upon the contribution from a working wife.

Unanticipated purchasers (group *B*) were more likely to be older (forty-five and over), in social class A and with incomes of £4000 and over. They were less readily able to increase their incomes temporarily and had reported rather lower confidence at the start of the year especially on those attitude variables dealing with durable purchasing expectations. Besides making unpredicted durable purchases they were also more likely to have taken an overseas holiday.

As a further indication of the internal consistency of the information collected throughout the surveys, we found that, at the end of the year, group *A* informants were likely to have reported that they had spent less on consumer durables than they had originally anticipated, while group *B* informants were more likely to report that they had spent more on durables than they had initially anticipated. This is therefore further reason for thinking that the purchase probability data are a meaningful source of information about buying expectations, all other things being equal.

This investigation of deviations in buyer behaviour from that which the respondents had initially predicted for themselves emphasises the question of the extent to which, with the benefit of hindsight, we can say that some types of respondent (especially distinguishable in terms of their age and socio-economic status) were over-confident or unduly cautious in their initial expectations. The influence of unexpected events or windfalls on purchaser behaviour over the survey year was less than might have been anticipated and this is consistent with a similar finding in Chapter 6. However, an apparent dependence on the ability to supplement a basic income which may be sensitive to overtime opportunities or to the ability of the spouse to work seems to be an important reason why purchases are not made as planned. It may also be the case that purchases are made or not made for reasons associated with the condition of the stock of items already owned by the household. Respondent explanations of their actual durable purchase decisions will therefore be discussed in Chapter 10.

Purchase expectations at the re-interview stages

The first parts of this chapter dealt with purchase probability information based on a 0–10 scale administered by an interviewer at the initial interviews in April 1972. We were anxious to continue to collect purchase expectations information for individual commodities during the four postal re-interviews over the following twelve months in order to allow a run of observations to be collected. But there was concern that a purchase probability scale as used in the initial interview would prove too complicated for a self-completion questionnaire. It was therefore decided that purchase expectations information on the postal re-interviews would relate only to a twelve month time horizon and should be collected by means of a seven-point scale, which used verbal descriptions rather than asking the respondent to make numerical estimates of probability. The question asked 'We are interested to know how likely you think it is that within the next twelve months from now you, or a member of your household, will have bought any of the goods listed below. Would you please consider what the likelihood is for each good and circle the number under the answer you consider most likely'. The seven points on the scale were: 'would certainly not buy', 'unlikely to buy', 'possibly won't buy', 'fifty-fifty chance of buying', 'possibly will buy', 'quite likely to buy', 'will certainly buy'. The answer categories were numbered from one to seven.

Each informant answered this question for each of the fifteen items over the four successive postal follow-ups. The distributions of the responses in aggregate for each survey are set out in Table 9.9. Comparing these with the distributions of the purchase probabilities in Figure 9.1, it seems that the extent to which the distribution peaks at the mid-point relative to the proportions of observations at the surrounding points was somewhat reduced. It is also apparent that with this form of verbal scale, there was no tendency for the distribution to turn up at the extreme point indicating certainty of making a purchase. The proportion indicating that there was no chance they would buy was considerably lower than when a purchase probability scale was used.

It is less easy to convert a verbal scale into a prediction of the number of purchases that would be expected. However, in order to offer some comparison between the purchase probability data from the first survey

TABLE 9.9 Distributions of responses to twelve month purchase expectations questions, Surveys II-V

Answer category	Survey			
	II	*III*	*IV*	*V*
	July 1972	*October 1972*	*January 1973*	*April 1973*
Would certainly not buy	66	62	63	64
Unlikely to buy	18	20	19	18
Possibly will not buy	3	4	4	4
Fifty-fifty chance	5	6	6	5
Possibly will buy	4	4	4	4
Quite likely to buy	3	3	3	3
Will certainly buy	1	1	1	1

and the expectations data from the second to the fifth surveys, some conversion of verbal responses to quantitative values was attempted. Thus it was assumed that an answer 'would certainly not buy' was equivalent to a purchase probability of 0; 'unlikely to buy' was equivalent to a probability of .17; 'possibly will not buy' had a value of .33; 'fifty–fifty chance' had a value of .50; 'possibly will buy' had a value of .67; 'quite likely to buy' had a probability value of .80 and 'will certainly buy' indicated a probability of 1.0. Using these values, equivalent mean twelve month purchase probabilities were calculated for each item for surveys II–V and are set out together with the purchase probabilities from the first survey in Table 9.10. While direct comparisons would be unwise, it will be observed that, notwithstanding the different distributions of responses obtained from the two forms of question, the estimated mean purchase probabilities from surveys I and II are very close. However, small changes in the values may be very important and it is not possible to say how far the values reflect an actual change in purchase expectations between the two surveys and how far they are influenced by the different method of collecting the information. Comparisons of the values in surveys II–V are justified as they were collected in the same way each time.

As these were questions relating to expected buyer behaviour over twelve months we do not have a further full year's evidence against which to assess the predictive value of this information. However, it is possible to look at the pattern of relationships between the stated purchase expectations and buyer behaviour over the remaining quarters of the survey year. Thus we can compare the proportion buying in the second, third and fourth quarters with the expectations stated at the beginning of the second quarter, those buying in the third and fourth quarter with expectations stated at the beginning of the third quarter and fourth quarter purchases against expectations at the beginning of the fourth quarter. As the time periods over which purchases are observed successively decline the ratio of purchases to expectations will also be expected to decline. The results are set out in Table 9.11. This analysis, as with that in the early part of this chapter, is based on the number of households who recorded a purchase and so excludes the effects of multiple purchases of the same item by a household.

TABLE 9.10 Mean twelve month purchase probabilities from Survey I and estimates of equivalent mean twelve month purchase probabilities from Surveys II-V

Item	*Mean Purchase Probability: Survey:*				
	I *April* *1972*	*II* *July* *1972*	*III* *October* *1972*	*IV* *January* *1973*	*V* *April* *1973*
Black and white television	.08	.07	.07	.07	.09
Central heating	.06	.07	.09	.08	.08
Carpets	.21	.24	.26	.27	.22
Colour television	.08	.12	.13	.11	.12
Cooker	.10	.12	.12	.14	.11
Deep freeze	.08	.12	.13	.14	.13
Dishwasher	.02	.04	.05	.04	.04
Furniture	.22	.26	.27	.29	.28
New Car	.13	.16	.12	.14	.14
Used Car	.14	.19	.15	.18	.17
Record player	.07	.11	.13	.13	.14
Refrigerator	.07	.10	.11	.09	.09
Tape recorder	.03	.07	.09	.09	.09
Vacuum cleaner	.13	.11	.13	.12	.15
Washing machine	.12	.11	.12	.14	.14

TABLE 9.11 Proportions purchasing at each twelve month purchase expectation level

Answer category	Purchases per cent of observations in each category		
	Expectations Survey II, Purchases in Quarters 2, 3 and 4	Expectations Survey III, Purchases in Quarters 3 and 4	Expectations Survey IV, Purchases in Quarter 4
Would certainly not buy	4	2	1
Unlikely to buy	7	4	2
Possibly won't buy	15	12	3
Fifty-fifty chance	23	18	7
Possibly will buy	34	18	11
Quite likely to buy	53	47	18
Will certainly buy	86	71	52

Table 9.11 indicates that the verbal purchase expectations scale also has substantial ability to predict which households were likely to make a purchase. Only four per cent of those who said they would certainly not buy a particular item over the following twelve months actually recorded a purchase in the ensuing nine months over which they were surveyed, whereas eighty-six per cent of those who said they would certainly buy in the next twelve months had already done so within the next nine months. Similar patterns exist for purchases over six and three months when analysed by twelve month purchase expectations in Table 9.11. The proportions who, having said they were certain to buy within the next twelve months had actually done so within the next nine and six months were particularly high. Indeed, if judged by the extent to which stronger subjective purchase expectations were accompanied by higher proportions actually making a purchase, it might be claimed that, comparing the results in Table 9.11 with those in Tables 9.4 and 9.6, a seven-point verbal scale is even more effective than an eleven-point purchase probability scale.

It is also of interest that whereas on a purchase probability scale over fifty per cent of all purchases were made by those stating zero purchase probabilities, with the verbal scale only twenty-five per cent of all purchases were made by those who had stated that they would certainly not buy a particular item.

Both purchase probability scaling and a verbal rating scale seem to predict actual purchases more effectively than dichotomous buying intentions data. A multi-point verbal scale has the disadvantage that it is less easy to produce a quantitative estimate of demand from it. However, on the basis of this limited exploration it does seem that, compared with a probability scale, a verbal scale produces a different distribution of responses which may offer even greater cross-sectional predictive accuracy. Its superiority seems most marked at the two extremes of the rating scale. Clearly, further investigation of these issues is required and a direct comparison of the predictive performance of the two scales from one or more surveys undertaken at the same point in time would be required for validation.

10 *Qualitative explanations of purchase behaviour*

In the previous chapter we paid particular attention to the predictive value of purchase probability information. In this chapter we shall consider the reasons given by respondents for their actual purchase behaviour, both in making a purchase and in not doing so when a purchase had been anticipated. There is always a danger in such an approach of undue rationalisation of reasons, a possible reluctance to admit the main motivation or even an inability to recall the reason for a particular decision. However, the recording arrangements adopted in the surveys and the nature of the information given by informants which was in many cases detailed and personal, does give ground for believing that the information collected was likely to be reliable.

At each postal follow-up survey, informants were asked to indicate which of the fifteen durable items under consideration they had purchased during the preceding quarter. They were then asked, in relation to the items purchased, to say why they had made those purchases at that particular time. They were also asked whether there were any items they had thought they might have purchased during the previous three months but did not do so and to indicate in respect of such items why they had not made the purchase. Answers were written in by the informants and were post-coded. The information obtained from these questions is of interest in that it indicates the sort of considerations that were apparently uppermost in consumers' minds not only in deciding to purchase a consumer durable but also in some cases in deciding not to make a purchase that had been under consideration. Variations in the reasons given for different durables and by different types of consumer will be of interest. In particular, we might look to see whether informants who stated low purchase probabilities but made a purchase gave different reasons from those who bought after having stated high purchase probabilities and whether non-purchasers who had stated high purchase probabilities were prone to give different reasons for not purchasing than other respondents.

TABLE 10.1 Informant explanations of reasons for purchases of durables analysed by product

Replacement Considerations	Previous product worn out/broken down	Previous product old, unreliable	Better product available	Needed different size	Change regularly	Other
TOTAL	219	79	41	26	22	3
Washing machine	13	8	2	1	0	0
Vacuum cleaner	27	5	1	1	0	0
Tape recorder	3	0	0	0	0	0
Refrigerator	2	2	0	5	0	0
Record player	8	2	5	1	0	0
Used car	24	24	5	5	9	0
New car	14	20	4	7	13	1
Furniture	60	1	8	3	0	1
Dishwasher	1	0	0	0	0	0
Deep freeze	0	0	1	3	0	0
Cooker	13	4	2	0	0	0
Colour television	9	3	2	0	0	1
Carpets	36	5	7	0	0	0
Central heating	1	2	4	0	0	0
Black and white television	8	3	0	0	0	0

																Total
General Incentives to buy																
Moved, extended, redecorated house	0	5	35	0	4	2	0	28	0	0	0	1	0	3	1	79
Save time/money, for convenience	0	5	1	0	1	15	2	2	1	2	0	1	1	2	4	37
Wants, needs	2	4	11	2	2	2	0	14	1	6	2	1	2	1	4	54
Bought as a gift	1	0	1	0	2	0	0	0	2	8	14	0	14	0	2	45
Business use	0	0	0	0	0	0	0	0	12	0	2	0	2	0	0	18
Other	5	0	1	3	2	0	1	4	1	5	1	1	0	1	3	28
Specific Influences on timing of purchases																
Could then afford	2	2	8	2	1	1	1	5	6	5	5	0	0	0	3	42
Bargain prices	3	0	8	1	2	3	1	2	7	9	9	1	3	1	1	51
Tax reasons	0	0	1	0	4	4	0	4	2	3	0	0	0	0	0	18
Change gas to electricity or to North Sea gas	0	7	0	0	11	0	0	0	0	0	0	2	0	0	0	20
Impulse	1	1	3	2	0	0	0	5	2	1	5	0	3	0	0	23
Other	0	3	2	2	0	1	0	3	1	3	3	2	2	0	1	23
Total	25	34	119	27	48	33	6	140	85	117	59	19	31	42	43	828

Note: Up to two reasons were coded for each reported purchase.

Explanations of purchases

Details of the reasons given, analysed by product, are set out in Table 10.1 and are analysed by different types of consumer in Table 10.2. While some purchasers did not give a reason for a purchase, others gave two reasons and overall the number of reasons is in excess of the number of recorded purchases. Altogether, nearly forty different types of reason were given by respondents but these may be categorised under three heads – reasons relating to replacement purchase decisions; indications of the general influence of particular incentives to purchase; and specific influences relating to the timing of the purchase. The demarcation between these groups of influence is not altogether distinct.

Replacement considerations were the most frequently noted and were important reasons for most items, especially, of course, those with high ownership levels. It is not necessarily inappropriate to find that non-owners of an item may have given a reason that was primarily explaining a replacement purchase. For example a person buying a colour television for the first time may give a reason that indicated he was replacing an old black and white set with a colour set. For most products it seems that households waited until a product actually broke down or wore out completely before making a replacement purchase but in the case of cars especially it appeared that the replacement decision was more likely to be based upon a view that the product had become old and/or unreliable. Undoubtedly the operation of a second-hand market for cars encourages replacement purchases to be made before the existing vehicle is completely worn out. Car buyers were also quite likely to say that it was their policy to replace their existing vehicle regularly.

General incentives to purchase covered a wide range of different considerations. The most important in this category was the effect of house moves, decorations or extensions, in encouraging purchases, particularly of carpets, furniture and central heating. The perceived economic advantages of deep freezes were emphasised in the explanation that a deep freeze offered savings in time and money and the advantages of greater convenience. Record players and tape recorders were particularly likely to be purchased as gifts.

The timing of purchases was primarily influenced by financial considerations – the availability of bargains, the ability of the household to afford the purchase at that time and the opportunity that some people felt (often erroneously) they were taking to avoid higher prices in the future by purchasing before the introduction of VAT. The effects of changes in type of fuel, either from gas to electricity or from town gas to North Sea gas were often the cause of purchases of central heating and cookers.

TABLE 10.2 Informant explanations of reasons for purchases of consumer durables analysed by type of informant.

	By owner-ship		By twelve months purchase probability			By probability of major attention (owners only)		
	Own	Not own	0-2	3-6	7-10	0-2	3-6	7-10
Replacement Considerations								
Previous product worn out, broken down	114	9	119	34	64	36	44	35
Previous product old, unreliable	69	4	45	13	21	31	19	19
Better product available	21	5	25	8	8	9	7	1
Needed different size	20	3	17	5	4	13	6	1
Change regularly	22	0	14	3	5	11	8	3
Other	1	2	2	0	1	1	0	0
General Incentives to buy								
Moved, extended, redecorated house	12	9	49	5	26	5	2	0
Save time, money, for convenience	9	24	15	13	7	5	1	0
Wants, needs	17	15	24	7	26	10	0	8
Bought as a gift	32	12	33	6	6	20	7	6
Business use	17	1	13	0	5	8	3	6
Other	15	7	16	3	8	7	4	4
Specific Influences on timing of purchases								
Could then afford	18	11	16	7	18	4	8	4
Bargain prices	28	11	30	6	14	12	9	8
Tax reasons	9	4	12	2	4	5	3	1
Change gas to electricity or to North Sea gas	20	0	14	1	5	9	2	2
Impulse	8	4	16	3	3	4	1	1
Other	13	5	18	1	7	5	5	3
Total	445	126	478	117	232	195	129	102

Notes: There are no observations for carpets or furniture under the headings by ownership or by probability of major attention. Central heating purchases were also not analysed by probability of major attention.

In Table 10.2 the reasons are analysed for different types of consumers. Owners are distinguished from non-owners, answers from informants that had initially stated low, medium and high twelve month purchase probabilities for each item are separately tabulated and so are the replies from owners that had stated differing probabilities of major attention on the items they owned at the time of the initial survey. Naturally, replacement considerations were proportionately much more important purchase reasons for owners than for non-owners of a particular item, although, as has already been pointed out, it is possible that one item may be replaced by a different consumer durable that had not previously been owned. In contrast, incentives to buy were proportionately much more important explanations of purchases by non-owners than by owners.

There is no evidence that people who had purchased unexpectedly (that is having stated a twelve month purchase probability in the range 0–2) had any different reasons for their purchases than those with higher probabilities. Product replacements were neither more nor less important and all three groups of respondents when distinguished by their purchase probabilities seemed equally responsive to financial considerations in respect of the timing of the purchase. When probabilities of major attention stated by owners are considered, those stating the lowest probabilities were less likely to explain their subsequent replacement purchases on the grounds that the previous product had become worn out.

Explanations of failure to purchase

This section deals with the reasons given by informants who had expected to make a particular purchase but in fact failed to do so. The information used here regarding the products people had thought they might purchase in the previous three months but had not in fact done so was based on respondent answers at the follow-up surveys. This does not allow us to analyse reasons for failure to purchase all the items for which at the initial interview the informant stated a high purchase probability. It also means that some cases of failure to purchase occurred where the initial purchase probability had been low.

In all, over 800 reasons were given for not making particular purchases. It is interesting to compare the number of reasons given for not purchasing each durable in Table 10.3 with the number of reasons for making a purchase of the same item, set out in Table 10.1. Reasons for purchases outweigh reasons for non-purchases in the case of central heating, carpets, furniture and used cars. Perhaps these are items where the consumer, having considered the possibility of a purchase, is more likely to go through with it. At the other extreme the ratio of reasons for not purchasing to the reasons for purchasing is highest in the case of colour televisions and deep freezes. Although the proportion of cases here where consideration of a purchase is actually turned into a purchase is low it may be that this is indicative of a high level of general interest in these products which will result in a higher level of purchases at some time in the future. For both colour televisions and deep freezes this interpretation is similar to that given to the high twelve to three month purchase probability ratio discussed in Chapter 9.

The types of reasons for not purchasing seem to fall into four main groups – absence of a need to make a purchase; financial reasons; changes of mind regarding the desirability of the product; and choice problems and delivery delays. As will be apparent from Table 10.3, the most important single reason was the decision that a particular item could not be afforded. This seems to be of almost equal proportionate relevance for all products. Absence of a need to buy because an existing item was still in use or had been repaired was a particularly important reason for not buying cars, vacuum cleaners and washing machines. Televisions were likely to be rented rather than purchased.

There was also quite strong evidence that many households had taken at least a temporary decision against a product not on financial grounds but for other reasons associated with the product itself. In some cases the decision not to buy reflected a change of priorities and a decision to buy something else instead. This reason was also more or less evenly distributed in proportionate terms across all durables. Decisions simply that the item was not worth buying or should not be bought as it was a luxury were also quite important. There was some tendency for these reasons to be given for colour televisions and deep freezes but they represent only a small proportion of the total reasons for not purchasing these two items. Among the reasons given that were related to one product only, we found five cases where informants said they had not purchased a car as they had either failed to pass a driving test or had lost their licence!

Many anticipated purchases are delayed rather than abandoned. It is unlikely that all such purchases would be completed in the fullness of time but a wide variety of reasons for the delays was recorded. These covered the effects of supplier delays, decisions to wait for new registration letters before buying a car, delays because of anticipated house moves or North Sea gas conversion, inability to find the required type or size of item and delays because of the difficulty of finding the article at a price the informant was prepared to pay. Such choice problems seem to be important in the case of all items, though they were

TABLE 10.3 Reasons for not purchasing a consumer durable, analysed by type of durable

	No need to purchase Existing product still in use	Existing product repaired	Other ways of acquiring	*Financial reasons* Could not afford to buy	Other
Black and white television	5	0	3	1	0
Central heating	0	0	0	8	1
Carpets	4	0	0	33	1
Colour television	3	0	19	31	0
Cooker	6	0	0	9	1
Deep Freeze	2	0	0	33	1
Dishwasher	0	0	0	4	0
Furniture	2	0	0	21	0
New car	12	0	0	17	0
Used car	7	0	0	22	0
Record player	5	0	1	7	0
Refrigerator	8	2	0	10	0
Tape recorder	0	0	1	1	0
Vacuum cleaner	14	9	0	16	0
Washing machine	21	7	0	14	0
TOTAL	89	18	24	227	4

Decision against the product																Total
Changed priorities	4	0	16	13	7	7	1	7	3	7	9	6	4	6	4	94
Not worth buying	2	1	3	11	1	15	0	1	8	4	5	0	4	2	0	57
Other	1	0	1	2	0	1	0	0	4	1	0	0	0	0	0	10
Choice problems																
Could not find at right price	0	1	3	2	1	4	0	4	7	6	3	1	0	0	1	33
Waiting for discounts	1	0	0	5	2	5	0	3	2	0	8	4	0	3	6	39
Delays by suppliers	0	4	6	1	5	4	0	6	7	0	2	0	0	0	2	37
Delayed due to house move or change to North Sea Gas	0	1	13	6	8	4	0	6	0	3	1	1	0	0	4	47
Could not make up mind	1	3	3	3	6	4	1	5	4	1	6	1	5	2	3	48
Could not find right design features	1	0	6	3	1	9	2	10	1	6	3	1	3	0	0	46
No time to choose	3	1	8	1	2	2	1	3	2	1	2	3	3	1	1	32
Total	22	20	97	100	49	91	9	68	67	58	52	35	21	53	63	805

Note: Up to two reasons were coded for each reported purchase.

TABLE 10.4 Reasons for not purchasing a consumer durable, analysed by type of consumer

	By ownership		By twelve months purchase probability			By probability of major attention (owners only)		
	Own	Not own	0-2	3-6	7-10	0-2	3-6	7-10
No need to purchase								
Existing product still in use	75	8	46	22	21	16	35	23
Existing product repaired	18	0	8	4	5	5	6	7
Other ways of acquiring	5	19	18	4	2	4	1	0
Financial reasons								
Could not afford to buy	86	90	124	43	60	36	26	20
Other	1	5	2	2	2	1	0	0
Decisions against the product								
Changed priorities	40	31	50	16	28	29	5	6
Not worth buying	19	37	30	18	9	8	4	4
Other	6	3	5	0	5	2	0	7
Choice problems								
Could not find at right price	17	9	19	7	7	7	5	5
Waiting for discounts	20	16	18	11	10	9	5	6
Delays by suppliers	17	8	25	3	9	9	3	3
Delayed due to house move or change to North Sea Gas	17	11	18	11	18	6	2	9
Could not make up mind	26	14	24	11	13	11	5	8
Could not find right design features	12	18	27	6	13	6	4	2
No time to choose	20	11	23	9	10	9	7	3
Other	2	1	0	0	3	2	1	0
Total	381	281	437	167	215	160	109	103

Notes: There are no observations for carpets or furniture under the headings by ownership or by probability of major attention. Central heating purchases were also not analysed by probability of major attention.

proportionately less so in the case of black and white televisions, vacuum cleaners and washing machines where the absence of a need to make a replacement purchase was found to be proportionately more important. The difficulty of finding items at what consumers considered to be the right price seemed to have mainly affected possible car purchases, while difficulties in finding an article with the right physical characteristics or in obtaining deliveries from the suppliers seemed to delay purchases of furnishings and cars. Problems of finding the right size of item also hindered purchases of deep freezes. Expected house moves or conversions to North Sea Gas appeared primarily to have delayed purchases of furnishings and cookers.

Differences in reasons analysed for different types of consumer are set out in Table 10.4. Owners were, naturally, much more likely to report that their existing products were still in use, and it was non-owners who were more likely to use rentals as an alternative means of acquiring a television. Non-owners were more likely to report that they had decided for financial reasons not to purchase an item.

There appears to be little difference in the reasons given when analysed by purchase probabilities. Owners who had stated medium and high probabilities that an item would require major attention were proportionately more likely to report that they had not needed to replace the item because it was still in use or had been repaired and owners were more likely to report a change of priorities as the reason for not buying if they had stated that their existing item had a low probability of requiring major attention. Presumably this also reflects the extent to which products in good working order will be less likely to be replaced and so allow alternative items to be purchased instead.

From this chapter we have a rather clearer indication of the sorts of factors that actually influence the timing of the purchase decision. Replacement considerations and hence the state of the existing durable stock loom large in explanations both of decisions to buy and not to buy; so too do financial considerations. House moves and other major developments will stimulate buying but expectations of such developments will cause delays in purchases. Unsatisfactory design features, price and delivery arrangements for particular durables all seem to discourage purchases and a change of priorities in the mind of the consumer may lead to the purchase of a different item instead.

While the pattern of reasons given does seem to differ in important respects between owners and non-owners, there does not seem to be as much variation in the way in which respondents who stated different probabilities of purchasing an item explain the reasons for their actual behaviour. This is of interest since it does indicate that the influences identified apply with equal effect whatever the initial expectations of the respondent. Owner estimates of the probability of major attention on an item seem to be consistently associated with the reasons subsequently given for replacement purchases. Products considered to be more likely to require major attention were proportionately more likely to have been replaced because they had broken down, while owners who had considered the probability of major attention to be quite high, but who did not make a replacement purchase, were proportionately more likely to say that the reason for not purchasing was because the product concerned was still in use.

11 *Analysis of purchasers of individual items*

The Approach

The purpose of this chapter is to identify the relevant characteristics of the purchasers of specific consumer durables and to investigate whether the information collected relating generally to the informant's socio-economic status and general confidence together with more product specific information is successful in predicting which individuals will actually make purchases. Such cross-sectional testing of the behaviour of individuals, not just in relation to their total expenditures (as is discussed in Chapter 6), but in relation to their purchases of specified items places an extremely high level of demand on the data. There will be many instances where people do not behave as the *ex ante* data about them suggests they would, and a high degree of precision is implied in actually predicting which particular durable will be purchased.

This process of analysis was begun in Chapter 9 where the predictive contribution of purchase probability data alone was considered and it was demonstrated that *ex ante* statements of purchase probabilities did have quite considerable cross-sectional predictive power. In this chapter we shall extend the analysis by incorporating other types of predictive variable as well. Almost all the variables were collected from the initial surveys and provide indicators of the ability, need and willingness of the informant to make a purchase. Some of these are general indicators of the respondent's status and attitudes while others are related to his attitudes, perceptions and expectations on specific products. In the initial analysis the variables were divided into five separate groups and they are therefore best described in terms of those groups. The last three groups relate to a willingness to buy.

1.   Ability to buy. This group incorporated information from each household about its social class (SOCL), age of the HoH (AGE), length of time the HoH had been married (TMRD), number of people in the household (PPL), whether household income could be temporarily increased (INCY) and by what amount (AMINCY), income of the head of the household (YHOH) and of the household (YHH), whether the household had any hire purchase commitments (HP), the total amount of credit the household had outstanding (TOTCRDT), change in the level of household savings over the previous year (DS), level of household savings (STOT), the number of people in the household working during the survey year (NOWK), total number of durables owned by the household (TOTG).

2.   *Need to buy.* This group was concerned with the state of the stock of existing durables and therefore only has predictive value in relation to replacement purchases. The variables here are product specific and relate to the age of the item (A), the length of time it had been owned (T), the probability that it would require major attention during the following year (PMA) and the replacement strategy that would be adopted – whether it would be repaired, replaced, or abandoned (RRA). Because the terms 'carpets' and 'furniture' cover a number of different items in the home it was not meaningful to collect information on the state of the stock of existing units of these items and so these variables are not included in respect of carpets and furniture. Since central heating once installed is not usually the subject of a replacement purchase this was also not included in this section.

3.   *General consumer confidence* based on the answers to the attitude scales AS 1 to AS 29 on the first survey (see Chapter 5).

4.   *Purchase expectations.* Purchase probabilities for specific items for three, six and twelve months ahead (P3, P6, P12), whether the informant was saving up to buy the particular item under consideration (SAVE), whether the informant expected to move house during the next twelve months (MOVE), the amount the informant expected to spend on consumer durables over the next three and twelve months (EXPSP 3, EXPSP 12), how the amounts that were expected to be spent in the next twelve months compared with what had been spent in the previous twelve months (ESMRLS 3, ESMRLS 12). In some cases, where appropriate, a variable was also included to reflect whether another durable that was shown to precede the one under consideration in the order of acquisition of durables was already owned (see Chapter 8). This was used particularly for low ownership items. For predictions of purchasers of colour televisions it was hypothesised that purchasers were likely already to own more than one car and/or a tape recorder; in

the case of deep freeze whether a washing machine and/or a colour television were already owned was included; in the case of dishwasher prior ownership of a deep freeze was included. In each of these cases this variable is shown as OWN.

5. Perceptions of the characteristics of particular durables. In an earlier paper (Pickering *et al* 1973b) we showed that different consumer durables could be grouped together on the basis of consumer perceptions of their characteristics as they relate to the durable purchasing decision. We have also demonstrated that certain characteristics help in distinguishing between buyers and non-buyers of cars (Isherwood and Pickering 1975). In the present study informants were asked to rate the characteristics of a sample of six of the durables on a battery of sixteen nine-point semantic differential scales. In addition, owners of particular items were asked to complete three further scales relating to perceptions of their existing item. Each scale was coded from one–nine from left to right across the scale.

Details of the semantic differential scales are included in the Appendix to this study. A summary of the concepts represented by each scale is as follows.

ES 1	Necessity	ES 9	Role of income
ES 2	Durability	ES 10	Relative running cost
ES 3	Impulse purchase	ES 11	Contribution to standard of living
ES 4	Convenience	ES 12	Peer group ownership
ES 5	Relative Cost	ES 13	New/second hand purchase
ES 6	Finance method	ES 14	Purchase expectation
ES 7	Functionality	ES 15	Rent/buy
ES 8	Importance of price	ES 16	Reliability

The additional scales, completed only by existing owners of an item were

ES 17 Existing model new/old
ES 18 Existing model up-to-date
ES 19 Existing model right size

This information is, of course, product specific and because of the repetitive nature of the exercise in completing a number of identical batteries of semantic scales it was felt that six was the maximum number of sets of scales that should be completed by each informant. The selection of products to be rated by each informant was randomly determined and the numbers completing a set of scales for each product tended to be very similar. A check of the proportion of owners rating each product showed that this was also very close to the actual proportion of owners of that item in the sample as a whole.

One consequence of the decision to have only some of the products rated by each informant is that the sample numbers on which the analysis of buyers and non-buyers of a particular product can be based when perceptions of product characteristics are included is less than the total number of informants providing information about their purchasing behaviour over the survey year. In practice, the number of observations on the perceptions of the characteristics of particular durables was in the range 160–190, with only two products having fewer than 170 observations. Since furniture and carpets are generic descriptions of a number of different items it was not appropriate to ask informants to rate the characteristics of these two products.

The listing of variables set out above is very extensive. Their use was in every case justified by *a priori* hypotheses that it was hoped to test in the research. There were however too many variables in total and also in relation to the number of observations to allow all to be included together in one analysis. Consequently a two-stage procedure was used in investigating the extent to which these variables could be used in predicting actual buyer behaviour.

First, an analysis was run using correlation and multiple regression techniques to establish which variables within each of the five groups specified at the beginning of this chapter had some association with actual buyer behaviour. The dependent variable in the multiple regression was in the binary form 0:1, either an individual did not make a purchase (0), or he did (1), over the survey year. The number of individuals used for each analysis at this stage was the maximum number for whom full information on the particular group of variables was available. Consequently, analyses using variables reflecting ability to make durable purchases, general economic confidence and purchase expectations of the informants were based on virtually all cases. Analyses of the predictive power of the need variables and perceptions of the characteristics of a particular durable were based respectively on the smaller number owning the item and completing the rating scales for that product.

Binary regression is not an ideal technique to use since it obviously cannot be assumed that the error term about the dependent variable is normally distributed and it is not a reliable technique when the average value of the dependent variable is very close to either 0 or 1. However, it does allow an effective identification of the significant variables as well as some comparison of the predictive power of the different types of variable. It is, of course, possible that a single variable can be significantly associated with a dependent variable but fail to be selected as significant in a multiple regression analysis. Since our primary purpose at this stage was to select for further analysis all those variables that might have some predictive power, we also used a matrix of zero order correlation coefficients as a means of identifying other variables that should not be discarded at this stage.

The second stage in the analysis was based on just those variables which were found in either the correlation or the multiple regression analysis to be significantly associated with purchase behaviour on that particular product. Since all types of variable were combined at this stage in just one analysis, the number of cases used here was restricted to those 160–190 individuals completing the rating scales on each particular item, except in the case of furniture and carpets on which, as already explained, rating scales were not completed. Once the relevant variables had been selected for each product their predictive power was tested using discriminant analysis. Discriminant analysis in the two group case is formally similar to multiple regression using a binary dependent variable but has certain statistical advantages in that it avoids the problems of the lack of homoscedasticity in the model and is not affected by the non-normal distribution of the dependent variable. It also has the practical advantage that by estimating the probability of membership of each group for each individual in turn, it allows the classificatory success of the discriminant function to be assessed through the 'hits and misses' table. The nature of the discriminant analysis used will be described in greater detail later in this chapter when we consider the overall classificatory power of the survey data. First, however, it is necessary to describe briefly the results of the initial selection procedure of the significant variables from the different groups of variables.

Correlation and regression analysis

As has already been explained, multiple regression is not an ideal technique for statistical investigations where the dependent variable takes a binary form. However, the use of correlation and multiple regression analysis allowed a fairly quick sift of the variables to establish which had some association with actual buyer behaviour for each of the individual products. More variables were found to have significant zero order correlations with buyer behaviour than were found to be statistically significant in the multiple regressions. This was to be expected, especially where a high degree of multicollinearity was to be observed, as with the purchase probability values for different time periods. There were only a few cases where a variable was found to be significant in the regression analysis but not to have a significant zero order correlation with the dependent variable. Variables significant in either or both of the tests are identified in Table 11.1 and all were used in the subsequent discriminant analyses on that particular product.

Before describing the results of the discriminant analysis it is worth looking briefly at the general patterns of association reflected in Table 11.1. Some rough indication of the explanatory power of the different groups of variables may be obtained from Table 11.2.

Ability to buy

There was a surprisingly low level of association between the variables reflecting the socio-economic status of the individual or his ability to buy consumer durables. Where they were significant we find that normally purchasers tended to be in higher social class groups, have larger incomes, were able to increase their incomes and owned more consumer durables already. The influence of life cycle variables is not well established but it was not altogether surprising to find that while people married less long were more likely to buy a record player, it was those married longest who were more likely to purchase cookers, which were in almost every case found to be replacement purchases.

Need to buy

Indicators of the need to make a purchase are relevant only in predicting replacement purchases. Again, their overall predictive power was not high. As was to be expected, purchases were more likely to be made where an item was older and owned longer; where the assessed probability of major attention was higher and where informants said they were more likely to decide to replace rather than repair it. The age of an item and the length of time it has been owned will normally be highly correlated. Both were included since the age of an item may be well in excess of the time it has been owned by the particular informant where the item was purchased second hand and this is particularly important in the case of the existing stock of motor cars. New cars tended to be purchased where an existing car was younger. This suggests, quite plausibly, that many new car buyers were more likely to replace a car before it became unduly old.

Willingness to buy – general economic confidence

While almost all the attitude scales were found to be significantly associated with buyer behaviour in the case of at least one product, it is appropriate to pay most attention to those variables that were found to be significant in the largest number of cases. The variable most frequently selected was the expectation of buying more durables in the next twelve months than in the past year (AS 24) which was significant with six items. Expectations for economic development (AS 4), expectations of buying a car (AS 14), expectations of buying a new durable (AS 15) and replacing an existing one (AS 16), responsiveness to a temporary income reduction (AS 21), the effect of prices of necessities on durable purchasing (AS 23), the ability to finance durable purchases from savings (AS 25) and the possibility that the household's income was being increased (AS 29) were all found to be significant with four or more products. The direction of association was not consistent in every case but it does appear that when initially interviewed, subsequent purchasers of particular consumer durables were more likely to have reported that they expected to buy more durables in the next twelve months, were more likely to expect to buy a consumer durable they had not previously owned, were more likely to expect to replace a durable (though not in the case of car purchasers), were more likely to be increasing their discretionary income, would be less affected by a temporary reduction in their income, would expect to be able to finance their durable purchases from their savings, and were less likely to consider that rising prices of necessities would affect their buying of consumer durables (though the converse was true in the case of buyers of carpets and used cars). While purchases of furniture and vacuum cleaners appeared to be associated with an anticipation that the development of the economy would become more favourable, purchases of carpets, record players and tape recorders were associated with an expectation that the economy would develop in a way that was unfavourable to the respondents concerned. Actual car purchasers (and also deep freeze purchasers) were more likely to have stated a stronger initial expectation of buying a car during the following twelve months but buyers of cookers and record players were more likely to have reported a lower expectation of buying a car over the following year.

While there are exceptions to the general pattern, it does seem reasonable to conclude that where the attitudinal variables had predictive power in relation to the purchases of individual durables, their direction of influence was such that more confident consumers were more likely subsequently to have purchased particular consumer durables. The majority of the variables that tended to occur as significant in several of the individual product analyses were concerned with durable purchasing expectations as such rather than general indications of economic confidence. It is interesting to observe, however, that there was also some tendency for purchases of particular

TABLE 11.1 Listing of significant variables from correlation and multiple regression analyses

Variable	Item														
	Black and white television	Central heating	Carpets	Colour television	Cooker	Deep freeze	Dishwasher	Furniture	New car	Used car	Record player	Refrigerator	Tape recorder	Vacuum cleaner	Washing machine
1. Ability to buy:															
SOCL					+				−	−	−				
AGE										−	+				
TMRD									−						
PPL									+						
INCY												+			
AMNCY															
YHOH								+	+						−
YHH								+	+						+

HP						+						
TOTCRDT						+						
DS			+			+						
STOT	−			+			+					
NOWK	+		+		+	+	+	+	+				
TOTG	−	+	+				+	+				
2. Need to buy												
A	+	+		+	+		−	/		+	/	
T		+		+	+		+	/		+	/	
PMA	+	+		+			+	/		+	/	
RRA	+	+		+		+	+	/	+	+	/	
3. Willingness to buy												
(a) General Economic Confidence										+		
AS 1						+				+		+
AS 2						−			−			+
AS 3						−		−				
AS 4				+	+					+	−	

Table 11. 1 continued overleaf

Variable	Item														
	Black and white television	Central heating	Carpets	Colour television	Cooker	Deep freeze	Dishwasher	Furniture	New car	Used car	Record player	Refrigerator	Tape recorder	Vacuum cleaner	Washing machine
AS 5						−		+			+				
AS 6	+														+
AS 7						+			−						+
AS 8				−	+						+				
AS 9										−				−	
AS 10	+		+								+				
AS 11													−		
AS 12			+												+
AS 13												−			
AS 14					+	−			−	−	+				

AS 15
AS 16
AS 17
AS 18
AS 19
AS 20
AS 21
AS 22
AS 23
AS 24
AS 25
AS 26
AS 27
AS 28
AS 29

(b) Purchase expectations

P3	+	+	+	+	+	+	+	+	+	+
P6	+	+	+	+	+	+	0	+	+	+
P12	+	+	+	+	+	+	+	+	+	+

Table 11. 1 continued overleaf

Variable	Washing machine	Vacuum cleaner	Tape recorder	Refrigerator	Record player	Used car	New car	Furniture	Dishwasher	Deep freeze	Cooker	Colour television	Carpets	Central heating	Black and white television	ES 1
SAVE	−	−	−		−	−	−	−	−	+	−	−	−	−	−	
MOVE			−					−				−	−	−		
EXPSP 3												+				
EXPSP 12						+		+				+		+		
ESMRLS 3	+					+	+									
ESMRLS 12				−				+				+				
OWN									−(1)							

(c) Perceptions of the Characteristics of Consumer Durables

ES 1	Tape recorder	New car	Furniture	Colour television	Carpets	Black and white television
	−	−	/	+	/	+

ES 2
ES 3
ES 4
ES 5
ES 6
ES 7
ES 8
ES 9
ES 10
ES 11
ES 12
ES 13
ES 14
ES 15
ES 16
ES 17
ES 18
ES 19

Notes: All variables indicated were significant at the 10% level. The signs + and − indicate the direction of association and are dependent on the direction of coding. An 'O' indicates that the signs were not consistent between the zero order correlation and the multiple regression analyses.
(1) the item owned in this case was a deep freeze.
/ indicates that observations on these variables were not collected for a particular item.

items to be associated with lower levels of confidence on some of the attitudinal variables. Thus buyers seemed to be people who were less likely to consider their financial position had improved, who had less confidence in economic policy and the prospects for economic progress. It is not necessarily surprising that people lacking in confidence in certain respects should be more likely to buy particular durables even though, as we saw in Chapter 6, when all expenditures are aggregated together, the heaviest spenders tended to be the more confident.

In passing, it is also relevant to comment that similar analyses were run to test the predictive power of the first three principal components of these variables. Their overall explanatory power was lower than that of the original twenty-nine attitude scales in combination. The second principal component, which it will be remembered from Chapter 5 was interpreted as a durable purchasing confidence component, was the one most frequently found to be significant, followed by the first principal component which was interpreted as a general economic confidence component. The third principal component was found to have little association with actual purchaser behaviour on individual products.

Willingness to buy – purchase expectations

The majority of the variables grouped here are directly concerned with the respondent's expectations of purchasing a specific product. The explanatory power here was higher than that for the other groups of variables considered so far. Purchase probabilities were consistently associated with actual buyer behaviour, the higher the stated probability the more likely was the purchase subsequently to have been made. This confirms the findings of Chapter 9. Actual purchasers of an item were also likely to have reported that they were saving up to purchase that particular item. Dishwasher purchasers (though very few in number) tended to own a deep freeze already, thereby confirming in this case the evidence and arguments of Chapter 7 about the predictability of orders of acquisition of consumer durables. Purchasers of durables generally were more likely to have anticipated spending larger sums of money. Purchases of several durables, including central heating, carpets and furniture were associated with stronger expectations of moving house.

Willingness to buy – perceptions of the characteristics of consumer durables

If consumers were likely to make a purchase of a consumer durable in the fairly near future, it was hypothesised that they would have a different perception of the characteristics and desirability of that item

TABLE 11.2 Coefficients of multiple determination (R^2) for groups of variables in multiple regression analyses on individual product purchases

Groups of variables	Black and white television	Central heating	Carpets	Colour television	Cooker	Deep freeze	Dishwasher	Furniture	New car	Used car	Record player	Refrigerator	Tape recorder	Vacuum cleaner	Washing machine
1. Ability to buy.	.000	.000	.000	.000	.002	.005	.044	.015	.080	.055	.013	.007	.023	.010	.047
2. Need to buy.	.024	/	/	.000	.076	.096	.000	/	.037	.017	.046	.048	.000	.040	.036
3a. General economic confidence.	.015	.037	.080	.065	.045	.068	.011	.084	.087	.087	.065	.019	.025	.021	.033
3b. Purchase expectations.	.076	.064	.238	.081	.135	.044	.143	.113	.147	.189	.097	.080	.088	.200	.131
3c. Perceptions of the characteristics of consumer durables.	.079	.103	/	.112	.183	.047	.150	/	.089	.174	.093	.068	.102	.084	.106

Note: / indicates that observations on these variables were not collected for a particular item.

from those who were less likely to buy it. Therefore, besides asking people directly whether they anticipated making a purchase of a particular item and whether they were saving up to buy it, consumers were also asked to rate particular durables on the basis of certain characteristics which were considered, in the light of depth interviews and other prior investigations, likely to relate to the purchase decision. As Table 11.2 indicates, the predictive power of these characteristics is, on average, as high as that of the purchase expectations variables and is considerably higher than that of the other groups of variables.

The most frequently significant variable was that dealing once again with purchase expectations (ES 14) and in the light of the evidence on purchase probabilities this is not surprising. Actual purchasers were more likely to have expected to buy these particular items than non-purchasers. Of the other variables which were frequently significantly associated with purchases, we found that buyers were more likely to consider an item a necessity than non-buyers (ES 1) (though buyers of televisions were more likely than non-buyers to consider a television a luxury); buyers were more convinced that an item generally contributed to the standard of living (ES 11) and that the item concerned was functional rather than pleasure giving (ES 7); buyers of dishwashers though not of other products were more likely to be part of a peer group that already owned the item (ES 12), and were more likely to expect to buy new rather than second hand (except for used car buyers) (ES 13). Replacement purchasers of an item they already owned were more likely to consider that they needed a different size (ES 19), to say that their existing item was older (ES 17) and to consider that more up to date models were available (ES 18).

The general impression from this analysis so far is that the different types of variables do appear to have some capacity to predict purchases of particular consumer durables. The relationships are plausible in that they suggest, by and large, that purchasers were most likely to be those who were better able to buy, most in need of making a replacement purchase and most willing to buy in terms of their general durable purchasing expectations, their expectations of buying that particular consumer durable and their favourable perceptions of the characteristics of the durable concerned. While all types of variable appeared to have some predictive power, at this non-aggregated level of analysis of the demand for individual commodities it appeared that variables that were product specific and reflected the willingness to purchase a particular item had the greatest success in this respect.

Discriminant analysis

Having identified the variables which, in terms of the statistical significance of their zero-order correlations with buyer behaviour, and/or their significance in multiple regression analysis, can be considered to have some association with purchase behaviour on a particular product, our next task was to investigate the predictive power of this combined subset of variables from each of the groups hitherto considered. The consequence of this selection procedure was that the number of independent variables available for use ranged between fourteen and twenty-nine according to the product concerned, the average number of independent variables was nineteen. As already explained, the number of observations on which the data could be tested was reduced to 160–190 for each product other than for carpets and furniture and was lower than this where an analysis was based on product owners only.

Rather than continue to use multiple regression analysis with the particular problems that it poses where the dependent variable is bi-variate in nature, discriminant analysis was used for this further stage in the investigation. As we have already noted, not only does this avoid the particular problems associated with multiple regression on a binary dependent variable, it also has the positive advantages that having estimated the optimal discriminant function it then calculates the probability of group membership for each individual informant; from this the actual classificatory success of the function can be estimated and those who were misclassified can be individually identified.

The primary purpose of discriminant analysis is to establish a linear discriminant function which maximises the difference between the centroids of the two groups (in this case the buyers and the non-buyers). The significance of the function and the significance of the difference between the two groups can be tested using statistical tests of Wilks λ and the F statistic. There are a number of discriminant analysis programs in use which produce different types of output. The one used in this particular case was a version of the BMD 07 M Stepwise Multiple Discriminant Analysis program. The actual discriminant function was not printed out, but details of the mean values for the two groups on the significant variables were reported.

From the discriminant function the probabilities were calculated for each individual that they would, on the basis of their characteristics on the significant variables, be classified as buyers or non-buyers. The overall classificatory success of the discriminant function can then be assessed by comparing the predicted classifications of each individual as either a buyer or a non-buyer with the actual classification, derived from our knowledge of how people behaved.

Where, as in the case of this research, there are substantially uneven groups of buyers and non-buyers and where the same data are used both to fit the discriminant function and to test its classificatory success, there is a need to compare the actual success rate with an expected success rate that takes account of these phenomena. This may be done using Morrison's proportionality criterion (Morrison 1969). The existence of uneven groups of buyers and non-buyers also means that the construction of a hits and misses table using a probabalistic criterion (i.e. that the predicted number of buyers should equal the actual number of buyers etc,) in fact tends to lead to an underprediction of the smaller group, in our case the buyers. We found that, on average, the predicted number of buyers was only about fifty-five per cent of the actual number of buyers. While the average overall success rate was high at ninety-two per cent, and sixty-five per cent of those predicted to be buyers were in fact buyers, only about thirty-six per cent of actual buyers were in fact predicted to be buyers, largely because the predicted number of buyers was well below the actual number. Since there is greater value in this research in positively identifying buyers than in establishing what sorts of people are likely to be non-buyers, this constitutes a serious drawback.

The problem, is however, not unknown and Morrison has suggested that it is appropriate to constrain the classificatory procedure to produce a predicted number of purchasers equal to the actual, or alternatively to constrain it so that a specified proportion (say seventy per cent) of actual buyers are correctly classified. In either case it is likely that this will be at the expense of the overall success rate but it may be considered worthwhile in the interest of improving the prediction of buyers of a product. As the discriminant analysis used printed out probabilities of membership of each group for all individuals it was possible to make manual adjustments to the hits and misses tables to investigate the consequences of adopting alternative classificatory criteria.

In the reporting that follows of the results of the discriminant analyses for individual products, the hits and misses tabulations are based on the criterion that the predicted number of purchasers should equal the actual number (except where the existence of several people with equal probabilities of group membership renders an exact equality impossible to achieve). In most cases, this has the expected effect of improving the overall ability to identify actual buyers and has only a marginal, though on balance adverse, effect on the overall classificatory success of the analysis. Using this approach across all products, on average fifty-three per cent of buyers were correctly classified and fifty-four per cent of those predicted to be buyers were in fact, correctly classified. The overall success rate was eighty-seven per cent.

If, however, we had tried to improve still further the identification of actual purchasers by requiring that seventy per cent of actual purchasers should be correctly classified, this would often have entailed a substantial increase in the total number of predicted purchasers and a further worsening of the overall success rate. For example, considering Table 11.10, an increase of fifteen in the number of correctly predicted purchasers of furniture would entail an increase of forty-nine in the number of non-purchasers who would also be classified as predicted purchasers, and in Table 11.16 to include the next three actual purchasers of tape recorders as predicted purchasers would necessitate increasing by forty-four the number of actual non-buyers who were incorrectly predicted to be purchasers. For all products, such an approach aiming to give seventy per cent of actual buyers correctly classified would mean that only thirty-nine per cent of predicted buyers were in fact actual buyers and the overall classificatory success would be eighty-one per cent.

Our purpose now is to take each consumer durable in turn and use the results of the discriminant analysis to establish the key characteristics in respect of which buyers of the product differed from non-buyers, and to offer some brief comment on the predictive quality of the data as indicated by the classificatory procedure based on the discriminant analysis. It should be remembered that these analyses are based on sub-samples who completed the rating scales on the characteristics of each particular consumer durable and that the variables included in each analysis are the small group of variables that were found in the correlation and regression analyses to be significantly associated with purchase behaviour on that particular item. Where necessary, two separate analyses are reported for a product, one relating to owners only and the other based on all informants in that sub-sample. In the latter case, variables relating to the state of the existing stock have had to be omitted. The significant variables shown in the various tables are set out in the order of their inclusion in the discriminant function, determined by their respective F ratios.

Black and white televisions

In the case of the analysis based on owners only, the six months purchase probability value (P6) was the only variable used in establishing the optimum discrimination. The mean values indicate that buyers had stated much higher purchase probabilities than non-buyers and the λ and F values indicate that the two groups of buyers and non-buyers were significantly different on this particular variable. The overall success rate (SRTOT) was just under ninety per cent, but that for buyers (SRB) was only thirty per cent. The expected overall success rate using Morrison's proportionality criterion (SRE) was just under eighty-seven per cent so the overall classificatory success was higher than a random procedure would have been expected to produce.

In the case of the analysis based on all respondents, whether owners or non-owners, the optimal discriminant function included two variables. The mean values on these variables showed that buyers had stated higher six month purchase probabilities than non-buyers (P6) and that they considered a black and white television to be more a luxury and less a necessity than did non-buyers (ES 1). This is perhaps a slightly surprising result and is not in keeping with our *a priori* notions that purchasers are more likely to consider an item to be a necessity than non-purchasers. A check revealed that none of this group of buyers owned or had bought a colour television and all but one already owned a black and white television. The most likely explanations of this phenomenon seem to be that there is a negative snob element associated with the ownership of such an item (see Pickering *et al* 1973b for further

TABLE 11.3 Results of discriminant analyses for black and white television

Differences of Means

	Mean Values			
	Owners		All Respondents	
Significant Variables	Buyers	Non-Buyers	Buyers	Non-Buyers
P6	2.80	0.51	3.00	0.44
ES1			6.64	5.26

Hits and Misses

	Owners Only Predicted		All Respondents Predicted	
Actual	Buyers	Non-Buyers	Buyers	Non-Buyers
Buyers	3	7	4	7
Non-Buyers	10	144	8	171

Statistics

Owners $\lambda=.927$; $F=12.83$ with DF1, 162 significance=0.05 per cent; SRTOT=89.6 per cent; SRB=30 per cent; SRE=86.9 per cent

All Respondents $\lambda=.889$; $F=11.68$ with DF2, 187, significance= 0.00 per cent; SRTOT=92.1 per cent; SRB=36.4 per cent; SRE=88.6 per cent

argument on this point) or that intending purchasers may experience some pre-purchase dissonance in their attitudes to this durable.

Carpets

TABLE 11.4 Results of discriminant analysis for carpets

| Significant Variables | Differences of Means | | Hits and Misses | | |
| | Mean Values | | | Predicted | |
	Buyers	Non-Buyers	Actual	Buyers	Non-Buyers
P12	5.10	1.18	Buyers	50	32
AS 4	4.02	3.61	Non-	32	241
SAVE	1.65	1.94	Buyers		
MOVE	2.60	2.85			
AS 19	4.50	4.24			

Statistics $\lambda=.719$; $F=27.226$ with 5,349 DF significance$=0.00$ per cent; SRTOT$=82$ per cent; SRB$=61$ per cent; SRE$=68.9$ per cent.

As this was considered to be a generic product group it was decided that it would not be appropriate to ask informants to rate carpets on the evaluative scales and data on existing ownership was not collected. Consequently those variables are not included for this product and the number of people for whom the analysis could be run was therefore the whole sample for whom complete information was available rather than just a sub-sample of it.

Buyers of carpets were more likely to have stated higher purchase probabilities (P12) and to have reported that they were saving up to buy carpets (SAVE). They had stronger expectations of moving house during the following twelve months (MOVE) and since we know that those who had expectations of moving were much more likely actually to have moved house during the survey year it is not surprising to find that there is a strong association between expected house moves and the purchase of carpets. Buyers of carpets were less sanguine about the possibility of benefiting from short term economic developments (AS 4) but slightly more hopeful about the trend in unemployment (AS 19).

Central heating

TABLE 11.5 Results of discriminant analysis for central heating

| | Differences of Means | | Hits and Misses | | |
| | Mean Values | | | Predicted | |
Significant Variables	Buyers	Non-Buyers	Actual	Buyers	Non-Buyers
P3	0.67	0.03	Buyers	5	10
AS 24	3.67	4.95	Non-Buyers	10	163
ES 1	2.53	4.27			
ES 11	1.47	2.20			
ES 16	2.47	2.09			
ES 6	3.80	5.40			

Statistics $\lambda=0.85$; $F=5.335$ with 1,186 DF significance$=0.17$ per cent; SRTOT$=89.4$ per cent; SRB$=33$ per cent; SRE$=85.3$ per cent.

Only a small proportion of households purchased central heating during the survey year and although the two groups are clearly defined, the overall classificatory success was not much better than a random procedure would have produced. Compared with non-buyers, central heating buyers had higher three month purchase probabilities (P3), expected to buy more consumer durables in the next twelve months (AS 24) and perceived central heating as being more of a necessity (ES 1), more likely to be financed from savings than on credit (ES 6), more strongly contributing to the standard of living (ES 11), but perhaps surprisingly, somewhat less reliable (ES 16). In general however, we can say that central heating purchasers had stronger durable purchasing expectations and a more favourable perception of the characteristics of central heating than non-buyers.

Colour television

Although the overall success rate was no better than a random allocation procedure would produce, the identification of actual buyers was quite successful. Buyers are characterised as having stronger expectations of buying this item (ES 14) and were more likely to have said they were saving up to purchase it (SAVE). They were more likely to think that a colour television contributed to their standard of living (ES 11) and were more confident that their purchases of consumer durables would not be affected by a temporary reduction in their income (AS 21).

The position of the three month purchase probability value (P3) in this set is difficult to explain. It will be observed on this variable that non-buyers had higher mean purchase probabilities than buyers and this is inconsistent with the evidence on ES 14. In fact if the mean twelve month purchase probabilities are considered, the mean value for buyers was 2.29 and the mean for non-buyers was 0.84. This is much more in keeping with the results that could be expected. That P12 was not selected as a significant variable in this set is probably due to the existence of multicollinearity between ES 14 and P12, since the correlation between the two was − .525. (The negative sign simply reflects the effects of the differing direction of coding of the two variables.)

TABLE 11. 6 Results of Discriminant Analysis for Colour Television

Significant Variables	Differences of Means		Hits and Misses		
	Mean Values			Predicted	
	Buyers	Non-Buyers	Actual	Buyers	Non-Buyers
ES 14	4. 65	7. 42	Buyers	9	8
AS 21	4. 82	3. 43	Non-Buyers	8	150
SAVE	1. 76	1. 97			
P3	0. 00	0. 12			
ES 11	2. 88	4. 87			

Statistics $\lambda=0. 77$; $F=9. 86$ with 5, 169 DF significance=0. 00 per cent; SRTOT=90. 9 per cent; SRB=52. 9 per cent; SRE=91. 2 per cent.

Cooker

Virtually all members of the sample owned a cooker, and this analysis relates only to replacement purchases. These were more likely to be made where the existing cooker was older (on average seven and a half years old at the start of the survey year) (A), and where the purchase expectation was greater (P3, P12), especially the expectation of purchasing over the following twelve months. Because of the nature of the item, the particular perceptions of its characteristics selected as significant do not appear to add much to our interpretative ability since

TABLE 11.7 Results of discriminant analysis for cooker

| | Differences of Means | | Hits and Misses | | |
| | Mean Values | | | Predicted | |
Significant Variables	Buyers	Non-Buyers	Actual	Buyers	Non-Buyers
P12	4.53	0.85	Buyers	8	7
ES 12	2.13	1.22	Non-Buyers	7	148
P3	0.20	0.18			
A	4.53	3.33			
ES 1	1.00	1.07			

Statistics $\lambda = 0.73$; F $= 11.84$ with 5, 164 DF significance $= 0.00$ per cent; SRTOT $= 91.8$ per cent; SRB $= 53.3$ per cent; SRE $= 83.9$ per cent

they indicate that buyers felt slightly more strongly than non-buyers that a cooker was a necessity, but appeared to be less convinced that their peer group owned one.

Deep Freeze

TABLE 11.8 Results of discriminant analysis for deep freeze

| | Differences of Means | | Hits and Misses | | |
| | Mean Values | | | Predicted | |
Significant Variables	Buyers	Non-Buyers	Actual	Buyers	Non-Buyers
P12	3.25	0.58	Buyers	6	6
AS 7	4.50	2.84	Non-Buyers	6	160
AS 22	5.25	4.18			
SAVE	2.00	1.98			
AS 15	3.08	4.50			

Statistics
  $\lambda = 0.80$; F $= 8.74$ with 5, 172 DF significance $= 0.00$ per cent; SRTOT $= 93.3$ per cent; SRB $= 50$ per cent SRE $= 87.4$ per cent

Buyers of deep freezes were much more likely to have stated higher twelve month purchase probabilities (P12) though they were not more likely to have been saving up to buy this item (SAVE). There was, however, little evidence that any members of the sub-sample were saving up to purchase a deep freeze and it is therefore surprising that in this case the SAVE variable should have been included as significant. Buyers were more likely to have indicated that there was a durable they did not own that they intended to buy (AS 15) and we know that deep freeze purchases by this sample were largely initial rather than replacement purchases. Purchasers were less concerned about the effects of economic policy on their financial position (AS 7) and less inclined to agree that because of rising prices they should buy quickly (AS 22).

Dishwashers

TABLE 11.9 Results of discriminate analysis for dishwashers

	Differences of Means		Hits and Misses		
	Mean Values			Predicted	
Significant Variables	Buyers	Non-Buyers	Actual	Buyers	Non-Buyers
SAVE	1.80	2.00	Buyers	3	2
OWN Deep Freeze	1.20	1.89	Non-Buyers	2	164
ES 1	5.60	8.13			
AS 19	2.40	3.99			
TOTG	10.20	7.51			

Statistics
$\lambda = 0.696$; F = 14.42 with 5, 165 DF significance = 0.00 per cent; SRTOT = 97.7 per cent; SRB = 60 per cent; SRE = 94.3 per cent

Dishwasher purchases were made by only a small proportion of the sample and were mainly initial purchases. They tended to be made by people who were saving up to buy a dishwasher (SAVE), and already owned a larger number of durables (TOTG) including a deep freeze (OWN Deep Freeze). It will be recalled that in the identification of acquisition patterns (see Chapter 8) it appeared that of the relatively new, low ownership durables deep freezes were more likely to be owned before a dishwasher. This analysis gives further confirmation that deep freeze owners are more likely than non-deep freeze owners to buy a dishwasher and so the analysis of acquisition patterns is shown in this case to have predictive value. Purchasers also considered dishwashers to be less of a luxury and more of a necessity than non-purchasers (ES 1) and they were more pessimistic about the future trend of unemployment (AS 19).

Furniture

TABLE 11.10 Results of discriminant analysis for furniture

Significant Variables	Differences of Means			Hits and Misses		
	Mean Values				Predicted	
	Buyers	Non-Buyers	Actual		Buyers	Non-Buyers
P3	2.00	0.43	Buyers		52	43
SAVE	1.73	1.93	Non-		43	217
AS 17	3.93	4.69	Buyers			
YHH	5.13	4.65				
AS 5	3.61	3.34				
MOVE	2.63	2.85				
AS 25	2.51	3.02				

Statistics
  $\lambda = 0.82$; F = 10.67 with 7,347 DF significance = 0.00 per cent;
  SRTOT = 76.4 per cent; SRB = 54.7 per cent; SRE = 60.8 per cent

As with carpets, this was a case where it was not appropriate to collect information on the state of the existing stock of products or perceptions of the characteristics of furniture. Consequently it is possible to base this analysis on all 355 people for whom full information was available. Furniture buyers were more likely to have stated higher purchase probabilities (P3), were more likely to be saving up to buy furniture (SAVE), and thought they were more likely to move house (MOVE). They had higher household incomes (YHH) and would be better able to finance durable purchases from their savings (AS 25), their purchases of durables would be responsive to a temporary increase in income (AS 17), but they were less likely to expect to have more money available to spend in the following twelve months (AS 5).

New car

TABLE 11.11 Results of discriminant analyses for new car

Differences of Means	Mean Values			
	Owners Only		All Respondents	
Significant Variables	Buyers	Non-Buyers	Buyers	Non-Buyers
SAVE	1.62	1.94	1.62	1.95
SOCL	1.82	2.52	1.82	2.69
ES 15	8.94	8.32	8.94	8.15
AS 23			4.56	3.75
Hits and Misses	Owners Only Predicted		All Respondents Predicted	
Actual	Buyers	Non-Buyers	Buyers	Non-Buyers
Buyers	13	21	16	18
Non-Buyers	7	112	15	124

Statistics

Owners only: $\lambda = 0.76$; $F = 15.88$ with 3, 149 DF significance = 0.00 per cent; SRTOT = 81.7 per cent; SRB = 38.2 per cent; SRE = 70.5 per cent

All Respondents: $\lambda = 0.73$; $F = 15.44$ with 4, 168 DF significance = 0.00 per cent; SRTOT = 80.9 per cent; SRB = 47.1 per cent; SRE = 69.4 per cent

Although car ownership was high among the particular sample used in this investigation, it is worth looking at the results for car owners and all respondents separately. As will be apparent from the tabulations, all new car purchases were made by previous car owners and are likely therefore to have been replacement purchases (though not inevitably so since the new car purchase may represent the acquisition of an extra item – a second or third car for the first time). The inclusion of non-owners does not have much effect on overall success rates, but does help, through the inclusion of one further variable, to improve slightly the proportion of correct predictions of actual purchasers. It will be observed that in this case the predicted number of purchasers could not be made equal to the actual number of purchasers since, at the margin, several respondents were calculated to have the same probabilities of group membership.

The variables that proved significant discriminators indicate that new car buyers had a higher social class status (SOCL), were more likely to be saving up to buy a new car (SAVE), were more likely to buy rather than rent (ES 15) and were less likely to consider that their durable purchases would be affected by the rising prices of necessities (AS 23).

Used car

TABLE 11.12 Results of discriminant analyses for used car

Differences of Means	Mean Values			
	Owners Only		All Respondents	
Significant Variables	Buyers	Non-Buyers	Buyers	Non-Buyers
P3	1.88	0.05	1.84	0.05
P12	2.83	0.59	2.77	0.55
A	3.26	2.50		
ES 2	3.24	4.43	3.28	4.33
ES 6	5.50	4.20	5.58	4.36
AS 9	2.86	3.31		
EXPSP 12			414.60	253.69

	Owners Only Predicted		All Respondents Predicted	
Hits and Misses				
Actual	Buyers	Non-Buyers	Buyers	Non-Buyers
Buyers	28	14	25	18
Non-Buyers	14	97	18	112

Statistics

Owners only: $\lambda = 0.65$; $F = 12.90$ with 6, 146 DF significance $= 0.00$ per cent; SRTOT $= 81.7$ per cent; SRB $= 66.7$ per cent; SRE $= 60.2$ per cent

All Respondents: $\lambda = 0.75$; $F = 11.07$ with 5, 147 DF significance $= 0.00$ per cent; SRTOT $= 79.2$ per cent; SRB $= 58.1$ per cent; SRE $= 62.6$ per cent

In the case of used cars, there was one instance of a non-owner making a purchase, so the vast majority of all used car purchases were also either replacements or additions to the household's stock of cars. The inclusion of the twenty non-car-owners leads to some change in the variables selected, while the age of an existing vehicle is, of course, only relevant to an analysis based on owners only.

Combining the information from the two sets of results, we may conclude that used car purchasers had stated higher probabilities of purchasing a used car (P3, P12), owned older cars (A), felt more strongly that it was a good time to buy durables (AS 9), expected to have larger sums of money available to spend on consumer durables in the following twelve months (EXPSP 12), were more likely to think that cars had to be replaced regularly (ES 2), but would buy on credit rather than from savings (ES 6).

New versus used cars

TABLE 11.13 Results of discriminant analysis, new v used car

| | Differences of Means | | Hits and Misses | | |
| | Mean Values | | | Predicted | |
Significant Variables	New Car Buyers	Used Car Buyers	Actual	New Car Buyers	Used Car Buyers
P3U	0.15	3.05	New Car Buyers	28	6
PPL	2.97	3.59			
ES 13	3.32	5.92	Used Car Buyers	15	24

Statistics
$\lambda = 0.69$; F = 10.48 with 3, 69 DF significance = 0.00 per cent
SRTOT = 71.2 per cent; SRNEW = 82.4 per cent; SRUSED = 61.5 per cent; SRE = 50.4 per cent

In an earlier paper, using a different set of data (Isherwood and Pickering 1975) we showed that it was possible, using similar sorts of variables, to distinguish effectively between new car buyers and used car buyers. The results set out in Tables 11.11 and 11.12 above on the discrimination between buyers and non-buyers of new cars and used cars respectively indicate that the significant variables tended to be different in the two cases. We therefore ran an extra analysis to test further the hypothesis that new and used car buyers could be distinguished on the basis of certain key characteristics. The results are set out in Table 11.13 and indicate that a successful discrimination between the two groups has been achieved. Four used car buyers had also purchased a new car over the survey year. For the purposes of this analysis they were categorised as actual new car buyers. On the basis of the significant variables in the discriminant set we can say that new car buyers can be distinguished from used car buyers in terms of their lower expressed probabilities of purchasing a used car (P3U), their smaller household sizes (PPL) and their stronger commitment to purchasing new rather than second hand (ES 13).

Record player

TABLE 11. 14 Results of discriminant analyses for record player

Differences of Means	Mean Values			
	Owners Only		All Respondents	
Significant Variables	Buyers	Non-Buyers	Buyers	Non-Buyers
ES 14	5. 80	7. 51	6. 04	7. 44
ES 7	6. 24	7. 73	6. 30	7. 79
SAVE	1. 92	2. 00	1. 93	2. 00
AS 4			4. 59	3. 63
AS 14	6. 00	4. 56	6. 07	4. 60
AS 5	4. 08	3. 23	4. 19	3. 26
PPL	3. 96	3. 56	3. 93	3. 43
P3	0. 44	0. 09	0. 41	0. 08
AS 8	4. 76	3. 67		

Hits and Misses	Owners Only Predicted		All Respondents Predicted	
Actual	Buyers	Non-Buyers	Buyers	Non-Buyers
Buyers	16	9	16	11
Non-Buyers	9	115	11	149

Statistics

Owners Only: $\lambda = 0.68$; $F = 7.96$ with 8, 140 DF significance = 0. 00 per cent; SRTOT = 87. 9 per cent; SRB = 64 per cent; SRE = 72. 1 per cent

All Respondents: $\lambda = 0.71$; $F = 8.95$ with 8, 175 DF significance = 0. 00 per cent; SRTOT = 88. 2 per cent; SRB = 59. 3 per cent; SRE = 75. 3 per cent

Of thirty-eight non-owners in this sub-sample two made an initial purchase of a record player, and so it is useful to report separately the results of analyses for owners only and for all respondents. The significant variables were largely similar in the two analyses (though the order in which they entered the analysis was rather different). They indicate that record player purchasers tended to have stated a higher expectation of purchasing such an item (P3, ES 14), were more likely to be saving up to buy a record player (SAVE), they had larger families (PPL), were rather less likely to think of a record player as pleasure giving (ES 7), they were less confident about economic development prospects (AS 4) and about their financial situation (AS 5), thought they were less likely to buy a car (AS 14) and their durable purchasing was more likely to be affected by the way the economy was being run (AS 8).

Refrigerator

TABLE 11.15 Results of discriminant analyses for refrigerator

Differences of Means	Mean Values			
	Owners Only		All Respondents	
Significant Variables	Buyers	Non-Buyers	Buyers	Non-Buyers
P12	2.86	0.47	2.86	0.46
PMA	3.57	1.40		
AMINCY	1.57	0.63	1.57	0.63

Hits and Misses	Owners Only		All Respondents	
Actual	Buyers	Non-Buyers	Buyers	Non-Buyers
Buyers	3	4	2	5
Non-Buyers	4	149	5	155

Statistics

Owners Only: $\lambda = 0.88$; F = 7.29 with 3,156 DF significance = 0.01 per cent; SRTOT = 95 per cent; SRB = 42.9 per cent; SRE = 81.2 per cent

All Respondents: $\lambda = 0.91$; F = 8.01 with 2,164 DF significance = 0.05 per cent; SRTOT = 94 per cent; SRB = 28.6 per cent SRE = 92 per cent

The proportion of buyers of refrigerators was extremely small and so a random classificatory procedure would be expected to produce a high overall success rate. However, although the proportion of buyers correctly classified remains low, it is well in excess of that which a random procedure would yield. All refrigerator purchases were reported by existing owners and the analysis indicates that buyers can be distinguished from non-buyers by the higher probabilities they had stated of purchasing a refrigerator (P12), the greater chance they estimated there would be of their existing model requiring major attention during the following twelve months (PMA) and the larger amounts by which they estimated they could increase their regular income by working overtime etc. (AMINCY).

Tape recorder

TABLE 11.16 Results of discriminant analysis for tape recorder

	Differences of Means		Hits and Misses		
	Mean Values			Predicted	
Significant Variables	Buyers	Non-Buyers	Actual	Buyers	Non-Buyers
ES 1	5.50	7.76	Buyers	3	5
			Non-Buyers	4	148

Statistics

$\lambda = 0.94$; $F = 10.36$ with 1,158 DF significance = 0.16 per cent. SRTOT = 94.4 per cent; SRB = 37.5 per cent; SRE = 91.1 per cent

There is no advantage in distinguishing owners and non-owners in this case. The proportion of buyers was again low but it appears that buyers' perceptions of tape recorders as less of a luxury and rather more of a necessity than non-buyers would think is an important basis for discriminating between the two groups.

Vacuum cleaner

Although there were some non-owners of vacuum cleaners and one purchase was reported by a non-owner, the results were sufficiently similar that it is not necessary to report the two analyses separately.

TABLE 11. 17 Results of discriminant analysis for vacuum cleaner

Significant Variables	Differences of Means		Hits and Misses		
	Mean Values			Predicted	
	Buyers	Non-Buyers	Actual	Buyers	Non-Buyers
P3	2. 65	0. 22	Buyers	8	9
ES3	7. 65	5. 52	Non-		
AS 21	2. 71	3. 68	Buyers	11	146

Statistics

$\lambda = 0.78$; $F = 15.56$ with 3, 170 DF significance = 0.00 per cent
STROT = 88. 5 per cent; SRB = 47. 1; SRE = 81. 5 per cent

Consequently the results shown relate to all respondents. Vacuum cleaner buyers had stated much higher purchase probabilities than non-buyers (P3), they considered themselves likely to make the purchase decision more rapidly (ES 3) but they considered their purchases of durables more likely to be affected by a temporary decrease in income (AS 21).

Washing machine

Of the twenty-nine non-owners in this sub-sample, seven bought a washing machine during the survey year and so the balance between replacement and initial purchases was more even than for many other items. The significant variables suggest that buyers of washing machines had lower incomes, especially of the HoH (YHoH), but were increasing their discretionary incomes (AS 29), initial purchasers were more likely to be saving up to buy a washing machine (SAVE) and had stronger purchase expectations (ES 14). Buyers of washing machines as replacements emphasised the convenience of a washing machine rather than regarding it as vital (ES 4). However, first-time buyers appear to have taken a different view. If we calculate mean values on variable ES 4 for non-owners only, we find that the mean for non-owners who purchased a washing machine during the survey year was 3.71 and the mean for non-owners who did not buy was 2.91. Thus prospective first-time buyers were more prone to take the view that a washing machine was relatively more vital to them and non-owners who did not buy were much more likely as a group to emphasise its convenience rather than its importance to them.

TABLE 11.18 Results of discriminant analyses for washing machine

Differences of Means	Mean Values			
	Owners only		All Respondents	
Significant Variables	Buyers	Non-Buyers	Buyers	Non-Buyers
AS 29	2.82	4.70	3.22	4.81
ES4	3.27	5.49	3.44	5.14
SAVE			1.83	2.00
ES 14			4.72	7.11
YHOH	3.64	4.52	3.39	4.45
YHH	4.91	4.93	4.83	4.83

Hits and Misses	Owners Only Predicted		All Respondents Predicted	
Actual	Buyers	Non-Buyers	Buyers	Non-Buyers
Buyers	6	5	11	7
Non-Buyers	5	133	7	153

Statistics

Owners Only: $\lambda = 0.87$; $F = 5.37$ with 4,144 DF significance = 0.46 per cent SRTOT = 93.3 per cent; SRB = 54.5 per cent; SRE = 86.3 per cent

All Respondents: $\lambda = 0.69$; $F = 12.68$ with 6,171 DF significance = 0.00 per cent; SRTOT = 92.1 per cent; SRB = 61.1 per cent; SRE = 81.8 per cent

Although household income (YHH) is a significant variable in the optimum discriminant functions, there does not seem to be any ground for concluding that on average buyers and non-buyers were substantially different on this variable. Its presence in the discriminant functions together with the income of the HoH (YHoH) serves to indicate that buyers of washing machines tended to have larger incomes from members of the household other than the HoH. In most cases this suggests that working wives were more strongly represented among households who bought washing machines than in the sample as a whole. This is also supported by the presence of AS 29 as the most significant variable in the discriminant function.

General comments on the results

The results show that each analysis successfully distinguished between the two groups – the groups of buyers and non-buyers of each product were significantly different from each other. The particular problems of testing the predictive power of the data have already been discussed and dealt with in the way advocated by others working in this field. After taking account of this we can still say that almost without exception the classifications reported here are better than those which would have been expected from a purely random allocative procedure. Although the prediction of buyers was far from perfect, the success achieved was much greater than a random procedure would have yielded. Consequently it may be claimed that the variables used in the discriminant analysis (which it will be remembered amounted at this stage to less than twenty on average for each product) do make a useful predictive contribution in the study of buyer behaviour.

The variables included in each discriminant analysis were those which in the earlier correlation and regression analyses had been shown to have some significant association with actual buyer behaviour. In almost all cases, the variables selected in the optimum discriminant function for each product had substantially different mean values for buyers and for non-buyers. Consequently it is possible not only to identify which variables contributed to the discrimination between the two groups but also to establish how the buyers of an item differed from the non-buyers on the selected characteristics.

Whereas in an anlysis of aggregate expenditures we would expect to find that recorded expenditures were higher where people were more wealthy, had greater confidence etc, in the case of the analysis of individual product demand different influences may apply. Purchases of items long established in the market place and having high market penetration may be associated with low socio-economic status in the case of initial purchases and with the ownership of older, worn out models in the case of those making replacement purchases. It is not therefore necessarily surprising that, for example, washing machine purchasers were found to have lower incomes than non-purchasers.

In fact, socio-economic variables, reflecting an ability to make consumer durable purchases, do not appear to have a strong influence on buyer behaviour for individual products. Indications of the state of the stock of existing items and hence of likely replacement demand have some influence in the case of new car, cooker and refrigerator purchases. Consumer confidence as represented by the AS variables retained some significance, though the selection of variables was dispersed and not as concentrated as might have been hoped. Generally speaking, purchases were associated with expressions of confidence – buyers felt that economic policy was not affecting their family or their buying of durables, purchases would not be affected by a temporary fall in income, but would respond to an increase, buyers were increasing their discretionary household income, they could afford to finance purchases from savings, they felt it was a good time to buy durables, expected to buy a new item and to buy more durables, and they were less concerned about the effects of rising prices of either durables or necessities.

In certain cases buyers were more pessimistic about likely future economic developments and the amounts they expected to have available to spend in the following twelve months; their expectations of buying a car; likely changes in the level of unemployment; and the effects of a temporary fall in their incomes on their purchasing of durables. Several of these examples related to purchases of furnishings and record players in particular and it may be that such purchases are made at a lower level of confidence than purchases of other sorts of consumer durable. In general, however, it is clear that most individual items are more likely to be purchased by people with greater economic confidence and a stronger commitment to durable purchases generally.

Purchase expectations variables tended to be the most frequently significant and as would be expected we find that purchasers of a particular durable were those who had stated higher purchase probability values on that item or were more likely to have said that they were saving up to buy it.

A number of the scales reflecting respondent perceptions of the characteristics of consumer durables were also significant. Compared with non-buyers of a product, we find that buyers rated the items they subsequently bought as more of a necessity and less of a luxury; functional rather than pleasure-giving; to be replaced regularly; bought rather than rented; the purchase decision could be made quickly; the item contributed to the standard of living; was owned by the peer group; and buyers had said they were more likely to buy that item in the following twelve months. In all these respects, it can be safely concluded that buyers were distinguished from non-buyers in terms of a perception of the characteristics of consumer durables that was more favourable to the purchase decision. There were also some exceptions to this picture. Central heating buyers appear to have concluded that central heating was more unreliable than did non-buyers, washing machine replacement purchasers were less convinced of the essential nature of the product than non-buyers and black and white television purchasers considered this item more of a luxury than non-buyers. As regards the financing of purchases, central heating buyers were more likely to finance their purchase from their savings but used car buyers were more likely to buy on credit. Again, this is not particularly surprising.

12   *Concluding comments*

In this study we have dealt with a number of different aspects of the household's demand for consumer durables. It is hoped that the preceding chapters have offered some relevant suggestions, especially as regards considerations of the methodology of the collection of expectational and attitudinal data, the analysis of the influences upon consumer discretionary behaviour and in understanding the determinants of individual household durable purchasing decisions.

The limitations imposed by a relatively small sample size and non-response (although from the first reinterviews onwards the response rate held up extremely well) serve to emphasise that the evidence reported here should be viewed as arising from a pioneering cross-sectional investigation, suggesting hypotheses and offering tentative conclusions which need further confirmation. In general, however, the results appear to offer good support for the original hypothesis that the demand for consumer durables is a function of the consumer's willingness to buy as well as his ability to do so. Thus they support the conclusions of other researchers in this field and also confirm the findings of our own earlier studies. The emphasis adopted here on the cross-sectional testing of the predictive performance of such data is unusual but we believe the results demonstrate that it is unnecessary for the advocates of such a 'behavioural' approach to the demand for consumer durables to be so defensive about the cross-sectional validation of their models.

The methodology used for data collection in this study appears to have worked well and there seems no reason why the more sophisticated scaling techniques advocated here could not be adopted more generally for forecasting purposes. While the eleven-point probability scale is not new, there may be a case for further investigation of the possible advantages (at least from a cross-sectional point of view) of using either this or a verbal scale. Either way, it is clear that consumer attitudes and expectations are measurable and can readily be converted to index number form. The attempt to derive some measure of desired stock adjustment from survey data also seems to have proved effective and could be developed further. The techniques mentioned so far are perhaps most appropriate for short term forecasting. It would appear, however, that the analysis of orders of acquisition and priority patterns on the one hand and changes in consumer perceptions of the characteristics of particular durables on the other are more useful for medium and long term forecasts.

More economists have recently become interested in the role of expectations in influencing economic behaviour. We have shown that there are several different types of consumer expectations and that different clusters of attitude variables can be identified. Both general economic confidence and durable purchasing expectations seem normally to be positively associated with higher levels of expenditure by individual consumers, although the influence of general economic confidence variables was not as strong as might have been anticipated.

It seems that an explanation for this is to be found in the divergence, during the survey year, in the movements of the index of economic confidence and the durable purchasing confidence index, with durable purchasing expectations remaining more buoyant while economic confidence declined further. It is interesting to note that Katona has commented that in the USA in 1973, for the first time since the Korean war in 1950, the traditional relationship between consumer confidence and durable purchasing broke down and durable demand was buoyant despite falling confidence (Katona 1975). It may well be that a similar situation existed in Britain in 1972–3 and this might help to explain the relatively low cross-sectional explanatory power of the economic confidence variables. Either because of increasing concern about inflation or because of increasing ability to make purchases due to higher incomes and easier credit, or both, consumers as a whole were making durable purchases which their general level of economic confidence would not normally have supported. This is exactly the sort of situation that the use of two indices of consumer confidence as described in Chapter 5 would be expected to handle more effectively than the more usual single index measure. It is encouraging that their overall movements tend to support the interpretation in this particular case.

The role of price expectations is worthy of some comment. In both the present study and our earlier survey (Pickering and Isherwood 1975) it was found that price attitudes were not significant predictors over a twelve or fourteen month period. In both cases, however, price attitudes seem to be associated with purchases over a shorter, three or four month, period from the initial expression of the attitude. Seemingly, therefore, concern about future price trends leads to a speedy purchasing reaction or as Katona has put it '. . . advance or excess buying represents an immediate response to a specific threat' (Katona 1975 p.148). While uncertainties and concerns about price trends seem to have stimulated durable purchases but contributed to a decline in economic confidence, there is also strong evidence that the Government's imposition of pay and price controls in November 1972 led to a significant improvement in economic confidence in the early part of 1973.

One of the outcomes of intensive cross-sectional investigations of the sort reported here should be a clearer understanding of the determinants of the behaviour of the individual consumer. In terms of aggregate expenditure, heavy spenders on durables were better able to afford to buy through their higher social class and ownership of more durables already. They were more likely to have expected to move house and actually to have done so during the survey year. They were more confident about their personal future economic prospects and had stronger durable purchasing expectations. They spent more if, by the end of the survey year, their household's income had increased substantially and their real financial position had improved, their general economic confidence had improved but their durable purchasing expectations had declined (having already been achieved). They spent more than would have been predicted if they had increased their usage of credit and had installed central heating during the survey year. They were likely to have recognised they had spent more than they had initially anticipated.

Initial acquisitions of particular durables seem to be made in a reasonably consistent order and any variations in that order, where estimated from historic orders of acquisition, present ownership patterns, or intentions to acquire next, can offer interesting insights into changes through time in consumer tastes. From the results of the present survey, it appeared that the prospects for colour televisions and deep freezes looked promising. Subsequent trends, however, in the demand for consumer durables in general and colour televisions in particular serve to emphasise that such analyses are based on assumptions of other things being equal and will not hold if relative prices or other objective economic conditions are substantially altered.

Purchasers of a particular consumer durable were most likely to have indicated strong expectations of purchasing that item, in many cases reported that they were saving up to buy it, and had a more favourable perception of its characteristics. Replacement demands tended to occur where existing items were older (except in the case of new cars) and where the estimated probability of major attention was higher.

Generally speaking, most durables tended to be purchased by more confident consumers. There were, however, exceptions to this which suggest that there may be a hierarchy of consumer durables, some of which are systematically more likely to be purchased by less confident consumers (although they were sufficiently confident or able to make at least some durable outlay). Socio-economic status did not normally appear to be closely associated with the demand for individual consumer durables.

The actual explanations of decisions to purchase or not to purchase seem to rationalise into a few key considerations. Owners were more likely to buy when their existing item had to be replaced and not before. Demand from non-owners for a particular item was much more sensitive to financial inducements and to considerations of their ability to afford the purchase. Problems of choice and the anticipation of future house moves were likely to discourage purchases while actual house moves appeared to encourage purchases.

Appendix Listing of variables used in the analysis

Variable Name	Variable Description and Coding	Comments
a) Socio-economic status variables		
SOCL	Social class status of informant household A = 1; B = 2; C_1 = 3; C_2 = 4; D = 5; E = 6	From Survey I
AGE	Age of the head of household 16–24 years = 1; 25–34 years = 2; 35–44 years = 3; 45–54 years = 4; 55–64 years = 5	From Survey I
MARST	Marital status of HoH Single = 1; Married = 2; Widowed/separated/divorced = 3	From Survey I
TMRD	Length of time HoH has been married less than 5 years = 1; 5–9 years = 2; 10–20 years = 3; over 20 years = 4	From Survey I
PPL	Number of people in household 1 = 1; 2 = 2; 3 = 3; 4 = 4; 5–7 = 5; 8 and over = 6	From Survey I
YHoH	Income of the HoH in £ less than £1000 = 1; 1000–1499 = 2; 1500–1999 = 3; 2000–2499 = 4; 2500–2999 = 5; 3000–3999 = 6; 4000–5999 = 7; 6000 and over = 8;	From Survey I
YHH	Total income of the household in £ less than £1000 = 1; 1000–1499 = 2; 1500–1999 = 3; 2000–2499 = 4; 2500–2999 = 5; 3000–3999 = 6; 4000–5999 = 7; 6000 and over = 8	From Survey I

Variable Name	Variable Description and Coding	Comments
INCY	Whether family income can be readily and temporarily increased. Yes = 1; No = 2 The different methods by which this could be achieved were also recorded.	From Survey I

AMINCY	Amount by which family income can be readily and temporarily increased, in £
	    up to £5 per week = 1; 5–10 per week = 2;
	    11–20 = 3; 21–40 = 4; over 40 = 5
		From Survey I

NOWK	Number of members of the household that had been working (full or part-time) over the survey year Actual numbers reported	From Survey V

b) Financial circumstances and expectations of the household

CRDT	Whether there was any bank credit outstanding Yes = 1; No = 2	From Survey I
HP	Whether there were any hire purchase commitments Yes = 1; No = 2 Information was also collected regarding the items on which HP was outstanding	From Survey I

TOTCRDT	Total credit outstanding excluding mortgages in £
	    Nil = 1; 1–50 = 2; 51–100 = 3;
	    101–500 = 4; over 500 = 5
		From Survey I

STOT	Total savings of household Small (less than £100) = 1; Medium (a few hundred pounds) = 2; Quite Large (£1000 or more) = 3 Details were also collected on the methods of savings used.	From Survey I

DS	How savings of the household had changed over the previous twelve months
	    Substantially decreased = 1;
	    Decreased = 2; Remained the same = 3;
	    Increased = 4; Substantially increased = 5
		From Survey I

HPEND	Whether any hire purchase agreements were due to end in the following three months Yes = 1; No = 2	From Survey I

Variable Name	Variable Description and Coding	Comments
HPEARLY	Whether any hire purchase agreements were likely to be ended early Yes = 1; No = 2	From Survey I
HPEXP	Expected change in the usage of hire purchase over the next three months Substantially less = 1; Less = 2; The same = 3; More = 4; Substantially more = 5	From Survey I
EXPDS	Expected changes in the level of the household's savings over the following twelve months Substantially decrease = 1; Decrease = 2; Remain the same = 3; Increase = 4; Substantially increase = 5	From Survey I
MRLSCR	Whether more or less bank credit was expected to be used over the next three months Substantially less = 1; Less = 2; The same = 3; More = 4; Substantially more = 5	From Survey I
EXPSP 3	Amount of money expected to be spent on consumer durables in the next three months Actual cash sums	From Survey I
EXPSP 12	Amount of money expected to be spent on consumer durables in the next twelve months Actual cash sums	From Survey I
ESMRLS 3	Whether amount in EXPSP 3 is more or less than the amount spent at the same time in the previous year Substantially less = 1; Less = 2; The same = 3; More = 4; Substantially more = 5	From Survey I
ESMRLS 12	Whether amount in EXPSP 12 is more or less than the amount spent in the previous twelve months Substantially less = 1; Less = 2; The same = 3; More = 4; Substantially more = 5	From Survey I
SAVE	Whether the household was saving up to purchase a specified consumer durable or for certain other types of outlay. The items and expenditures covered were: black and white television, carpets costing more than	From Survey I

Variable Name	Variable Description and Coding	Comments
	£50, central heating, colour television, cooker, deep freeze, dishwasher, furniture costing more than £50, holidays, home improvements and decorations, new car, used car, record player, refrigerator, tape recorder, vacuum cleaner, washing machine	
MOVE	Whether the household expected to move house during the next twelve months Yes = 1; Uncertain = 2; No = 3	From Survey I

c) The ownership of specified consumer durables

OWN	Whether specified durables were in the household. The durables covered were: black and white television, car, central heating, colour television, cooker, deep freeze, dishwasher, record player, refrigerator, tape recorder, vacuum cleaner, washing machine In home = 1; Not in home = 2	From Survey I
Q	Number of units of each specified consumer durable in the household (asked for all durables in the household listed in OWN except central heating) Actual number	From Survey I
T	Length of time the item had been in the household (asked for all durables in the household listed in OWN except central heating) Less than 1 year = 1; 1–2 years = 2; 3–4 years = 3; 5–9 years = 4; 10 years and over = 5	From Survey I
A	Age of item (asked for all durables in the household listed in OWN except central heating) Less than 1 year = 1; 1–2 years = 2; 3–4 years = 3; 5–9 years = 4; 10 years and over = 5	From Survey I
OBT	How the item was obtained (asked for all durables in the household listed in OWN except central heating) Bought personally = 1; Gift = 2; Rented/hired = 3; Provided by employer = 4; Obtained with coupons, trading stamps = 5; Other = 6	From Survey I

Variable Name	Variable Description and Coding	Comments
PMA	Probability that the item would require major attention within the next twelve months (asked for all durables in the household listed in OWN except central heating) Probability values from 0–10	From Survey I
RRA	Action that would be adopted if major attention was required (asked for all durables in the household listed in OWN except central heating) Repair = 1; Replace = 2; Abandon = 3	From Survey I
TOTG	Total number of units of different consumer durables. Actual number	Derived from data from Survey I
ACQ	Historic order in which specified durables were first acquired. The durables covered were: black and white television, first car, second car, third car, colour television, cooker, deep freeze, dishwasher, record player, refrigerator, tape recorder, vacuum cleaner, washing machine.	From Survey V
NXT	The one durable which the household would most like to acquire next, of those not at present owned. The durables covered were as in ACQ and a further category was added for those households not wishing to own any further durables.	From Survey V

d) Consumer confidence variables

	All AS variables were set out as seven point semantic differential scales, the scale points were labelled: Agree strongly; Agree; Agree slightly; Agree with neither or both equally; Agree slightly; Agree; Agree strongly. Answers were coded from one for 'Agree strongly' to the left hand statement to seven for 'Agree strongly' to the right hand statement. The polar opposite statements are set out below, the first statement in each pair was the left hand statement, the second statement was the right hand statement.	Collected in Surveys I, II, III, IV, V, subscripts 1 to 5 in the text refer to the particular survey

Variable Name	Variable Description and Coding	Comments
AS 1	Financially, we as a family are better off than we were a year ago/ Financially, we as a family are less well off than we were a year ago.	
AS 2	Financially, we as a family expect to be better off next year than we are now/ Financially, we as a family, expect to be worse off next year than we are now.	
AS 3	My employment opportunities look good for the next year/ My employment opportunities do not look good for the next year.	
AS 4	The development of the economy is likely to be favourable to us as a family over the next year/ The development of the economy is not likely to be favourable to us as a family over the next year.	
AS 5	I expect to have more money available to spend in the next twelve months than I had in the last year/ I expect to have less money available to spend in the next twelve months than I had in the last year.	
AS 6	There are now good prospects of continuous economic progress in this country/ Prospects for continuous economic progress are not good at the present time in this country.	
AS 7	The way in which the economy is being run is affecting my financial position and that of my family/ The way in which the economy is being run is not affecting our financial position.	
AS 8	The way in which the economy is being run does not affect my personal buying of durable goods/ The way in which the economy is being run does affect my buying of durables.	
AS 9	This is a good time to buy durable goods/ This is not a good time to buy durable goods.	
AS 10	This is now a good time to build up savings/ This is not a good time to build up savings.	

Variable Name	Variable Description and Coding	Comments
AS 11	This is now a good time to buy stocks and shares and unit trusts/ This is not a good time to buy stocks and shares and unit trusts.	
AS 12	I have confidence in the way the economy is being run at present/ I have no confidence in the way the economy is being run at present.	
AS 13	I expect prices to rise over the next twelve months/ I don't expect prices to rise over the next twelve months.	
AS 14	I expect to buy a new or a used car in the next twelve months/ I do not expect to buy a car in the next twelve months.	
AS 15	There is a durable good which I do not already own that I intend to buy in the next twelve months/ I do not expect to buy any additional durable goods in the next twelve months.	
AS 16	There is a durable good which I already own that I expect to replace in the next twelve months/ I do not expect to replace any of the durables I own in the next twelve months.	
AS 17	My purchases of durable goods would be affected by a temporary increase in income/ My purchases of durable goods would not be affected by a temporary increase in income.	
AS 18	We are currently saving up to purchase a particular durable good/ We are not saving up at present to buy a particular durable good.	
AS 19	I expect the level of unemployment to rise on average over the next twelve months/ I expect the level of unemployment to fall on average over the next twelve months.	
AS 20	Prices of most goods are rising at the moment/ Prices seem to be pretty stable at the present time.	

Variable Name	Variable Description and Coding	Comments
AS 21	My purchases of durable goods would be affected by a temporary decrease in income/ My purchases of durable goods would not be affected by a temporary decrease in income.	
AS 22	Because prices of the durables I want to buy are rising I ought to buy quickly/ There is no need to rush into durable purchases just because prices are rising.	
AS 23	Because prices of foodstuffs and other things I have to buy and spend money on are rising I am less able to buy the durable goods I would like/ The prices of foodstuffs and other things I have to buy have no effect on my ability to buy the durable I would like.	
AS 24	I expect to buy more durable goods in the next twelve months than I have done in the last year/ I do not expect to buy as many durable goods in the next twelve months as in the last year.	
AS 25	I would expect to be able to pay for any durable I particularly wanted from my savings in the next twelve months/ I would not be able to pay for a durable from my savings in the next twelve months.	
AS 26	I would expect to be able to pay for anything I particularly wanted on credit/ I would not be able to finance the purchase of a durable on credit.	
AS 27	I expect my financial commitments to increase in the next year or two/ I expect my financial commitments to decline in the next year or two.	
AS 28	As a country, we are doing well at the moment/ As a country, we are *not* doing so well at the present time.	
AS 29	We are currently increasing our household income e.g. by overtime or my wife going out to work/ We are not increasing our household income at present.	

Variable Name	Variable Description and Coding	Comments
OPT 1, OPT 2, OPT 3,	The OPT variables were respondent scores on the first three principal component combinations of the attitude scales from the relevant survey.	
DAS 1_{1-5} to DAS 29_{1-5}	The DAS variables were created by subtracting the code on each AS variable in Survey V from the code on the same variable in Survey I.	

e) Purchase probabilities

P3	Probabilities of purchasing each durable item in the following three months. The durables covered were: black and white television, carpets (costing £50 or more), central heating, colour television, cooker, deep freeze, dishwasher, a major item of furniture (costing £50 or more), new car, used car, record player, refrigerator, tape recorder, vacuum cleaner, washing machine. Actual probability values from 0–10	From Survey I
P6	Probabilities of purchasing each durable item in the following six months. The durables covered were as for P3. Actual probability values from 0–10	From Survey I
P12	Probabilities of purchasing each durable item in the following twelve months. The durables covered were as for P3. Actual probability values from 0–10	From Survey I
PV	Expectations of purchasing each durable item in the following twelve months recorded on a seven-point verbal scale. Would certainly not buy = 1; Unlikely to buy = 2; Possibly won't buy = 3; Fifty-fifty chance of buying = 4; Possibly will buy = 5; Quite likely to buy = 6; Will certainly buy = 7.	From Surveys II, III, IV, V.

f) Perceptions of the Characteristics of particular durables

	All ES variables were set out as nine-point semantic differential scales, the scale points were not labelled. Answers were coded	From Survey I

Variable Name	Variable Description and Coding	Comments
	from one at the extreme left hand end of the scale to nine at the extreme right hand end. The polar opposite statements are set out below, the first statement in each pair was the left hand statement, the second statement was the right hand statement. Respondents rated a randomly determined sample of six durables on these scales. The durables were drawn from: black and white television, car, central heating, colour television, cooker, deep freeze, dishwasher, record player, refrigerator, tape recorder, vacuum cleaner, washing machine. ES 17, ES 18, ES 19 were only rated by owners of the durable concerned.	
ES 1	Necessity/Luxury	
ES 2	Have to be replaced regularly/Long lasting	
ES 3	Have to plan purchase carefully/Buy fairly quickly	
ES 4	Convenient/Vital	
ES 5	Relatively expensive/Relatively cheap	
ES 6	Buy from savings/Buy on credit	
ES 7	Functional/Simply gives pleasure	
ES 8	Have to wait for the right price/Price irrelevant	
ES 9	Need an increase in income to buy/Can afford out of present income	
ES 10	Relatively high running costs/Low running costs	
ES 11	Contributes to standard of living/Does not contribute to standard of living	
ES 12	The majority of my friends and neighbours own one/The majority of my friends and neighbours do not own one	
ES 13	Likely to buy new/Likely to buy second hand	
ES 14	Will probably buy within the next 12 months/Would not consider buying within the next 12 months	
ES 15	Would rent/Would buy	
ES 16	Reliable/Unreliable	
ES 17	Ours is fairly new/Ours is getting old	

Variable Name	Variable Description and Coding	Comments
ES 18	More up-to-date models than ours are available/ More up-to-date models than ours are not available	
ES 19	Size of our present model is adequate for our needs/ We could do with a different sized model	

g) Change in household circumstances during the survey year

DYHoH	How income of the HoH had changed in the previous three months. Declined substantially = 1; Declined = 2; Not changed = 3; Increased = 4; Increased substantially = 5	From Surveys II, III, IV, V.
DYHH	How income of the household had changed in the previous three months. Declined substantially = 1; Declined = 2; Not changed = 3; Increased = 4; Increased substantially = 5	From Surveys II, III, IV, V.
DSHH	How savings of the household had changed in the previous three months. Declined substantially = 1; Declined = 2; Not changed = 3; Increased = 4; Increased substantially = 5	From Surveys II, III, IV, V.
EXPCFD	Respondent comparison of his assessed expenditure on durables over the survey year compared with the amount he had expected to spend in that year. Considerably less = 1; Less = 2; About the same = 3; More = 4; Considerably more = 5	From Survey V
DYHoHYR	Change in income of the HoH over the survey year. Considerably less = 1; Less = 2; About the same = 3; More = 4; Considerably more = 5	From Survey V
DYHHYR	Change in income of the household over the survey year. Considerably less = 1; Less = ; About the same = 3; More = 4; Considerably more = 5	From Survey V

Variable Name	Variable Description and Coding	Comments

DSYR	Change in household savings over the survey year.
	    Considerably less = 1; Less = 2;
	    About the same = 3; More = 4;
	    Considerably more = 5
		From Survey V

DHPYR	Change in the household's use of HP and other credit over the survey year.
	    Considerably less = 1; Less = 2;
	    About the same = 3; More = 4;
	    Considerably more = 5
		From Survey V

DSHYR	Change in the level of the household's shareholding over the survey year.
	    Considerably less = 1; Less = 2;
	    About the same = 3; More = 4;
	    Considerably more = 5
		From Survey V

ANTD	Whether the changes indicated in DYHoHYR, DYHHYR, DSYR, DHPYR and DSHYR had been anticipated. No = 1; Yes = 2	From Survey V

DFAV	Whether unanticipated changes referred to in ANTD were more favourable or less favourable than had been expected.
	    Substantially less favourable = 1;
	    Less favourable = 2; About the same = 3;
	    More favourable = 4; Substantially more favourable = 5
		From Survey V

WMOVD	Whether, during the survey year, the household had moved house. No = 1; Yes = 2	From Survey V
WBCAR 2	Whether, during the survey year, a second car had been purchased for the first time. No = 1; Yes = 2	From Survey V
WBCAR 3	Whether, during the survey year, a third car had been purchased for the first time. No = 1; Yes = 2	From Survey V
WRETD	Whether, during the survey year, the informant had retired from work. No = 1; Yes = 2	From Survey V
WINCHH	Whether, during the survey year, the size of the household had increased. No = 1; Yes = 2	From Survey V
WHOLS	Whether, during the survey year, an overseas holiday had been taken. No = 1; Yes = 2	From Survey V

Variable Name	Variable Description and Coding	Comments
WDEC	Whether, during the survey year, home redecorations or improvements costing over £100 had been undertaken. No = 1; Yes = 2	From Survey V
WCH	Whether, during the survey year, central heating had been installed. No = 1; Yes = 2	From Survey V
WFIN	Whether, during the survey year, substantial and continuing new financial commitments had been entered into. No = 1; Yes = 2	From Survey V
WHXP	Whether, during the survey year, heavy, unexpected expenses had been incurred. No = 1; Yes = 2	From Survey V
WGN	Whether, during the survey year, any large unexpected payments had been received. No = 1; Yes = 2	From Survey V
WCC	Whether, during the survey year, a credit card had been received for the first time. No = 1; Yes = 2	From Survey V
FPCFD	Comparison of financial position in real terms, compared with a year before. Substantially worse off = 1; Worse off = 2; About the same = 3; Better off = 4; Substantially better off = 5	From Survey V
OPF; OPD	Opinion on actual level of prices for food and durable goods, compared with what would have been expected a year earlier. Substantially higher than expected = 1; Higher than expected = 2; About the same = 3; Lower than expected = 4; Substantially lower than expected = 5	From Survey V
PNB	Whether the level of prices had actually prevented a purchase that would otherwise have been made during the survey year. No = 1; Yes = 2	From Survey V
	Details of the actual items that had not been purchased for this reason were also recorded.	From Survey V
PERL	Whether, during the survey year, the anticipation of future price increases had	From Survey V

Variable Name	Variable Description and Coding	Comments
	caused an item to be purchased earlier than had otherwise been planned. No = 1; Yes = 2 Details of the actual items that had been purchased for this reason were also recorded.	

h) Durable purchasing activities during the survey year

Variable Name	Variable Description and Coding	Comments
BNB	Whether a particular durable had been purchased in the previous three months. The durables concerned were: black and white television, carpets (costing over £50), central heating, colour television: cooker, deep freeze, dishwasher, a major item of furniture (costing over £50), new car, used car, record player/radiogram, refrigerator, tape recorder, vacuum cleaner, washing machine. No = 0; Yes = 1	From Surveys II, III, IV, V.
RB 1/RB 2	Reasons for purchasing the particular durable recorded in BNB at that time. Actual reasons were recorded and subsequently categorised.	From Surveys II, III, IV, V.
RNB 1/ RNB 2	Reasons for not purchasing any particular durable specified in BNB which the household thought they might have purchased in the previous three months but did not in fact do so. Actual reasons were recorded and subsequently categorised.	From Surveys II, III, IV, V.
QEXP	Total expenditure on the durables listed in BNB in the previous three months, net of trade-in allowances. Actual expenditure levels.	From Surveys II, III, IV, V.
EEXP	Informant estimate of the expenditure of his household on the durables listed in BNB over the survey year. Actual expenditure levels.	From Survey V
EXPYR	Actual expenditure level on the durables listed in BNB over the survey year based on the summation of the quarterly expenditures recorded in QEXP. Actual expenditure levels.	Derived from data from Surveys II, III, IV, V.

Bibliography

ADAMS FG (1964) 'Consumer attitudes, buying plans and purchases of durable goods: a principal component time series approach' *Review of Economics and Statistics* Vol 46 p.347

ADAMS FG (1965) 'Prediction with consumer attitudes: the time series – cross section paradox' *Review of Economics and Statistics* Vol 47 p.367

ADAMS FG and GREEN EW (1965) 'Explaining and predicting aggregative consumer attitudes' *International Economic Review* Vol 6 p.275

ADAMS FG and KLEIN LR (1972) 'Anticipations variables in macro-econometric models' in B Strumpel, JN Morgan and E Zahn eds. *Human Behavior in Economic Affairs* (Elsevier) p.289

ANGEVINE GE (1974) 'Forecasting consumption with a Canadian consumer sentiment measure' *Canadian Journal of Economics* Vol 7 p.273

BEHREND H (1966) 'Price images, inflation and national incomes policy' *Scottish Journal of Political Economy* Vol 13 p.273

COHEN CD (1971) *British Economic Policy 1960 – 1969* (Butterworth)

DUNKELBERG WC (1969) *Forecasting Consumer Expenditures with Measures of Attitudes and Expectations* unpublished Ph.D thesis, University of Michigan.

DUNKELBERG WC (1972) 'The impact of consumer attitudes on behavior: a cross-sectional study' in B Strumpel, JN Morgan and E Zahn eds. *Human Behavior in Economic Affairs* (Elsevier) p.347

FERBER R (1962) 'Research on household behaviour' *American Economic Review* Vol 52 p.19

FRIEND I and ADAMS FG (1964) 'The predictive ability of consumer attitudes, stock prices and non-attitudinal variables' *Journal of the American Statistical Association* Vol 59 p.987

GABOR A and GRANGER CWJ (1972/73) 'Ownership and acquisition of consumer durables: report on the Nottingham consumer durables project' *European Journal of Marketing* Vol 6 p.234

GOODMAN LA (1959) 'Simple statistical methods for scalogram analysis' *Psychometrika* Vol 24 p.29

GUTTMAN L (1945) 'Questions and answers about scale analysis' Research Branch, Information and Education Division, Army Service Forces *Report D-2*

GUTTMAN L (1954) 'A new approach to factor analysis: the radex' in P
    Lazarsfeld ed *Mathematical Thinking in the Social Sciences* (The Free
    Press) p.258
HEALD GI (1970) 'The relationship of intentions to buy consumer durables with
    levels of purchase' *British Journal of Marketing* Vol 4 p.87
HEBDEN JJ and PICKERING JF (1974) 'Patterns of acquisition of consumer
    durables' *Oxford Bulletin of Economics and Statistics* Vol 56 p.67
HYMANS SH (1970) 'Consumer durable spending: explanation and prediction'
    Brookings Papers on Economic Activity Vol 2 p.173
IRONMONGER DS (1972) *New Commodities and Consumer Behaviour*
    (Cambridge University Press)
ISHERWOOD BC and PICKERING JF (1975) 'Factors influencing individual
    purchases of motor cars in Great Britain' *Oxford Bulletin of Economics
    and Statistics* Vol 37 p.229
JUSTER FT (1964) *Anticipations and Purchases* (Princeton University Press)
JUSTER FT (1966) *Consumer Buying Intentions and Purchase Probability*
    (National Bureau of Economic Research).
JUSTER FT (1969) 'Consumer anticipations and models of durable goods
    demand' in J Mincer ed. *Economic Forecasts and Expectations – Analysis
    of Forecasting Behaviour and Performance* (National Bureau of
    Economic Research) p.167
JUSTER FT and WACHTEL P (1972a) 'Anticipatory and objective models of
    durable goods demand' *American Economic Review* Vol 62 p.564
JUSTER FT and WACHTEL P (1972b) 'Inflation and the consumer' *Brookings
    Papers on Economic Activity* Vol 4 p.71
KATONA G (1951) *Psychological Analysis of Economic Behaviour* (McGraw
    Hill)
KATONA G (1960) *The Powerful Consumer* (McGraw Hill)
KATONA G (1964) *The Mass Consumption Society* (McGraw Hill)
KATONA G (1972) 'Theory of expectations' in B Strumpel, JN Morgan and E
    Zahn eds *Human Behavior in Economic Affairs* (Elsevier)
KATONA G (1974) 'Psychology and consumer economics' *Journal of
    Consumer Research* Vol 1 p.1
KATONA G (1975) *Psychological Economics* (Elsevier)
KENDALL MG (1955) *Rank Correlation Methods* (Griffin)
KLEIN LR and LANSING JB (1955) 'Decisions to purchase consumer durable
    goods' *Journal of Marketing* Vol 20 p.109
LANCASTER KJ (1966) 'A new approach to consumer theory' *Journal of
    Political Economy* Vol 74 p.132
LANCASTER KJ (1971) *Consumer Demand, A New Approach* (Columbia
    University Press)
LEMON N (1973) *Attitudes and Their Measurement* (Batsford)
McFALL J (1969) 'Priority patterns and consumer behaviour' *Journal of
    Marketing* Vol 33 p.50
MORRISON DG (1969) 'On the interpretation of discriminant analysis' *Journal
    of Marketing Research* Vol 6 p.156

MUELLER E (1963) 'Ten years of consumer attitude surveys: their forecasting record' *Journal of the American Statistical Association* Vol 58 p.899

NATIONAL INSTITUTE OF ECONOMIC AND SOCIAL RESEARCH (1972) *National Institute Economic Review* No 60 May

NATIONAL INSTITUTE OF ECONOMIC AND SOCIAL RESEARCH (1973) *National Institute Economic Review* No 64 May

ODLING-SMEE JC (1968) 'The private short term demand for vehicles in the United Kingdom 1955-66: a preliminary investigation' *Bulletin of the Oxford University Institute of Economics and Statistics* Vol 30 p.189

PAROUSH J (1965) 'The order of acquisition of consumer durables' *Econometrica* Vol 33 p.225

PAROUSH J (1973) 'Efficient purchasing behaviour and efficient order relations in consumption' *Kyklos* Vol 26 p.91

PICKERING JF, HARRISON JA and COHEN CD (1973a) 'Identification and measurement of consumer confidence: methodology and some preliminary results' *Journal of the Royal Statistical Society* Series A Vol 136 p.43

PICKERING JF, HARRISON JA, HEBDEN JJ, ISHERWOOD BC and COHEN CD (1973b) 'Are goods goods? Some empirical evidence' *Applied Economics* Vol 5 p.1

PICKERING JF and ISHERWOOD BC (1974) 'Purchase probabilities and consumer durable purchasing behaviour' *Journal of the Market Research Society* Vol 16 p.203

PICKERING JF and ISHERWOOD BC (1975) 'Determinants of expenditure on consumer durables' *Journal of the Royal Statistical Society*, Series A Vol 138 p.504

PICKERING JF (1975) 'Verbal explanations of consumer durable purchase decisions' *Journal of the Market Research Society* Vol 17 p.107

PYATT FG (1964) *Priority Patterns and the Demand for Household Durable Goods* (Cambridge University Press)

SAGI PC (1959) 'A statistical test for the coefficient of reproducibility' *Psychometrika* Vol 24 p.19

SCHIPPER L (1964) *Consumer Discretionary Behaviour* (North Holland)

SHAPIRO HT and ANGEVINE GE (1969) 'Consumer attitudes, buying intentions and expectations: an analysis of the Canadian data' *Canadian Journal of Economics* Vol 2 p.230

SHAPIRO HT (1972) 'The index of consumer sentiment and economic forecasting' in B Strumpel, JN Morgan and E Zahn eds. *Human Behavior in Economic Affairs* (Elsevier)

SMITH RP (1975) *Consumer Demand for Cars in the USA* (Cambridge University Press).

STRUMPEL B, NOVY K and SCHWARTZ MA (1969) 'Consumer attitudes and outlays in Germany and North America' paper read to the Ciret Conference 1969.

SURREY MJC (1971) *The Analysis and Forecasting of the British Economy* (Cambridge University Press)

THEIL H and KOSOBOD RF (1968) 'How informative are consumer buying intentions surveys?' *Review of Economics and Statistics* Vol 50 p.50

TOBIN J (1959) 'On the predictive value of consumer intentions and attitudes' *Review of Economics and Statistics* Vol 41 p.1

Index